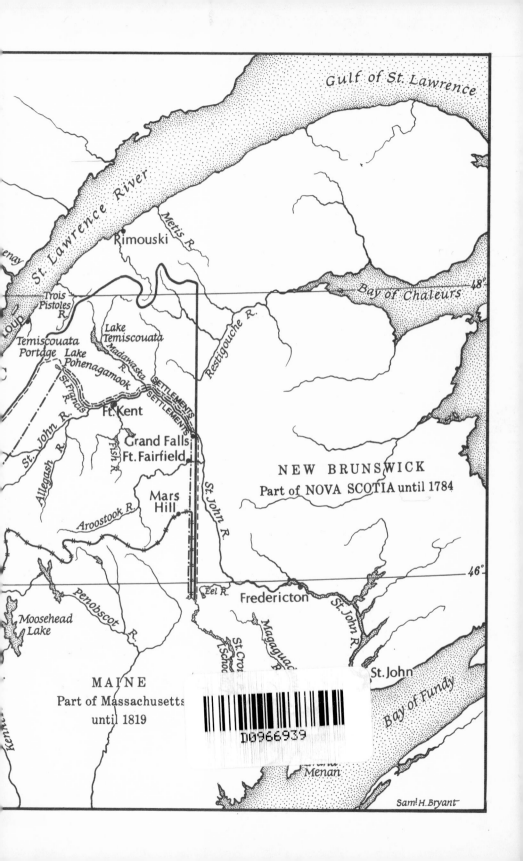

Gulf of St. Lawrence

St. Lawrence River

Metis R.

Rimouski

Bay of Chaleurs

48°

enay

Trois
Pistoles
R.

Loup

Lake
Temiscouata

Temiscouata
Portage Lake
Pohenagamook

Madawaska

Restigouche R.

St. Francis R.

SETTLEMENTS
SETTLEMENTS

Ft. Kent

St. John R.

Allegash R.

Fish R.

Grand Falls
Ft. Fairfield

NEW BRUNSWICK
Part of NOVA SCOTIA until 1784

Mars
Hill

Aroostook R.

St. John R.

46°

Penobscot R.

Eel R.

Fredericton

St. John R.

Moosehead
Lake

Magaguad R.

St. Croix
1. Schoo

St. John

Bay of Fundy

MAINE
Part of Massachusetts
until 1819

Kenn

Menan

Sam! H. Bryant

Fruits of Propaganda in the Tyler Administration

Fruits of Propaganda in the Tyler Administration

Frederick Merk

with the collaboration of
Lois Bannister Merk

Harvard University Press
Cambridge, Massachusetts
1971

Foreword by John Tyler

The question of [the Northeastern] boundary . . . had assumed a politico-party aspect and seemed . . . to be almost impossible to settle; and yet . . . the negotiator encountered and overcame all difficulties. True . . . the British government [evinced] every possible desire to settle the long pending difficulties . . . yet the causes of complaint were numerous and as much skill was required to reconcile conflict of opinion at home, as that which existed between the two governments.

On the other hand no difficulty of serious moment stood in the way of a successful negotiation of the Texas treaty. It required only the assent of the Presidents of the two Republics to negotiate . . . The difficulties arose afterwards, and the people had to interpose their authority in order to crown the measure with success, an interposition, the necessity for which . . . had not been anticipated.

Extract from a lecture delivered by John Tyler in 1856 and published in the *Southern Literary Messenger* for August of that year.

Acknowledgments

I am indebted to many friends and institutions for help in preparing this volume. I have received repeated assistance concerning problems of maps from Helen Wallis and Edward J. Miller of the Map Division of the British Museum. Mrs. Edith L. Hary, Law Librarian of the Maine State Library, patiently responded to my inquiries regarding votes of the Maine legislature found only in Senate and House manuscript journals. John J. Janitz, Manuscript Librarian of the Maine Historical Society, gave me much personal help in addition to opening to me the rich resources of the library. Philip A. Putnam, Associate Librarian of the Harvard Law Library, repeatedly gave me the benefit of his detailed knowledge of its resources. M. O. Gustafson and M. G. Eckhoff of the National Archives came often to my assistance. Dr. Frances Gregory of Westhampton College, Richmond, gave me bibliographical aid. I am indebted to the staff of the Massachusetts Historical Society, the Boston Public Library, the New-York Historical Society, the New York Public Library, the Library of Congress, the libraries of the College of William and Mary and of the University of Virginia, the Pennsylvania Historical Society, the Bangor Public Library, and, especially, the staff of the Harvard College Library. The Maine Historical Society has given permission to publish the documents from its Francis O. J. Smith Papers, from its Miscellaneous Letters of F. O. J. Smith on the Northeastern Boundary, and from its John Fairfield Papers, which figure so prominently in the section of Documents in this book. The Massachusetts Historical Society has given permission to publish the letter from President Tyler to Edward Everett of April 27, 1843, quoted in the Introduction, which is from its Edward Everett Papers. The Organization of American Historians has granted permis-

Acknowledgments

sion to republish my article "A Safety Valve Thesis and Texan Annexation," which appeared initially in the *Mississippi Valley Historical Review*, XLIX (Dec., 1962). I owe much to Professor Holman Hamilton of the University of Kentucky, who read the entire manuscript and gave me the benefit of his valuable and detailed appraisal of it. My greatest indebtedness is to my wife, Dr. Lois Bannister Merk, without whose help in research, analysis, and scholarly criticism this book could never have been written.

F. M.

Cambridge, Massachusetts
May 1970

Contents

Illustrations

Introduction

Propaganda under John Tyler

In the decade of the 1840s two American Presidents, John Tyler and James K. Polk, transformed the boundaries of the United States. By diplomacy they converted contested lines into peaceful ones, and by annexation and war they extended others to transcontinental proportions. They were able, in this process, to add territories to the United States exceeding in dimension those that had come with national independence. This was the remarkable achievement of half a dozen years.

John Tyler initiated the process. In 1842 he obtained, by negotiation, an agreement regarding the boundary between the United States and British possessions in North America from the source of the St. Croix River at the east to the "most northwestern point" of the Lake of the Woods in present-day Minnesota. By the Webster-Ashburton Treaty of that year he converted this line, which had been threatening to erupt into an armed clash at a number of points, into a symbol of peace.

A year later he wakened the dormant issue of annexing Texas and extending the southwestern boundary to the Rio Grande. This renewed a bitter sectional controversy over the extension of slavery. In the course of this controversy he pressed upon Congress a Joint Resolution inviting Texas, with boundary undefined, into the Union. Congress complied in the closing hours of his administration, and the boundary issue soon afterward produced a war with Mexico. The line in this latitude became a symbol of conflict.

At the north the line went back in its history to the Treaty of 1783,

3

closing the War of the American Revolution. It had been described in detail in the treaty, but without requisite knowledge. Its geographic anchors, named as boundaries, could not be located or they did not fit the surveys. One problem—that of identifying the St. Croix River named in the treaty as part of the boundary—was resolved by a mixed commission in 1798, and the river's source was marked by a monument. But other uncertainties remained on the long line between the monument and the most northwestern point of the Lake of the Woods; for forty-four years they generated controversy. One zone of controversy particularly threatening in the late 1830s lay between Maine and New Brunswick. By 1841 the continuing border affrays and tensions there made the governments of Great Britain and the United States realize that peace could no longer be preserved without a full stabilization of the entire line.

On April 4, 1841, Tyler became President of the United States. He had been elected Vice-President on the ticket headed by William Henry Harrison in the so-called "frolic campaign" of 1840. Harrison, an Indian fighter and territorial governor, had won the presidential nomination in preference to leaders of the party who were considered too closely identified with such policies as internal improvements at federal expense, a protective tariff, and a bank chartered by the federal government—policies defensible only under a "broad construction" of the Constitution. Tyler had been named for the vice-presidency on the strength of his ability to gather votes among Southerners partial to a strict construction of the Constitution and opposed to the measures desired by the Whig leaders. He had once been a follower of Andrew Jackson, but had rebelled against Old Hickory's arbitrary leadership and had thrown in his lot with the Whigs as the lesser of two evils. The ticket, so artfully constructed, had easily won the election, and on March 4 Harrison had become President. A month later he was dead.

When Tyler became President on April 4, the skies were dark, and so were Whig forebodings. One Whig accustomed to confiding forebodings to his diary was John Quincy Adams, then a member of Congress from Massachusetts. On that day he wrote this dour comment:

> The influence of this event upon the condition and history of this country can scarcely be foreseen. It makes the Vice-President of the United States, John Tyler, of Virginia, Acting President of

the Union for four years less one month. Tyler is a political sectarian [states' rights believer] of the slave-driving, Virginian, Jeffersonian school, principled against all improvement, with all the interests and passions and vices of slavery rooted in his moral and political constitution—with talents not above mediocrity, and a spirit incapable of expansion to the dimensions of the station upon which he has been cast by the hand of Providence, unseen through the apparent agency of chance. To that benign and healing hand of Providence I trust, in humble hope of the good which it always brings forth out of evil. In upwards of half a century this is the first instance of a Vice-President's being called to act as President of the United States, and brings to the test that provision of the Constitution which places in the Executive chair a man never thought of for it by anybody. This day was in every sense gloomy—rain the whole day.[1]

Even more anxious regarding the event of the day was Henry Clay. He firmly believed in a broad construction of the Constitution. He had found it hard to have Harrison preferred as the Whig's choice for President, and the succession of Tyler seemed worse yet. Daniel Webster was less upset. He had become Secretary of State in Harrison's cabinet and expected to be a power in the new administration.

Tyler soon exhibited a determination to maintain his "sectarian" or strict constructionist views. He began by vetoing two measures, shepherded by Clay through Congress, one to create a "fiscal bank," another to create a "fiscal corporation." In retaliation he was read out of the party. All the members of the cabinet resigned in September 1841, except Webster, who remained in the hope of extinguishing the embers smouldering on the northern border. Tyler became that anomaly of American politics, a President without a party. As chief executive he wielded greater authority in the conduct of foreign affairs than he did in domestic ones, and he early turned his energies to a search for a solution of the Northeastern boundary problem—the most pressing of the day. He carried this forward while the wreckage of party piled up around him.

The uncertainties remaining on the Northeastern boundary after the St. Croix River had been located were inherent in other terms of the

1. Charles F. Adams (ed.), *Memoirs of John Quincy Adams* (12 vols., Boston, 1874–1877), X, 456–457.

Treaty of 1783. One such term was "highlands." The treaty provided that the boundary should follow the highlands separating streams flowing into the St. Lawrence River from those flowing into the Atlantic Ocean. In 1763 those highlands had been named by British administrators as the line separating the province of Quebec from the provinces of Nova Scotia and New England, as then constituted. But the highlands had never been found or surveyed. Another troublesome term was "northwest angle of Nova Scotia." Even the meaning of the terms "Atlantic Ocean" and "Gulf of St. Lawrence" made trouble. The highlands were to be the boundary as far as the Connecticut River's "northwesternmost head," another troublemaker. A portion of the line—from the Connecticut River to the St. Lawrence—was the forty-fifth parallel, but that also caused problems for surveying reasons. And between the St. Lawrence and the Lake of the Woods added problems were uncovered as settlement advanced on both sides of the line in the half century between the Treaty of 1783 and the Tyler administration.

Efforts to solve these problems were not lacking. In 1802 the Jefferson administration opened negotiations in London for a convention under which a mixed commission would be established to find the highlands and the northwesternmost head of the Connecticut River. Such a convention was drawn up and signed in London, and Jefferson asked the Senate to ratify it in October 1803. But the Senate failed to do so.

Another endeavor to solve these problems came out of the negotiations for peace at Ghent following the War of 1812. The negotiators wrote into the peace treaty a series of clauses referring disputes on segments of the line between the St. Croix monument and the Lake of the Woods to joint commissions for settlement. If agreement were not so reached, the disputes were to be submitted to arbitration by friendly sovereigns or states. An award by an arbitrator on any segment was to be binding on both sides. No arbitrations, however, resulted.

In 1827 a convention applying arbitration specifically to the Northeastern dispute was agreed upon. The King of the Netherlands was chosen as arbitrator with the approval of President John Quincy Adams. In 1831 the King handed down a judgment that the line described in the Treaty of 1783 could not be ascertained, and he suggested a compromise line to replace it. His award was rejected by the American Senate (to the lasting regret of President Jackson) on the ground that it went beyond the authority conferred upon the arbitrator by the terms of the Treaty of Ghent and the Convention of 1827.[2] The award was then also declined by the British.

Eight years of futile correspondence between the two governments followed. These were years of disagreement as to whether a new negotiation, if held, should set up procedures for another attempt to find "on the face of the earth" the line intended by the words of the Treaty of 1783, or whether that approach should be abandoned and an effort be made to find a conventional line—one arrived at by an exchange of equivalents and meeting the needs and wishes of the two parties.

The British refused to consider any further attempt, whether by joint survey or joint commission, to find the treaty line, unless advance assurance was given by the American government that Maine would be bound by the result. The American government sought to induce Maine to give up its search for the treaty line and to agree to a negotiation for a conventional one, but failed. Believing that the treaty line could be found, the government of Maine proposed a new survey, run either by itself or by some joint arrangement. It believed the federal government was committed to finding the line intended by the treaty and that the proposals of the British were based on sophistries in interpretation of its terms.

In the late 1830s both sides resorted to direct action. Lumbermen and settlers moved into the contested area from Maine and from New Brunswick. Timber thieves were active on both sides; arrests were made, and ejections occurred. A civil posse from Maine was brought into the contested area, and the state's militia was summoned. British troops were called in. Congress authorized a war credit of ten million dollars and empowered the President to enroll fifty thousand volunteers. But President Martin Van Buren still hoped for a peaceful settlement and sent General Winfield Scott into the disturbed area with pacific orders. He and the Lieutenant Governor of New Brunswick arranged a truce in 1839. The truce only temporarily lessened the tensions, however; they reappeared during the next year.

Maine had acquired by now in both the United States and in Great Britain a reputation for intransigence. The state was in a strategic posi-

2. The terms of reference are in Article 1 of the Convention of 1827, which in turn refers to article 5 of the Treaty of Ghent. See [Albert Gallatin and William P. Preble,] *North Eastern Boundary Arbitration* (Washington, 1829–1831), Statement of the United States, Appendix 1, 29–34.

tion to have its way. As a state, it claimed political jurisdiction in the disputed area. It possessed, also, ownership of half of the public land under the agreement of separation made with Massachusetts in 1819 prior to separate statehood. It had abundant theoretical support for intransigence in the states' rights doctrine and took full advantage of it. Yet other states of the Union felt that a single state should not assert boundary claims with an aggressiveness that might involve the remaining twenty-five in war.

In 1841 the governments of the United States and Great Britain became inclined toward a friendly settlement. In the United States Daniel Webster, Secretary of State in the Harrison-Tyler administration, was an Anglophile. In Great Britain the ministry of Melbourne, which had supported the truculent Palmerston as Secretary for Foreign Affairs, was overthrown, and the Conservative party took office with the pacific Aberdeen controlling foreign relations. Tyler and Webster were determined to use this opportunity to bring the nagging Northeastern dispute to a peaceful conclusion.

A peaceful conclusion, they believed, was dependent on Maine's acceptance of the principle of a negotiation for a conventional line. The idea was far from new. President Jackson's Secretary of State had sought to convert Maine to acceptance of this principle in 1832, but had failed. What was new in the Tyler presidency was a new mode of implementing the idea. Maine was to be converted to the principle by a program of statewide propaganda secretly directed by the administration and paid for out of an executive fund, authorized by Congress for secret use in foreign intercourse.[3] The public in Maine was to be persuaded that any attempt to reach the treaty line without war would be futile and that the state would win greater benefits peacefully in a negotiation based on the principle of an exchange of equivalents. The propaganda was to appear to be local in origin, of nonparty character, and was to create the impression that it was a

3. The secret fund of Presidents for missions in the conduct of foreign relations was provided for by Congress in 1810. See *Laws of the United States vol. 10* (Washington, 1811), Chap. LXI. A distinction was drawn in Chap. LXI, sec. 3, between expenditures that could be made public and those "by certificates" that need not be made public. A good discussion of the fund, including its earlier history, may be found in a special message of President Polk to the House of Representatives on April 10, 1846, in response to a request of the House regarding Webster's use of the fund. See James D. Richardson (comp.), *Messages and Papers of the Presidents* (10 vols., Washington, G.P.O., 1896–1898), IV, 431–436.

manifestation of religious sentiment in the state eager for the preservation of peace.

This plan was proposed to Webster in the spring of 1841 by Francis O. J. Smith, a well-known Maine politician and newspaper publisher, who had earlier sought to interest President Van Buren in a comparable plan. Like Webster and Tyler, Smith was a "man between parties." He had once been an ardent Democrat and a defender of the treaty claim of Maine. He had fallen away from the party, however, and in the campaign of 1840 had supported the Harrison-Tyler ticket. He had economic interests in the settlement of the Maine issue.

In an interview with Webster in the latter's home, he offered himself as the unseen director of the plan. He followed this with a statement of his terms in a letter dated June 7, 1841. Webster engaged him with Tyler's approval. His compensation was agreed upon, and arrangements were made for the employment of assistants. He went promptly to work. He converted editors of newspapers and local political leaders by private interviews, by confidential correspondence, by articles written under a nom de plume in a strategically placed religious journal, and by memorials printed and extensively circulated and signed, addressed to the governor of the state and the legislature, asking that the boundary dispute be brought to an early conclusion by a negotiation for a conventional line.

The unfolding of this plan appears below in "Daniel Webster and the Search for Peace," and in the appended documents. It is evident in the correspondence between Smith and Webster, in the letters of Smith to confidants in Maine, and in the exchanges between Smith and the editor of the *Christian Mirror* of Portland. It is most intriguingly described in later depositions of Tyler and Edward Stubbs, the disbursing clerk of the President's secret fund, before a special committee of the House of Representatives, appointed in 1846 to investigate charges made against Webster. A report of the committee was published at the time in the *Congressional Globe* and in the House documents. But, as published, it was a heavily censored version of the testimony of the former President and the depositions of the disbursing clerk. The deleted testimony, buried since then in the manuscripts of the House of Representatives in the National Archives, is made public in this volume, reintegrated into the committee report. These letters and archival materials shed new light upon the Webster-

9

Ashburton Treaty of 1842. They illustrate the Tyler administration's yearlong program of preparatory propaganda in Maine, which came to fruition in Washington in the boundary provisions of the memorable treaty negotiated by Webster and Lord Ashburton, with the acquiescence of Maine.

One of the documents published here in facsimile, as an illustration, is a copy of a "Memorandum" of payments made by Webster from the President's secret fund. It was laid before the investigating committee by the disbursing clerk and exhibits, among other payments, those made to Smith and to others of Webster's agents who were to influence the governor and members of the Maine legislature to cooperate in the plan for an agreement on a conventional line. Among the agents were Jared Sparks, Peleg Sprague, Albert Smith, and C. S. Daveis. These individuals were employed to cast doubt on the interpretation of the treaty line that Maine had been fighting for.

In the "Memorandum" an item of payment appears, not directly related to the boundary issue. It refers to an issue on the New York frontier and is noticed here for the light it casts on the means that Webster and Tyler were ready to use to resolve Anglo-American controversies. The item is $1,000 paid to a Mr. Crittenden. The reference is to John J. Crittenden, the Attorney General of the United States from March to September 1841. The issues with which he had dealt were the *Caroline* affair and the case of Alexander McLeod.

The *Caroline* was an American steamboat plying the Niagara River, which separates New York from what was then called the province of Upper Canada. It was employed in 1837 during the Mackenzie Rebellion in Upper Canada to run recruits, supplies, and ammunition from sympathizers on the American side to the rebels operating from Navy Island on the Canadian side. Late that year a force of Canadian volunteers, with the approval of Canadian authorities, crossed the river to the American side, seized the *Caroline,* set it on fire, and pushed it out into the river to sink. In the melee an American, Amos Durfee, was killed.

Three years later, Alexander McLeod, a Canadian sheriff, while on a visit in upstate New York, was arrested on the charge of having participated in the attack on the *Caroline* and with having shot Durfee. He was alleged to have boasted in a saloon of having participated in the affair. Other Canadians in that part of New York had also been arrested on like charges. The evidence brought against McLeod in the court indicting him was all questionable, including that of two witnesses who swore they had seen him in the affray.

The affair became a threat to peace as a result of the British government's assumption of responsibility for the attack across the border. The British Foreign Office under Palmerston maintained that the attack had been a defensive measure on the part of the colonial authorities and that if McLeod were assumed to have been on the expedition he was part of an authorized force of Upper Canada and could not, therefore, be tried for murder. The British minister in Washington was ordered to give warning to the American government that a break in relations, and probably war, would follow if McLeod were convicted of murder and executed.

The juridical case lay clearly within the jurisdiction of the state of New York, for the charge against McLeod was murder within the confines of a state. Under the Constitution the federal government had no right to interfere with state authorities in such a case. Though Tyler was a staunch upholder of states' rights in domestic matters, he felt that the federal government ought not to be dragged into war by the action of a state. His predecessor, Harrison, had already requested Attorney General Crittenden to proceed to Albany to obtain the intervention of Governor William H. Seward in the case, in the interest of peace. Crittenden believed that the assignment was outside his duties, but it was the first request of importance made to him by the President, and he complied. In Albany he was told by Seward that McLeod had a thoroughly sound alibi, that he could prove he had been in his own Canadian community during the assault on the *Caroline,* and that if he were convicted he would be given a gubernatorial pardon. But no governor, Seward held, could interfere in a trial in a state court. This was reported by Crittenden to Webster, and it drew from Tyler a response marked by asperity.

In the trial the case against McLeod collapsed. Abundant evidence proved his absence from the scene of the attack on the *Caroline.* The two witnesses who had testified to having seen the accused in the melee did not appear. In October 1841 the jury trying the case declared McLeod innocent of the charge of murder twenty minutes after receiving it. Rumor circulated during the trial and afterward that the witnesses upon whom the prosecution had relied had somehow been kept

11

Copy of a Memorandum without date, in pencil.

(In agents writing)

Mr Webster to a/c for $9,200

Less payment to Mr Crittenden 1000

$ 8200

Payts certified by him 3610

$ 4590

(In Mr Webster's writing) except the footing figures.

Smith	1500	
——— (not legible) (it may be assistants)	500	500 r
Albert Smith	200	
Sparks	250	×
Sprague	250	×
Smith of (Va)	200	500 ~
C S Davies for map	200	× 300 r
for journey to Boston twice	400	
Various small items	100	× 100 ~
	3300	1400

This is all, unless the President should think something more ought to be allowed to Mr Sparks.

Copy of a memorandum of State Department expenses on the New York frontier 1841 and in Maine 1842. House Report 684, 29 Congress, 1 session (1846), "Report of the Select Committee on Charges against Mr. Daniel Webster," 126. Records of the House of Representatives, Record Group 233, National Archives.

Sir,

In reply to your note of yesterday. I can only say that I should regard $250 [...] to Mr. Sparks for the map fully enough. I do not doubt but that it will satisfy him. If otherwise we can see more about it.

Yr.

Signed J Tyler
Aug 25 1842

Mr Stubbs

Copy of a letter of John Tyler 1842 about compensation to Jared Sparks for aid in connection with the Northeastern Boundary dispute. House Report 684, 29 Congress, 1 session (1846), "Report of the Select Committee on Charges against Mr. Daniel Webster," 127. Records of the House of Representatives, Record Group 233, National Archives.

out of the way, either by the federal government or by the state government. After the trial the rumor reached the British minister in Washington, who reported it to the acting Lieutenant Governor of Upper Canada.

Still later, in 1846, Webster was charged in Congress with having interfered in the trial. The charge was part of a continuing Democratic assault on him. In the House the most vituperative of Webster's assailants was the chairman of the Committee on Foreign Affairs, Charles J. Ingersoll of Pennsylvania; in the Senate it was a New Yorker, Daniel S. Dickinson. Both were extreme Anglophobes and expansionists. Dickinson charged on February 25, 1846, that Webster's interference in the McLeod case "was a palpable and direct one, and an attempt, on the part of the authorities at Washington, to arrest the ordinary course of justice, and prevent a trial upon the merits." Webster made a devastating reply in a two-day speech in the Senate on April 6 and 7. He denied that the federal authorities had done anything prior to or during the trial except to comply with a requisition from McLeod's attorney for materials from the diplomatic files necessary to his defense. He challenged Dickinson to prove that the federal authorities had done any act "which the common sense of men holds to be a palpable and direct interference. I say there was none."[4]

A careful student of the McLeod case, Alastair Watt, in a detailed article appearing in the *Canadian Historical Review*, has cast deserved doubt on the surmises in Washington that witnesses against McLeod had been bought off by the federal authorities prior to the trial. He dismisses, as entirely without foundation, reports that McLeod's counsel was paid from funds provided by the American government. He cites evidence from reliable Canadian sources that all the expenses of the case were paid for out of the Military Chest of Upper Canada.[5] And

4. For Ingersoll's and Dickinson's charges against Webster, see *Cong. Globe*, 29 Cong., 1 sess., 343 (Feb. 9), 621 (Apr. 7), 627 (Apr. 8, 1846). Webster's reply is *ibid.*, 609–612 (Apr. 6), 616–621 (Apr. 7, 1846); also in *Works of Daniel Webster* (6 vols., Boston, 1853), V, 78–147.

5. See Alastair Watt, "Case of Alexander McLeod," *Canadian Historical Review*, XII (June 1931), 144–167, especially 158; James M. Callahan, *American Foreign Policy in Canadian Relations* (New York, Macmillan, 1937), Chap. 8; Albert D. Kirwan, *John J. Crittenden* (Lexington, University of Kentucky Press, 1962); Lyon G. Tyler, *Letters and Times of the Tylers* (3 vols., Richmond, 1884–1896), II, 208–211; Glyndon G. Van Deusen, *William H. Seward* (New York, Oxford University Press, 1967). For the correspondence between Seward and Webster on the McLeod case and the precautions being taken to prevent violence, see

yet the testimony appearing in the "Memorandum" of Tyler's disbursing clerk is that $1,000 was paid to Mr. Crittenden, which could hardly have been a mere travel allowance from Washington to Albany.

This money could conceivably have been used for the protection of McLeod against lynching, or for preventing sabotage of installations in Canada by overwrought patriots or fugitive Canadian rebels. These dangers were known to the state authorities, however, and the Governor had assured Webster that they had been fully guarded against. The President and Webster may have felt that supplementation of state activity was necessary, just as in Maine they felt that quiet reversal of state policy was necessary. In each case the results were pacific. On March 12, 1846, the former President described them succinctly in a letter to Webster: "The peace of the Country when I reached Washington, on the 6th day of April 1841, was suspended by a thread, but we converted that thread into a chain cable of sufficient strength to render that peace secure, and to enable the Country to weather the storms of faction by which it was in every direction assailed."[6]

Not only the subsidence of current "storms" but the future of Anglo-American peace was a paramount concern in the Webster-Ashburton negotiation. A major article in the concluded treaty (Article 10) provided for mutual extradition of fugitives from justice in specified types of cases and described the process of extradition to be employed. Also, Lord Ashburton, in a letter to Webster that became part of the settlement, recognized that his own government (of the Palmerston period) had not been blameless in the *Caroline* affair. And, finally, Webster obtained legislation from Congress, soon after the treaty was ratified,

---

New York Assembly Documents, 1842, I, No. 2, Doc. C. An issue of "conflict of interest" dogged the case. McLeod's attorney was Joshua A. Spencer of New York. He was made United States District Attorney for Northern New York while the McLeod case was moving through the state courts. Much of the correspondence between Seward and Tyler, and between Seward and Webster, consisted of argument as to whether it was seemly or safe to appoint, as a federal district attorney, the person serving as McLeod's attorney. Seward wished to know whether "there was not in fact a conflict between his [Spencer's] official duties and character, and his engagement as counsel for the accused"; also, "whether it could not have been thought important, in view of the peculiar circumstances of the case, to inquire whether it was indispensably necessary to assign the duties of district attorney to a person lying under such an assignment." *Ibid.,* 114, 115. For intriguing hints as to Crittenden's efforts to quiet the McLeod affair, see fn. 32 to Documents relating to the Maine boundary.

6. Claude H. Van Tyne (ed.), *Letters of Daniel Webster* (New York, McClure, Phillips & Co., 1902), 310–311.

permitting cases such as McLeod's, where subjects of foreign states were in the custody of state courts, to be removed to the federal courts.[7] These arrangements were of more than ordinary importance for the future because of the extent of the Anglo-American frontier and the turbulence of the frontier elements on both sides of it.

Respecting the Pacific Northwest the Tyler administration exhibited a like eagerness for compromise of Anglo-American controversies. There the problem was the peaceful partitioning of the Oregon Country. Extremists among American expansionists were insisting in Congress, and elsewhere, that the British had no rights in Oregon, were mere intruders there, and ought to be expelled. This seemed reckless to Tyler. In the Webster-Ashburton negotiation he had in mind a partition at the forty-ninth parallel to the Pacific. Indeed he would have agreed to a boundary less favorable to the United States; he would have accepted the lower Columbia as the boundary from the point where the forty-ninth parallel crosses it, provided part or all of Upper California could have been obtained from Mexico with British help. The harbor waters of Puget Sound and the Straits would have gone to the British in such a settlement, but the United States would have gained the superlative harbor of San Francisco. This was the "tripartite plan" intimated to Ashburton by Webster as soon as Ashburton revealed that he had no authority under his instructions to concede any territory north of the Columbia.

The tripartite plan seemed a happy one to Lord Ashburton and was recommended by him to his government. But it was derailed by adverse developments. One of these was a British decision not to exert pressure on Mexico for such a deal. Another was the hasty action of Commodore Thomas ap Catesby Jones, commander of the American naval squadron in the Pacific, and a Virginian like the President, who seized the important port of Monterey on October 19, 1842, on hearing that war with Mexico was about to begin. Jones did lower the flag

7. For the exchange of notes between Webster and Ashburton in 1842 on the *Caroline* and McLeod affairs, see William R. Manning, *Diplomatic Correspondence of the United States, Canadian Relations 1784–1860* (3 vols., Washington, Carnegie Endowment, 1940–1943), III, 189, 770. For the extradition article and the congressional act on cases similar to the McLeod case, see Albert B. Corey, *Crisis of 1830–1842 in Canadian American Relations* (New Haven, Yale University Press, 1941), 172–173; and Hunter Miller (ed.), *Treaties and Other International Acts of the United States of America* (8 vols., Washington, G.P.O., 1931–1948), IV, 461.

and sail away the next day on learning that his information had been incorrect, but his enterprise produced such a stir in Mexico that any possibility of a cession of territory to the United States was foreclosed. The Tyler strategy of winning peace in the Pacific Northwest and territory farther south for Southern institutions and American trade was thus defeated.[8]

The next spring the President prepared for a negotiation with the British on several related problems, Oregon, California, and a new commercial agreement—all of which were to be settled together. The negotiation was to be held in Washington, not London, where Edward Everett, the American minister, would have been the negotiator. To pave the way for the negotiation the President arranged with Duff Green, a close friend from Maryland, to proceed to London, ostensibly as a private citizen on business of his own, but really as an executive agent.

Green was a person of Southern views with a party history not unlike that of the President. He was a "man between parties." He had once been an ardent Jacksonian, but had broken with Jackson and with Van Buren and had joined the Whigs. He had supported Harrison for the presidency in 1840 and had been responsible in part for the naming of Tyler as the vice-presidential candidate. He was a land speculator, promoter of mining and railroad enterprises, and editor of a succession of newspapers in St. Louis, Washington, and New York. He was above all a restless manipulator and propagandist. He was ambitious to play the role of kingmaker. His allegiance to Tyler was temporary; he more persistently pressed Calhoun, to whom he was related by marriage, as a candidate for the presidential nomination. After the death of Calhoun in 1850 he turned his attentions to the archexpansionist, George M. Dallas of Pennsylvania. As to political issues, his abiding loyalties were to expansionism, protection of slavery, and states' rights.

The President prepared Edward Everett for Green's coming by a letter of April 27, 1843, in which he outlined his plans in foreign affairs and his proposals for realizing them. He had recently offered Everett a mission to China in exchange for the London post. He gave Everett

8. For a further account of the tripartite plan and its outcome, see Frederick Merk, *The Oregon Question* (Cambridge, Mass., Harvard University Press, 1967), 189–215.

friendly notice of Green's coming, advising him that it was for the purpose of quietly smoothing the way for a commercial treaty. But Everett, to whom Green had made himself obnoxious on an earlier mission to London for Tyler, was suspicious. The President did not discuss the Texas issue much in his letter. The Oregon question seemed to be more on his mind, but both Green and Everett knew the deep desire of the President for the annexation of Texas. The letter heralding Green is worth quoting at length for its revelation of the President's adeptness in combining issues and his desire for peace with the British.

> . . . The adjustment of the [Oregon question] is rendered the more difficult from the fact of its isolation. Hence I have been extremely anxious to introduce the subject of California & Texas so that as to any concessions which might be made on the Columbia, which standing alone would involve the administration in violent denunciations, we might present a counterpoise in territory of incalculable value elsewhere acquired. The accomplishment of this seems at the moment to be hopeless and leaves me in some state of anxiety as to the Oregon Question. There is a decided feeling getting up in the community for the immediate occupation of the country up to the 49th degree. A measure of that character was very near receiving favour from Congress at its last session. This is what I wish to avoid. I mean the adoption of any action on our part which might bring us in collision with England. Peace is my desire—peace on fair & honorable terms. Other considerations looking to the future & connected with the highest state of public prosperity, demand of us as far as practicable, to remove any probable cause of quarrel with England. The peace of Europe may depend on the life of a single monarch & should war take place, I wish this country to be in a condition to become the carrier of the world. I fear that the Oregon Question cannot be placed in a situation standing alone, to meet the sanction of the Senate. But if a commercial treaty could be connected with it, having the feature of moderate duties upon importations here, giving reasonable encouragement to our manufacturing labour at the same time that we substituted permanency in place of extravagant duties, and as correlative concessions on the part of England, a reduction of duties on tobacco, cotton & rice, and the abolition of all duties on Indian corn, salted provisions etc, & if possible a low duty exclusively in favour of America's flour & wheat, then

a circle of interests would be completed which embracing the whole Union & every interest, would secure us peace in any contingency and give new vigour to public prosperity. These are great objects & should you have declined the mission to China you may have a most important part to play in the great drama of politics.

Under the circumstances I have thought such a man as General Green, acting under limited countenance and known only as a private citizen, might be of great service in bringing facts to our knowledge, by holding consultations with persons possessing important interests in the trade & commerce of England. English public sentiment might thus be brought to bear upon the English Ministry. He will confer freely with you if it should be your pleasure & possess you of all the information he may acquire. You will perceive the interests involved in all this matter & be gradually feeling your way with the British Ministry.[9]

The plan of winning British goodwill by a reciprocal lowering of tariffs and thus paving the way to a pacific settlement of the Oregon question was, in a sense, a substitute for the ill-fated tripartite plan. It seemed to Tyler an ideal combination of elements—each attractive in itself to a Southern expansionist and low-tariff man. But its timing was hardly practicable. It ran counter to the settled high-tariff views of the Whigs who controlled the Senate and of the Conservatives who controlled the British Parliament. It prospered as little as had the tripartite plan.

The Texas issue, mentioned incidentally in the letter, had been in a state of relative quiescence until the spring of 1843. For five years it had been so because of differences over annexation between the sections and within parties in the United States. The South desired annexation because Texas would be an outlet for Southern institutions and energies, as well as for those of the nation. But proposals of annexation had led to differences. They had aroused widespread hostility in the North because of objection to the spread of slavery. Many North-

9. This letter is in the Edward Everett Papers, Massachusetts Historical Society, under date Apr. 27, 1843. Tyler entrusted its transmission to Duff Green. A thousand dollars was paid to Duff Green from the contingent fund for foreign intercourse on the day of this letter. The transaction is recorded in State Department Manuscripts, Record Group 59, Bureau of Accounts, National Archives, portions of which are depicted here. A valuable sketch of Duff Green by Fletcher M. Green appears in the *Dictionary of American Biography;* see also his "Duff Green, Militant Journalist," *American Historical Review,* LII (Jan. 1947), 247–264.

19

I hereby authorise the Agent of the Department of State to advance to the Secretary of State, out of the appropriation for the Contingent Expenses of Foreign Intercourse, One thousand dollars as requested in the within letter: the object not expedient now to specify.

John Tyler –

March 24" 1843.

Recd One thousand Dollars

Dsmd. Volatee

The above sum of one thousand dollars is brought into the acct for 2 Qur. of 1843 as paid for Special Agency by order of the President. It having been paid to D Green as this receipt annexed.

E. Stubbs, Agent
21 July 1843 –

Authorization of State Department funds for Duff Green in 1843. In "Letters to Presidents Requesting Authorization of Disbursements," Bureau of Accounts, Records of the State Department, Record Group 59, National Archives.

erners, however, had tastes for territorial acquisitions regardless of the spread of slavery.

In 1836, after Texas had won a smashing victory over the army of Mexico at the Battle of San Jacinto, its government applied for annexation to the United States. The application was not welcomed, however, by the American Congress during the Jackson and Van Buren administrations. Texas won only recognition and treaties of commerce from the United States and from European states. In July 1843 it withdrew its application and pressed instead for closer relations with the British and for a truce in the continuing war with Mexico. This change seemed ominous to Tyler and especially so to Abel P. Upshur, Webster's successor as Secretary of State, who was an enthusiast for annexation and an ultraist regarding slavery.

In this tense situation a sensational private letter from "General" Green, written in July 1843, reached Upshur in Washington. It brought "authentic" information that Lord Aberdeen had agreed, on behalf of the British government, to guarantee interest on a commercial loan to be made to Texas, which would have as its sole condition that Texas would abolish slavery. The letter was the principal outcome of Green's "private" mission to London.

The "authentic" information, which several months later Everett reported, after careful investigation, to have been anything but authentic, was accepted at once as truth by Upshur and Tyler. It was immediately passed on to the American representative in Texas. The result was the opening of a very secret negotiation with the government of Texas for a treaty of annexation.[10] The negotiation was thrown into momen-

10. The Green letter of July 1843 was followed by a second, written on August 3. The second is preserved in the State Department archives in the National Archives under the label "Special Agents." The theme developed in both letters was a British "plot" to finance abolition in Texas by means of a loan, on which the British government would guarantee the interest. That theme proved short lived. It perished for lack of corroborative evidence and because the alleged plot failed to materialize. It did, however, have the effect of opening discussions concerning annexation with Texas. A more plausible theme, which dominated subsequent diplomatic correspondence, was that Lord Aberdeen had openly confessed in Parliament a British wish for abolition in Texas. This, and Green's explanation of British motives in it, was accepted by Upshur and incorporated in his diplomatic correspondence and in editorials anonymously appearing in the *Madisonian*, the organ of Tyler in Washington; see particularly those of Sept. 23, 25, 28, and Nov. 3, 1843; see also Green to Calhoun, Oct. 18, 1843, in American Historical Association, *Annual Report, 1929* (Washington, G.P.O., 1930), 188–190; and Claude H. Hall, *Abel Parker Upshur* (Madison, State Historical Society of Wisconsin, 1964), Chap. 8.

tary disorder by the accidential death of Upshur, but was resumed with even greater energy by Upshur's successor, John C. Calhoun. In the meantime Green had spread in London and sent to American journals, notably to the expansionist *New York Herald,* then a supporter of Tyler, the thesis that the governing classes in England had a selfish reason for their drive against slavery in the world.[11] In 1833 Parliament, yielding to what Green felt was a misguided philanthropy, had destroyed slavery in the British colonies. Then had come an abrupt decline in production, especially of sugar, in the British West Indies. Free Negroes did not produce sugar as efficiently or cheaply as did slaves. The government could not well re-establish slavery because of public opinion in England. Instead, it adopted a program of overthrowing slavery in the rest of the world, especially in Cuba, Brazil, Texas, and the United States. That program would be popular in England and would comport well with British economic interests. It would depress the competitive power of the rivals of England to the low British level. Then England, through its dominance in manufacturing, commerce, and sea power, would regain its supremacy. The program was to begin in Texas and follow on in the United States. Upshur and, after him, Calhoun readily accepted this thesis. They incorporated

11. The journals in the United States containing an early letter of Green to this effect were the *Boston Post,* Oct. 10, the daily *New York Herald,* Oct. 12, and the weekly *New York Herald,* Oct. 14, 1843. A reprint appeared in *Niles' Register,* LXV (Oct. 21, 1843), 123. Green sent a later letter repeating these views to the London *Times,* whose editor scornfully rejected it. This was then sent to the *Boston Post,* where it appeared in installments on December 14, 15, 1843. Everett reported confidentially to Upshur on November 16, 1843, a conversation with Lord Aberdeen on the subject of Green's views. He wrote: "In speaking in my interview with Lord Aberdeen . . . of the uneasiness, which had been excited in the United States, in reference to the measures supposed to be pursued by Great Britain to effect the abolition of Slavery in Texas, I told him that there were persons in the United States who firmly believed, that Great Britain was pursuing this object and resolved if possible to accomplish it, with a view to aggrandize herself and Colonies, at the expense of the United States in general and the Slave-holding States in particular; and I sketched to him briefly the plan of policy in this respect, which is ascribed to Great Britain in a letter recently addressed by General Duff Green to the Editor of the *Boston Post.*—Lord Aberdeen treated it as a notion too absurd and unfounded to need serious contradiction. He said, however, that bearing in mind the sensibilities that existed on this subject, he would endeavor hereafter to express himself with great caution, when it became necessary to speak of Slavery." For this "private" dispatch, see William R. Manning (ed.), *Diplomatic Correspondence of the United States, Inter-American Affairs, 1831–1860* (12 vols., Washington, Carnegie Endowment, 1932–1939), VII, 251.

the essentials of it into the diplomatic correspondence that went to the Senate with a treaty of annexation in the spring of 1844.[12]

The Green thesis was fortified by another as terrifying—that the British were intent on drawing a noose of strangulation about the United States. The noose would consist of British dominions in the north, their sea power along the coasts and in the Caribbean, and their satellite, Mexico. If Texas were to become a satellite the noose would be closed and the knot tightened.

These ideas did not harmonize with the earlier convictions of Tyler regarding the need for maintaining friendly relations with the British. They reflected the presence in the State Department of Upshur and Calhoun in place of Webster. They were designed to win a solid Southern vote in the Senate for ratification of a treaty with Texas.

A propaganda thesis to win the Northern vote in the Senate was also required. Northern opposition had defeated every earlier proposal of annexation, and a two-thirds majority was necessary in the Senate to ratify a treaty. To meet this need a striking, new thesis was developed, with the approval of Tyler. It was that slavery everywhere in the United States would be put on the road to extinction if Texas were annexed. Slavery, according to the thesis, was a soil-destroying institution. It destroyed the fields on which it prospered. The institution was already in flight from the seaboard areas of the South and from the border states. Slave owners were migrating from those worn-out soils to the virgin ones of the Southwest. If Texas were annexed its

12. The documents (including reference to Green's letter) which accompanied the treaty are printed in *Senate Docs.*, 28 Cong., 1 sess. (Ser. 435), No. 341. The Green mission of 1843 to England is described in the Duff Green Papers in the Southern Historical Collection of the University of North Carolina, now available in microfilm. Rolls No. 4–6 and 25 relate to the period of the 1840's; see especially Green to Tyler, May 31, 1843, Roll 4; Green to Sir Robert Peel, June 27, 1843, Roll 4; and Green to C. A. Clinton, Apr. 26, 1844, Roll 25. A body of papers covering Green's first mission to London and his participation in the Paris fight on the ratification of the Quintuple Treaty of 1841 is in the Library of Congress. An article by St. George L. Sioussat in American Antiquarian Society, *Proceedings*, XL (1930), 175–276, is based on these materials. See also Henry M. Wriston, *Executive Agents in American Foreign Relations* (Baltimore, Johns Hopkins Press, 1929), index under "Green, Duff." Revealing glimpses of government financing of Green's mission of 1841–1842 are in the Green Papers, Roll 4, especially C. A. Wickliffe to Green, Oct. 26, 1841, and Green to Benjamin Green, Nov. 26, 1842, Mar. 19, 1843; also in Calhoun to Tyler, June 14, 1844, in American Historical Association, *Annual Report, 1899* (2 vols., Washington, G.P.O., 1900), II, 597. This letter states that Green received a thousand dollars from the contingent fund for his 1841–1842 mission.

rich soils would draw to it the slave population of all the remainder of the Union. Then would occur the inevitable exhaustion of the soil. Planters would be faced by bankruptcy. To save themselves from this fate they would emancipate their slaves. The Negroes would move happily across the Rio Grande to freedom in Mexico and in Central and South America. Texas, if annexed, would serve the nation as a safety valve. Through that valve would disappear, not only slavery, but the Negroes themselves and the entire problem of race relations.

This ingenious concept was Robert J. Walker's contribution to the Texas cause. It appeared in a sizable pamphlet entitled *Letter of Mr. Walker of Mississippi, Relative to the Annexation of Texas,* published in Washington early in February 1844 and is reprinted as the final document in this volume. Its publication was timed to make its full impact on the vote in the Senate upon the anticipated Texas treaty. Walker was a close associate of Tyler and was the leader in the Senate of the annexation forces. He knew intimately Northern and Southern attitudes and prejudices regarding slavery, the Negro, and race relations. He was by birth and upbringing a Northerner; by vocation he was a Southern planter devoted to politics. He had reservations regarding the righteousness of slavery and had hopes that, someday, in the future, it would disappear.

Tyler had held similar views for many years; indeed, he had presented them to Congress as early as 1820. The measure then under discussion was a bill preliminary to the admission of Missouri to statehood, which had been brought into the House on February 13, 1819. It had been met at once by an amendment, proposed by James Tallmadge of New York, that would have imposed, as a condition of admission, a congressional prohibition on the further introduction of slavery into the state and would have provided that children born to slaves after admission should be free at the age of twenty-five. The amendment had been promptly approved, and this had emboldened another antislavery New Yorker to propose that slavery also be excluded from the territory of Arkansas, lying to the south of Missouri. The session of Congress had come to an end before a final decision was reached on either the original bill or the proposals following it. But they had raised a sectional controversy, described by Thomas Jefferson as a "firebell in the night," involving not only the extension of slavery into the territories, but, equally significant, the balance of power in the Senate.

In the next Congress the struggle was resumed. On February 16, 1820, Jesse B. Thomas of Illinois proposed in the Senate a compromise to be written into a new admission bill. It would have permitted slavery in the state of Missouri, but would have prohibited it and involuntary servitude forever, except in punishment of crime, in all the remainder of the Louisiana Purchase north of the line of 36°30'. On the following day, while the Senate was acting favorably on the amendment, Tyler, in the House, delivered a fighting speech against any congressional measure which, in establishing a state, would require it, as a condition of admission, to give up its right to slavery. He pointed out that the right to slavery is a right of the state, protected by the Constitution, and he challenged encroachment on it by the measures proposed.

Tyler further believed that the western territories should be left open to slavery. Left open, they would draw to themselves the slaves from the worn-out soils of the southeastern states. A sparsity of slaves would ensue in the southeastern states, which, in turn, would be an incentive to emancipation, just as the sparsity of slaves had been an incentive to emancipation in the Northern states. If legislation closing the western territories to slavery were enacted, this beneficent development would be blocked.

Diffusion of slaves over the western territories would, moreover, be of immediate service to the slaves, both to those taken west and to those left behind: the former would share in the productiveness of virgin soils; the latter would have better care, since their sparsity would have increased their value to their masters.

Yet another glimpse of the future had moved Tyler in 1820 to ask the House not to close the western territories to slavery. If those territories were closed and the slaves remained cooped up in the Southeast, a "dark cloud" would form over those states before long. "Will you permit the lightnings of its wrath to break upon the South when by the interposition of a wise system of legislation you may reduce it to a summer's cloud?"[13]

---

13. Tyler's speech of Feb. 17, 1820 is in *Annals of Congress*, 16 Cong., 1 sess., vol. 2, 1382–1394. Throughout his life Tyler condoned and supported slavery though he was troubled about its righteousness. He held the British responsible

A precedent for Tyler's speech had been provided the year before by Henry Clay when he spoke to the House in opposition to the Tallmadge amendment. Clay was then Speaker of the House, which gave weight to his views. He believed that diffusion of slaves over the western territories would mitigate slavery's evils throughout the South. How it would do so is unclear, for the speech is not recorded in the *Annals of Congress*. Replies made to it by other members of Congress, however, show clearly that diffusion was Clay's remedy for the evils of slavery.[14]

This prescription was well known to Walker. What he contributed in his *Letter* of 1844 was to update it and apply it to the Texas issue. He envisaged the flow of slaves from east to west as ending in a concentration of them in Texas. The soil of Texas would ultimately be exhausted under the wasteful system of slave cultivation, and the plantation owners there would be obliged to emancipate their slaves. Texas would then, if admitted to the Union, make its final contribution to the solution of the nation's slavery problem: lying adjacent to Mexico, which forbade slavery, it would become a safety valve. The Negroes would simply cross the Rio Grande. All the explosive forces of slavery, free Negroes, and race relations would pass off quietly and automatically into Latin America. Northern humanitarians, concerned for the welfare of Negroes, would have special reasons for rejoicing, for in Latin America Negroes would find economic opportunities wide open, and, of even greater importance, an escape from the bars to racial equality, which in the United States would never come down.

The Walker *Letter* had an enormous distribution; according to a contemporary estimate, it had a circulation, in newspapers and pamphlets, of millions. Its distribution was said, in antislavery circles, to

---

for having fastened it on the colonies. He hoped to ameliorate it by spreading it thin over the western country. His anger was easily aroused, however, against Northern abolitionists who wished to eradicate it; he saw eye to eye with Northern doughfaces. At the time of the Mexican War he privately believed that Polk had thrust the fighting on Mexico, yet he gave public support to the war. His indignation was then directed toward Northern proponents of the Wilmot Proviso. His basic philosophy, like that of Northern expansionists, was that the solution of the slavery problem should be left to the future.

14. For press references to Clay's speech and excerpts from replies made to it in Congress, see James F. Hopkins (ed.), *Papers of Henry Clay* (Lexington, University of Kentucky Press, 1959–), II, 669–670.

have been stimulated by a "Texas fund" in Washington. It was the most cited of the writings on annexation in Congress and in the nation. If a vote on the treaty could have been taken in secret executive session, a majority sufficient for ratification, composed of Northerners and Southerners, might have been mustered.

The treaty came before the Senate on April 22, 1844. Its existence was, by then, an open secret. But neither its terms nor its accompanying documents, which contained intriguing references to the "authentic" information of Green and defenses of slavery by Upshur and Calhoun, were known to the public. All were sent to executive session of the Senate with a covering letter from Tyler, urgently recommending ratification.[15] Five days later an antislavery Senate Democrat betrayed the treaty and the correspondence to the press. In the revulsion of feeling that followed, the treaty was rejected on June 8 by a two-thirds vote. The issue then moved into the presidential campaign.

In the campaign the Walker *Letter* was spread before a wider audience and, if contemporary opinion is correct, tipped the balance in closely divided Northern states in favor of Polk—the annexation candidate—by holding wavering antislavery Democrats to party loyalty, while the Whig vote was split. Its ultimate effect appeared several months later when the Joint Resolution of annexation was passed by a lame-duck Congress in March 1845. The resolution was adopted by an ample margin in the House; in the Senate (which had overwhelmingly rejected the treaty eleven months before) it was adopted by a scant margin.

In 1847, in distributing credit to those who had brought annexation to fruition, Tyler gave prominent place to Robert J. Walker, "whose writings unveiled the true merits of the question, and, aided by the expositions of many editors of the newspaper press, brought the public mind to a just and sound decision."[16] The "just and sound decision"

15. Richardson (comp.), *Messages and Papers*, IV, 307–313.
16. *Niles' Register*, LXXIII (Sept. 11, 1847), 31. The President, according to his latest biographer, Robert Seager, *and Tyler too* (New York, McGraw-Hill, 1963), 215, never endorsed Walker's safety valve theory, "so far as it can be determined." This judgment ignores the letter here quoted and the public approval given the theory by at least two members of Tyler's cabinet, below, pp. 109–110. Seager observes on the same page that Tyler complained of Calhoun's having foolishly put the annexation negotiations on the narrow basis of slavery protection. This complaint, noted also by other biographers, came after the defeat of the treaty. Before that event the President did unquestionably appoint Upshur as

was the adoption by Congress of the Joint Resolution inviting Texas into the Union—the second of the rich fruits harvested from propaganda in the Tyler administration.

Propaganda as a tool in politics was not, in the Tyler administration, a new American development. It was as old at least as American history. Already in the clash between the American colonies and England preceding the American Revolution both contestants relied on it. In the contest over the formation and ratification of the Constitution it played a major role, as illustrated in the classic *Federalist Papers* of James Madison, Alexander Hamilton, and John Jay. In the controversy between the Federalists and Jeffersonians over the centralization of power in the federal government the famous Kentucky and Virginia Resolutions were a device employed by the Jeffersonians to crystallize issues for the voters. As the nation matured after the War of 1812 and turned its energies away from Europe, propaganda in politics became increasingly directed toward domestic issues.

The propaganda described in this volume was, however, of another type: it was directed toward issues at the same time foreign and domestic in character. The issue of Texas annexation was most clearly of this nature. It was foreign in that Texas, Mexico, and Great Britain were all foreign states; it was domestic in that it involved slavery and its extension, both subjects on which the sections and parties were bitterly divided. This was a combination offering an opportunity to defend annexation on the score of protection of slavery against foreign foes and at the same time to urge annexation upon the Northern audience on the score of the prospect of its effecting an early end to slavery.

The slavery protection thesis of the Green and Calhoun propaganda reflected a view of slavery that was gaining favor at the time among Southern slavery ultraists. Their view was that slavery, as maintained in the South, was far from being a necessary evil inherited from the

---

Secretary of State, knowing of his ultraism on the slavery issue, did approve Upshur's initiation of the negotiation with Texas on the ground of an alleged British threat to slavery in Texas, did name Calhoun thereafter, who reinforced Upshur's slavery emphasis, and did send to the Senate the telltale correspondence of both secretaries together with the treaty. Later, on April 17, 1850, Tyler wrote Webster (Tyler to Webster, John Tyler Papers, Library of Congress) a disavowal both of Upshur's and Calhoun's emphasis, but his inclusion of Upshur in the disavowal has not been much noticed by his biographers.

past, as had been commonly believed; it was, on the contrary, a positive good, both economically and morally. Green and Calhoun held that it was at least as beneficent in the returns it brought to labor as the wage system of the North and of Europe. Green compared slavery as it had existed in the British West Indies prior to 1833 with the system of free Negro labor following emancipation and showed that slavery had been superior in every respect. Calhoun compared the lot of Southern slaves with that of Northern free Negroes, greatly to the disadvantage of the latter. In one of the documents sent with the Texas treaty to the Senate he wrote: "On the other hand, the census and other authentic sources of information establish the fact, that the condition of the African race throughout all the States, where the ancient relation between the two has been retained, enjoys a degree of health and comfort which may well compare with that of the laboring population of any country in Christendom; and it may be added, that in no other condition, or in any other age or country, has the negro race ever attained so high an elevation in morals, intelligence, or civilization."[17]

A marked characteristic of the propaganda emanating from Tyler circles was its identification of Northern opposition to annexation with abolitionism, and of American abolitionism with British abolitionism. British activity was centered in London, where, in the early 1840s,

---

17. In the documents transmitted with the message to the Senate (see fn. 12) the evolution of the Tyler program of annexation is traced from the time of receipt of Green's "authentic" information to the submission of the treaty to the Senate. Upshur's dispatches are a full development of Green's thesis as to British materialism in seeking abolition of slavery in the world and in Texas particularly. They describe the disastrous effects upon the United States that would follow abolition of slavery in Texas and British dominance there. Calhoun's contribution was chiefly his defense of American slavery as a positive good, which appears in the famous letter from him to Richard Pakenham, British minister in Washington, written on April 18, 1844, four days prior to the submission of the treaty to the Senate. The letter took the form of comment on a dispatch from Aberdeen to Pakenham, of which a copy had been sent to the State Department at Upshur's request on February 26. Aberdeen had sought to make clear that, though the British government desired general abolition of slavery in the world, it would engage in no secret or underhand interference to further this humane purpose. He disavowed any improper interference in Texas, in particular, or any design of dominance there. Calhoun, in reply, turned the letter into an admission of improper British interference with slavery in Texas, which in turn made necessary the negotiation by the American government of an annexation treaty as a defensive measure. The view, quoted in the text, that American Negro slavery is a positive good, followed this argument.

world antislavery conventions were held, to which Americans were attracted. The presence of Americans at the conventions drew the fire of Green, who believed, as has been seen, that the British government was hypocritically using the antislavery feeling of its public as a cover for imperialistic and materialist designs and that the American abolitionists, cooperating with the British, were giving aid and comfort to the enemy. In a letter for the London *Times*, written in the autumn of 1843, he opened with a scurrilous reference to the Reverend Joshua Leavitt, a Boston abolitionist and editor of the *Emancipator* in attendance at one of the conventions in London, as a "degenerate American" and an "adjunct in manufacturing public opinion for England." He followed this with an assault on the genuineness of the British government's efforts to abolish slavery in Cuba and Brazil. An excerpt from the letter is worth citing as an indication of Green's aggressive spirit:

> You will here see that Sir Robert Peel places his refusal to repeal the discriminatory duty on slave grown sugar on the ground that it will aid you [British] in abolishing slavery, and is necessary to protect you from the imputation of being influenced by mercantile and pecuniary considerations; whilst Mr. Calhoun (and, I may add, such will soon be the opinion of the continental powers of Europe) looks to the manner in which that question is treated by your government, as conclusive proof that your persevering efforts to abolish slavery in Cuba and Brazil are attributable, not to any benevolent desire to ameliorate the condition of the blacks, but to a conviction that your scheme of emancipation [in the British West Indies] has entirely failed, and that the abolition of slavery elsewhere is indispensable to the prosperity of your colonies.[18]

The editor of the *Times*, who had printed a long communication from Green defending American state governments in default, or in repudiation, of their state bonds, indignantly refused to print this letter. He wrote editorially that he had never before seen concentrated in any one individual so great a quantity of "brass." "The gentleman's impudence amounts to a talent . . . We stare . . . at the mode in

---

18. The letter appears in full in the *Boston Post*, Dec. 14, 15, 1843. The letter of Calhoun to Green, referred to by Green, is published in American Historical Association, *Annual Report, 1899*, II, 545–547.

which this advocate . . . of a confederation of public bankrupts coolly turns the tables, and, without having or pretending to have a word of valid defense, begins lecturing us, his creditors, on the hypocrisy of our pretensions to philanthropy and the selfishness of our exertions to abolish slavery and the slave trade."[19] Green, however, was not abashed. He sent the letter to the *Boston Post*, an anti-British journal in Massachusetts, which he considered the voice of the Tyler-Calhoun faction of the Democratic party, and there it was promptly published.

A characteristic of the annexation propaganda flowing from Tyler circles was its selectivity as to audience. The audience to which Tyler sent the Calhoun thesis—that the Senate was obligated under the Constitution to protect slavery by ratifying the Texas treaty—was a secret session of that body. The expectation was that the public would not hear of the thesis until after the treaty had been ratified. On the other hand, the Northern public heard early and late the Walker thesis that annexation would produce an ultimate emancipation of the slaves, combined with present and future opportunities for its own enrichment.

Walker again exhibited this selectivity as to audience in a later publication. A few weeks prior to the close of the presidential canvass of 1844, while his *Letter* describing the wondrous potential of Texas as a "safety valve" was circulating everywhere in the North, a pamphlet appeared under the auspices of the Democratic Association of Washington, designed for reading by Southern Whigs. Entitled *The South in Danger*, it maintained that Clay was the candidate of Northern abolitionists, pledged to the destruction of slavery, and that any Southern Whig, interested in preserving that institution, should move to the party pledged to the annexation of Texas and its candidate. The pamphlet was not signed by Walker, but was immediately recognized as his and was reprinted by Northern Whigs (with their own prefaces) in four large editions for distribution in the North. The intent was to show the hollowness of his argument on the future of slavery in his earlier *Letter*.[20]

19. London *Times,* Nov. 14, 1843.
20. [Robert J. Walker,] *The South in Danger* (Washington, Sept. 25, 1844). For a list of the Whig reprints see Thomas W. Streeter, *Bibliography of Texas 1795–1845* (5 vols., Cambridge, Mass., Harvard University Press, 1955–1960), Part III, vol. 2, 450–452. One Whig reprint was published by a Whig congressman, Willis Green of Kentucky, chairman of the Whig Congress Committee. It contained a foreword by Green, dated October 1, 1844, naming Walker as the author and

The same tailoring of propaganda to audience was evident in the case of Maine. The boundary there was an internationally explosive issue, made more so because it was complicated by the doctrine of states' rights which had been, and might easily become again, explosive in American politics. The solution for the problem adopted by the administration was to defuse the states' rights doctrine—which the President normally considered basic—by a local application of propaganda financed by the secret fund of the executive for foreign intercourse. It was a strange solution for a President who prided himself on political consistency, but it did have the merit of preserving peace.

On the other hand a national audience was always chosen for selected topics of propaganda. One such topic was the wrongs and barbarities that the American people had suffered in the past at the hands of the British and would suffer again if they were allowed to press closer upon the United States through their relationship with Texas and their position in the Oregon Country. If annexation should fail, Texas would become a British dependency, then a colony. It would be abolitionized and would, thereafter, be a base for the incitation of slaves in the South to insurrection. The wild Indians of Texas would become a scourge on American settlements throughout the Southwest, inflicting on them the accustomed Indian atrocities. Likewise, if the British were allowed to remain in the Oregon Country, the savages there and on the route to Oregon would destroy the trappers and

---

distributor of the pamphlet. It declared that Walker had "carried large numbers of it in person to the folding room of the United States Senate, and superintended the enveloping of them, with a watchful eye to prevent the escape of a single copy; and after the folding was completed, had the whole . . . sent to his boarding house. Having received several copies of this document, and understanding that Mr. Walker intended to circulate it only in the South, and to prevent, if possible its appearance in the North, I thought this surreptitious and partial circulation of it would be a fraud upon the American people." This statement was printed on October 2 in the *National Intelligencer,* the great Whig daily. Walker replied to it in a long letter appearing in the Washington *Globe,* on October 3, 1844, acknowledging his authorship of the pamphlet but protesting that the distribution of it was not intended for the South alone. At a later date Southern historians, confusing the appeal of September 25 with Walker's earlier *Letter,* spread the baseless tale of two versions of the *Letter,* one for Northern and the other for Southern consumption. See John D. Shields, *Life and Times of Seargent Smith Prentiss* (Philadelphia, 1884), 348; and James E. Walmsley, "Presidential Campaign of 1844 in Mississippi," *Mississippi Historical Society Publications,* IX (1906), 192–193.

pioneers bound for that country. Walker was especially adept in spreading this type of fear propaganda.

In disclosing to the Senate that he had concluded an annexation treaty with Texas, the President sought to give the impression that he wished it to be ratified on broad national, not on sectional, grounds. Taking a cue from Walker, he stressed the material advantages that annexation would bring the North, but he took care, in describing Southern interests in the treaty, to refer to the documents that accompanied it.

Also, in submitting the treaty, the President developed a theme he had touched upon earlier in messages to Congress. He declared: "Our right to receive the rich grant tendered by Texas is perfect and this Government should not, having due respect either to its own honor or its own interests, permit its course of policy to be interrupted by the interference of other powers, even if such interference were threatened. The question is one purely American."[21] Any interference by other powers would, he implied, be British and would, if tolerated, violate the principles established by President James Monroe.

Once again, on June 10, 1844, after the annexation treaty had been rejected by the Senate, the President, in a message asking the House of Representatives for action by a joint resolution on annexation, declared: "The Government and people of the United States have never evinced nor do they feel any desire to interfere in public questions not affecting the relations existing between the States of the American continent. We leave the European powers exclusive control over matters affecting their continent and the relations of their different States; the United States claims a similar exemption from any such interference on their part."[22]

The President was clearly seeking a bond to unite the country in support of his policy of acquiring slave territory, by quoting the words and program of the celebrated declaration of President Monroe.

---

21. Richardson (comp.), *Messages and Papers,* IV, 311. Earlier references to these interferences are in the annual messages of Tyler to Congress of 1842 and 1843, *ibid.,* 197, 261–262. For congressional speeches repeating the theme, see the debate over the Texas treaty in 1844 in *Cong. Globe,* 28 Cong., 1 sess., Appendix, 531, 721, 762; see also Dexter Perkins, *The Monroe Doctrine 1826–1867* (Baltimore, Johns Hopkins Press, 1933), 68–70; and *Mr. C. J. Ingersoll's View of the Texas Question* [Washington, 1844], 12–15.
22. Richardson (comp.), *Messages and Papers,* IV, 326.

When he was no longer President, Tyler offered revealing comments on his role as chief executive in the field of foreign affairs. He pointed out suggestively that in this field he had been freer of the furies of factional politics than he had been in domestic affairs. He took full credit for the favorable outcome of his foreign policy. He believed the Webster-Ashburton settlement was principally his contribution. Webster had done well, but had acted in all important matters under his direction. With regard to the ill-fated annexation treaty, he felt its failure had been due to Calhoun, who had overplayed the theme of the protection of slavery in the diplomatic correspondence concerning Texas. The successful Joint Resolution of annexation had been his recommendation to Congress.

Lyon Gardiner Tyler, son of the President, inherited these views and incorporated them in his *Letters and Times of the Tylers,* Volume II, published in 1885. They were carried into subsequent biographies of Tyler, but they did not impress biographers of Webster and of Calhoun, or, in many cases, writers on American foreign policy.

The reticences of the former President are as revealing as his claims to credit. He was reticent concerning his use of the secret fund for foreign intercourse to convert the public and government of Maine to a course he felt desirable. A congressional committee probed that subject in 1846, but aimed its questions at the activities of Webster, who was then still worth attacking. The complicity of the former President was doubtless suspected, and he did testify, but clear evidence to establish it remained hidden for a century and a quarter in the House manuscripts at the National Archives. Tyler's financing of Green's mission to London in 1843 was concealed from the Senate and from the public by Tyler's fiction, in response to repeated Senate inquiries, that Green had gone to England as a private citizen.[23] Not

23. For the unsuccessful efforts of the Senate to draw from Tyler the facts regarding Green's mission of 1843 to London and its financing, see *Senate Docs.,* 28 Cong., 1 sess. (Ser. 436), No. 351; and Richardson (comp.), *Messages and Papers,* IV, 327, 328, 360. An illustration of Calhoun's evasiveness on this issue is his letter to Tyler of June 3, 1844: "In reply, the undersigned has the honor to report to the President that, after diligent inquiry, no letter of the character referred to [Green's to Upshur] can be found on the files of the department, nor any evidence that such has ever been placed on them. He is unable to ascertain the name of the writer in question, from any documents in possession of the department; and presumes that the letter referred to in the resolution of the Senate, being 'private,' is amongst the private papers of the late Mr. Upshur." *House Docs.,* 28 Cong., 1 sess. (Ser. 444), No. 271, pp. 98–99.

until 1847, in a defense of himself against charges of critics, did Tyler make public his warm approval of Walker's *Letter*.

Tyler's aims and methods had a significance beyond the years of his administration. They remained as models and inspiration for Presidents of expansionist temper for the rest of the era preceding the Civil War. They served Polk particularly well; he sought, as did Tyler, to keep the peace with the British. His loud talk of "All Oregon" was no more than a political and diplomatic tactic. He was inexorable in pressures for territory southward. He relied, as did Tyler, on the help of Northern expansionists. Also, in directing propaganda and diplomacy, he depended on deep secrecy which sometimes failed him.[24] He outdid Tyler in one respect: he developed to the full the theme broached by Tyler and usable in both sections of the Union—that European interference in the New World, in violation of the principles of Monroe, imperiled the safety and republicanism of the United States and that security required the expansion of the United States over the endangered areas. Tyler had applied this rationalization to Texas; Polk extended it to most of the perimeter of the United States.[25]

The emphasis of Tyler and of his successor on southward as compared with northward expansion entailed risks. It aroused suspicion in the North, especially in antislavery circles. In these circles it seemed to fly in the face of world trends toward emancipation. It seemed a turning away from the unionism emphasized by Andrew Jackson. It prepared the way for the sectionalism represented by Jefferson Davis. All this was ominous for the peace of the Union.

24. Polk's reliance on secrecy is described in Frederick Merk, *The Monroe Doctrine and American Expansionism* (New York, Alfred A. Knopf, 1966), Chaps. 5, 9.

25. The London *Times*, the traditional thunderer against the expansion of slavery and demagogism of American Democratic Presidents, anticipated a rerun by Polk of the Tyler course. On reading Polk's inaugural address, its editor observed on March 28, 1845: "It must be acknowledged that Mr. Polk treads very closely upon his predecessor's heels. In the inaugural address . . . we find faithfully reproduced all the worst characteristics of the American statesmen who have been in power since the withdrawal of Mr. Webster from the cabinet . . . If Mr. Polk was chosen as the thorough representative of the party which makes slavery, repudiation and foreign aggression its claims to distinction, we are bound to acknowledge that he has not swerved from the intentions of his constituents. His language on all these subjects has the same unblushing impudence which belonged to his predecessors, and which we had fondly imagined no one else could rival; but in his mouth it has this very serious aggravation, that it convinces us he is prepared to begin where the others leave off."

Part One.
Propaganda for
Stabilizing the
Northern Boundary

Daniel Webster
and the Search
for Peace, 1841-1842*

In the first and second articles of the Treaty of 1783 closing the War of the American Revolution two prime aims of the United States were won: independence and a favorable set of boundaries. The boundaries appeared in Article 2, prefaced by the hope that, as drawn, they would serve to prevent all disputes on the subject in the future. That hope proved vain.

The northern boundary, as described in the treaty, took its departure from the source of the "St. Croix River," whence it was to go "due north" to the "highlands" separating streams flowing into the St. Lawrence River from those flowing into the Atlantic Ocean. In 1763 British administrators had designated these highlands as the line separating the province of Quebec from the provinces of Nova Scotia and New England. The due north line had been made Nova Scotia's western boundary in instructions to the Royal Governor of Nova Scotia in 1763. But neither the highlands nor the line had been surveyed.

The 1783 treaty line, after intersecting the highlands, was to run along their crest southwestwardly to the "northwesternmost head" of the Connecticut River then go down the middle of that river until it reached the forty-fifth degree of north latitude. Thereafter it was to follow this latitude until it intersected the St. Lawrence River. It

---

* A portion of this paper was read at a meeting of the Massachusetts Historical Society in Boston on February 9, 1956. No portion of it has been previously published.

was next to take the course of the St. Lawrence to Lake Ontario, then the middle of Lakes Ontario, Erie, and Huron (and the middle of their connecting waters) to Lake Superior, then northward of Isle Royal to the "Long Lake and the water communication between it" and the most northwestern point of the Lake of the Woods. Finally, it was to go, on a due west course, to the Mississippi River.[1] So clear did this line seem that no misunderstanding of it in the future seemed possible.

A standard map was used to make sure that the line would coincide with the topographic features of the country. It was a Mitchell map of 1755 which had been brought by later editions to 1775. Whatever defects were in the map were due to the wilderness character of the area apportioned and to lack of detailed knowledge of its topography. Principal rivers appeared on it in the right places, but their tributaries, even in the northeast, were approximated. Nomenclature was uncertain, and relief features such as "highlands" were vague. In the northeast streams were shown flowing in one direction to the St. Lawrence, and, in another, to the Atlantic, but how they were separated, whether by mountains or by watersheds that might, indeed, be swamps, was not revealed. Such omissions were major elements in producing the disputes that followed.

A dispute soon arose over which of the rivers flowing into Passamaquoddy Bay was the St. Croix shown on Mitchell's map and named in the treaty. In that locality two rivers flow into the bay, each at some time called "St. Croix." Of these the Schoodic, which lies to the west, was favored by the British; the Magaguadavic, which lies to the east, was favored by the Americans. Since the sources of these rivers were far apart, the dispute would ultimately involve thousands of square miles of territory. To settle the issue the two governments created a mixed commission, under the authority of the Jay Treaty of 1794, one member British, another American, and a third selected by the others. After several years the commission came to the conclu-

---

1. The treaty, with valuable commentaries, is published in Hunter Miller (ed.), *Treaties and Other International Acts of the United States of America* (8 vols., Washington, G.P.O. 1931–1942), II, 96–107. Mitchell's map is John Mitchell, "Map of the British Colonies in North America," described *ibid.*, III, 328–333. Miller quotes largely from the work of Colonel Lawrence Martin, then chief of the Map Division of the Library of Congress.

sion, based on archaeological evidence, that the Schoodic was the St. Croix intended by the treaty. At its source a monument was erected in 1798.

The next problem was to extend the line from the monument due north to the highlands. If those highlands could be located, the intersection of the due north line with them would be the northwest angle of Nova Scotia. This problem engaged the attention of the Jefferson administration in the spring of 1802. At that time James Madison, the Secretary of State, consulted James Sullivan, a native of the Maine district of Massachusetts, who had earlier been employed by the federal government as its agent on the St. Croix commission. He was a trusted public servant of Massachusetts and later its governor. In replying to Madison's inquiry he wrote that the highlands named in the treaty were those which the Royal Proclamation of 1763 had named as the southern boundary of Quebec. But commissioners sent to find them, he added, had found none. One of the commissioners had informed Sullivan that as far west as the upper waters of the Chaudière there were no highlands on the south side of the St. Lawrence, that the whole region was a vast high flatland, much of it swamp, from which rivers flowed in opposite directions, some to the St. Lawrence, others to the Atlantic Ocean. This description had been confirmed to Sullivan by Indians acquainted with the region. Should these accounts be found correct, nothing could be done, Sullivan wrote, but to appoint a commission to ascertain the location of the line of the highlands. He believed that, though no chain of mountains meeting the requirement of highlands in the treaty was to be found, yet there were eminences from which a horizon could be made to fix the latitude from quadrant observations. He added a wry comment, which proved to be one of the understatements of the age, that the line would not be "easy to discover."[2]

In the light of this testimony, and more to the same effect, Madison undertook to obtain a convention with the British providing for commissions to run surveys and to settle all the boundary controversies, from the one in the east concerning the highlands to the one in the west concerning a "boundary gap" between the Lake of the Woods

2. *American State Papers Foreign Relations* (4 vols., Washington, 1832–1834) [hereafter cited as *A.S.P., F.R.*], II, 586–587.

and the Mississippi River. He wrote the American minister in London on June 10, 1802, by way of instruction, that the highlands in the northeast are "now found to have no definite existence." He wished the point to be determined at which the line from the St. Croix monument reached the highlands, with due regard to the general idea that the highlands meant the "elevated ground dividing the rivers falling into the Atlantic from those emptying themselves into the St. Lawrence." He desired adjustments to be made, also, in the treaty provisions regarding the northwesternmost head of the Connecticut River and the boundary gap in the Northwest.[3]

The American minister and the British Secretary for Foreign Affairs drew up a convention on May 12, 1803, authorizing the appointment of commissions for these purposes, which Jefferson approved. In a message to Congress of October 17, 1803, he recommended ratification of the convention, observing that new knowledge of the ground in the northeastern and northwestern parts of the United States had "evinced that the boundaries established by the Treaty of Paris between the British territories and ours in those parts were too imperfectly described to be susceptible of execution." He believed the procedure of the new convention promised "a practical demarcation of those limits to the satisfaction of both parties."[4] His endorsement did not satisfy the Senate, which rejected the section of the convention relating to the Northwest boundary gap, and in doing so rejected the entire instrument.[5] The boundary problems remained unresolved, and, in the meantime, other problems produced the War of 1812.

During that war the British found themselves more than normally dependent on overland communication from the Bay of Fundy to the city of Quebec. The St. Lawrence, which served them well during the open season, was closed by ice during the winter, and the winter was long. Along the lower St. John the overland road ran through settled territory where it was sufficiently guarded, but along the upper

---

3. *Ibid.*, 585. The boundary gap lay between "the most north-western point of the Lake of the Woods" and the Mississippi River. The Lake of the Woods lies well to the north of the source of the Mississippi, and a line drawn due west from any point on that lake would meet no part of the river. The issue was settled in the Treaty of 1818, Article 2. See Miller (ed.), *Treaties*, II, 659.

4. James D. Richardson (comp.), *Messages and Papers of the Presidents* (10 vols., Washington, G.P.O., 1896–1898), I, 359.

5. *Journal of the Executive Proceedings of the Senate* (Washington, 1828–   ), I, 463.

river it was less so.[6] It ran there along the northern bank of the St. John to the Madawaska River, followed that stream and the west bank of Lake Temiscouata to the Temiscouata Portage, and thence to the St. Lawrence. That road would be severed if the American claim, under the treaty of 1783, were to be recognized as projecting northward beyond the St. John toward the St. Lawrence. In the peace negotiations at Ghent the British sought a "rectification" of the highlands provision of the treaty, but they found the American delegates wary of the idea.

In the peace treaty the boundary problems on the northern frontier were referred to a series of joint commissions—a commission for each disputed segment of the line from the St. Croix monument to the Lake of the Woods.[7] The treaty was remarkable in Anglo-American diplomacy for the number of its authorizations of commissions to resolve boundary disputes. If an authorized commission should fail to come to an agreement on the issue assigned to it, the next step was to be arbitration by some friendly sovereign or state. No authorized commission was directed to a more pressing problem than that of the Northeastern boundary.

To that commission the American appointee was Cornelius P. Van Ness, a Vermont jurist and politician. His British counterpart was Thomas Barclay, earlier associated with the St. Croix commission. These two labored from 1816 to 1821 with exploratory surveys, conferences, and preparation of reports. Their only achievement was further confusion.

Van Ness drew a line from the monument at the source of the St. Croix due north to the highlands, which he considered to be grounds sufficiently elevated to send waters both to the St. Lawrence River and to the Atlantic Ocean. Highlands were not, he thought, necessarily mountains or hills. His due north line went to the elevated grounds from which the Metis River flowed into the St. Lawrence and the Restigouche flowed into an arm of the Atlantic, known as the Bay of Chaleurs. The length of the line from the monument was 144 miles. The highlands so reached were followed southwestward to the north-

6. In the terminology of the period the upper St. John was that part of the river above Grand Falls, and the lower river was the part below the Falls. The lower river flowed southeastward, through British territory, to the Bay of Fundy.

7. John B. Moore, *International Arbitrations* (6 vols., Washington, G.P.O., 1898), I, 69–70; Miller (ed.), *Treaties*, II, 574–582.

westernmost head of the Connecticut River. This left to the British, in the north, where as much room as possible was desired, a narrow space indeed. In some places the line was not more than thirteen miles from the St. Lawrence.

Barclay believed highlands could mean only mountainous elevations in a series. He thought the series need not necessarily lie in a continuous line. His line ran north from the St. Croix monument, a distance of only forty miles, to an elevation called "Mars Hill." Then it passed from hill to hill, in a rather zigzag course, westward to Metjarmette Portage, then southwestward along highlands, upon which he and Van Ness were agreed, to the headwaters of the Connecticut. There he chose as the northwesternmost head the one more advantageous to the British than that chosen by Van Ness.

The lines set up by these conflicting reports fixed the claims of the two governments at their full. The claims remained in that state to 1842, representing a dispute over territory amounting to 12,027 square miles.[8]

The economic goals the Americans particularly sought in the disputed area were, in the first place, the basin of the Aroostook, a western affluent of the St. John, attractive for lumbering and very fertile in soil. Its population was American—loggers and farmers. Other goals were the Madawaska settlements which lay on both sides of the upper St. John, stretching eastward for a distance of forty miles from the entrance of the Madawaska River. Though its people were Acadians, brought to the region after the American Revolution by Sir Frederick Haldimand, the Governor-General of Canada, to guard the route to Quebec, they were believed by American expansionists to wish escape from British dominion. Their lands were rich and were used both for farming and for lumbering. Other tributaries of the St. John desired especially for lumbering by Americans were the Fish, the St. Francis, and the Allegash. One of the prime American objectives lay outside the part of Maine actually claimed: free navigation of the lower St. John, which seemed of particular importance to settlers in the Aroos-

8. Moore, *International Arbitrations,* I, 136, 171–190. For later use of the Van Ness and the Barclay reports, see [Albert Gallatin and William P. Preble,] *North Eastern Boundary Arbitration* (Washington, 1829–1831), *passim;* and Albert Gallatin, *The Right of the United States to the North-Eastern Boundary Claimed by Them* (New York, 1840).

took Valley.[9] This could be obtained only if, by agreement, the United States were to acquire a footing on the upper St. John.

The assets most sought by the British in the disputed area were, in order of importance, an extent of territory north of the St. John sufficiently wide to provide safety, in time of war, for the route connecting the Bay of Fundy with the city of Quebec—nothing was more important than that route—the only all-year connection from the ocean to inland Canada. The area necessary to ensure its safety was thought by the military experts to be everything from the northern bank of the St. John to the southern bank of the St. Lawrence. Next in order, the Madawaska settlements, clinging to the upper St. John on both its banks above the Grand Falls, seemed to British imperialists necessary to hold as a matter of honor inasmuch as their people were subjects of the Crown.[10] The timber remaining on the upper St. John and its tributaries was an asset, but of less importance.

Since division of these assets by the commission procedure had failed, the next step, as prescribed under the Treaty of Ghent, was arbitration by some friendly sovereign or state. Neither side pressed this vigorously. But in 1827 a new convention was concluded in London, which Albert Gallatin, a signer of the Treaty of Ghent, accepted for the United States. It provided that an arbitrator, yet to be chosen, should decide two unsettled issues named in Article 5 of the Treaty of Ghent: the northwest angle of Nova Scotia, involving location of the highlands; and the northwesternmost head of the Connecticut River. The convention provided, also, that each side submit its evidence to the arbitrator and that his decision be binding.

The words of the convention indicated an awareness of the complications and magnitude of the arbitrator's work. They did so in describing the preceding commission's efforts: "The Reports and Documents of the Commissioners appointed to carry into execution the 5th Article of the Treaty of Ghent, being so voluminous and complicated, as to render it improbable that any Sovereign or State should be willing or able to undertake the office of investigating and arbitrating upon them, it is hereby agreed to substitute for those Reports, new and

9. The confluence of the Aroostook and the St. John rivers was in undisputed British territory.

10. Thomas Le Duc, "The Maine Frontier and the Northeastern Boundary Controversy," *American Historical Review*, LIII (Oct. 1947), 30–41.

separate Statements of the respective cases severally drawn up by each of The Contracting Parties in such form and terms as each may think fit."[11]

This convention was ratified by both sides, and the King of the Netherlands was chosen as arbiter.[12] Late in 1827 President Adams appointed Gallatin to be head of the delegation to prepare the American case, with William Preble, a justice of the Maine Supreme Court, as his associate. Gallatin gave to the preparation of the case two years of intensive labor, to say nothing of Preble's labor.

The principal thesis of his case when submitted was that the line named in the Treaty of 1783 was, indeed, ascertainable; it was the line already laid out in the Van Ness report. The line ran from the St. Croix monument to the highlands, which Gallatin thought lay where a stream tributary to the St. Lawrence (the Metis) and a stream flowing into the Atlantic (the Restigouche) moved in opposite directions. These highlands had been designated as separating Nova Scotia from Quebec already in 1763, in the Royal Proclamation of that year. They formed a leg of the northwest angle of Nova Scotia, the other leg being the line due north from the St. Croix monument. The northwest angle of Nova Scotia was reciprocal to the "northeast angle" of Maine. The apexes of both angles, Gallatin maintained, were identical. All maps published in England from 1763 to 1781 showed this to be the case.

Gallatin listed nineteen such maps.[13] His government, he declared, had found, among published maps of the period, none contradicting this mass of evidence. From this demonstration of the highlands as located at the northeast, Gallatin traced them through to the southwest. Throughout, they were shown to be elevated grounds separating streams flowing into the St. Lawrence River from those flowing into the Atlantic Ocean. A distinction was drawn between the St. Lawrence River and the Gulf of St. Lawrence which was an arm of the Atlantic. Flowing into the "river" in the northeast was the Metis. Into an arm

11. Miller (ed.), *Treaties*, III, 319–385. A more graphically written appraisal of the complications and laboriousness of the work appears in an instruction by John Quincy Adams to Richard Rush of June 25, 1823, *A.S.P., F.R.*, V, 523–527.

12. J. Q. Adams, though normally dubious of the goodwill of European monarchs toward the United States, nevertheless assented to the King of the Netherlands as arbiter.

13. [Gallatin and Preble,] *North Eastern Boundary Arbitration*, 30–31.

of the Atlantic—the Bay of Chaleurs—flowed the Restigouche. The elevation between them was the highlands of the treaty. Further inland, the upper waters of the Du Loup River, and those of the Chaudière, flowed into the St. Lawrence. The upper waters of the St. John, Penobscot, and Connecticut flowed into the bays, gulfs, and inlets of the Atlantic. It was the destination of the flow of waters from either side of the highlands that determined the location of the highlands. This was the essence of the American case.

As for the provision of the Treaty of 1783 regarding the northwesternmost head of the Connecticut River, Gallatin pointed out that the term recognized the existence of several heads and that, in making a choice among them, the northwesternmost had to be taken. This meant that Hall's Stream must have been the one intended by the treaty for the boundary.

The British case was a restatement of Barclay's report. It drew a line from the St. Croix monument northward to Mars Hill and thence westward so as to bring within the British claim the whole of the drainage basin of the St. John. The northern half of the basin would provide a space wide enough for the safety of the road connecting the maritime provinces with the city of Quebec. The southern half would give the British even the valley of the Aroostook, settled by Americans. The British case made claim, also, to all the western tributaries of the upper Connecticut.

In a counterstatement Gallatin was caustic as to Mars Hill and its line. That hill, he observed, was an isolated elevation. Neither it nor the line anchored to it was near the waters of any river other than tributaries of the St. John. It was at least a hundred miles distant from the waters of any river flowing into the St. Lawrence. The Gallatin case, in its positive and negative argument, was a model of research, penetration of analysis, and lucidity of presentation.

In a notable historical work Gallatin is criticized for having "bungled the whole affair." The chief criticism is: "The most obvious inquiries would have turned up copies of Mitchell's Map that would have proved the American case completely; for example, King George's own copy, then available in the British Museum. Gallatin, with all his experience in public affairs, neglected to search even that far."[14]

14. Samuel F. Bemis, *John Quincy Adams and the Foundations of American Foreign Policy* (New York, Alfred A. Knopf, 1949), 478.

This judgment raises the question whether King George's own copy of the map was actually available in the British Museum at the time of Gallatin's labors on the case for the arbiter. The King's collection was removed to the British Museum in the summer of 1828. On July 12, 1828, the Trustees of the Museum adopted a resolution that no one was to be admitted to that collection unless brought personally by a Trustee, until the arrangement of the books was completed. Gallatin was not then resident in England. He had returned to the United States in the autumn of 1827 at the end of his mission and remained there throughout his preparation of the case of the United States for the Dutch arbiter. Had he dreamed that the collection of George III contained a Mitchell map with a red line favorable to the United States, and had he returned to London to consult it or had sent an agent to do so, a confession of the reasons for the consultation to a Trustee of the Museum would have been necessary, which would probably not have facilitated entrance to the collection. Eleven years after the collection came to the Museum a member of the British Parliament gained admission to it and learned of the presence there of the map supporting the American case. Promptly thereafter the map was removed to the privacy of the Foreign Office, at Palmerston's request to the Trustees of the Museum.[15]

The decision of the King of the Netherlands, handed down in 1831, was that it was impossible to trace a line fulfilling all the conditions called for by the Treaty of 1783. The King took the stand taken earlier by Sullivan, Madison, and Jefferson, whose opinions had been in part included in the British case. He decided that the highlands of the treaty simply could not be located—that they were neither north of the St. John, as Americans contended, nor south of the river, as the British contended. He further found that rivers flowing into the Bay of Chaleurs and into the Bay of Fundy could not be considered flowing into the Atlantic and that therefore the Restigouche and St. John rivers could not be considered as entering that ocean. He took the still more

15. Henry Adams, *Life of Albert Gallatin* (Philadelphia, 1879), 628–629. For valuable aid in describing the administration of the King George III Library and of its Topographic Collection, I am indebted to Helen Wallis, Superintendent of the British Museum Map Room, and to Edward J. Miller, Assistant Keeper, who is working on a history of the British Museum. Gallatin is also criticized for not having specified in the case he prepared that the Mitchell map used in the peace negotiation of 1782–1783 was the 1775 edition.

discouraging ground that no fresh topographical evidence or new documentary evidence could be turned up that would permit finding the boundary line intended by the treaty. He suggested, as a compromise, a line that, in effect, split the difference between the contending claims. His proposal was to draw a line from the St. Croix monument due north until it met the St. John River. Then the line would go up the St. John and its tributary—the St. Francis—to and along the divide separating the waters of the St. Lawrence from the waters successively of the upper St. John, Penobscot, and Kennebec, and thence to the headwaters of the main Connecticut. The line would then go down that stream to an intersection with the forty-fifth parallel and follow this parallel to the St. Lawrence. But at Rouse's Point, where an American fort lay three-fourths of a mile north of the parallel, in consequence of an early surveying error, the award would permit the fort, and a radius of a thousand meters around it, to remain with the United States.[16]

This award was immediately attacked by Preble, who had become the American minister at The Hague. Preble challenged the right of the King to hand down such a decision under the terms of reference specified in the convention of 1827. The King's authority ended, Preble maintained, as soon as he had decided that the language of the treaty could not be made to fit the topography of the country. No sovereign, Preble maintained, would have been entrusted by the United States with a right to hand down a definitive decision if the decision meant replacing the treaty line. Preble also objected to the line on other grounds.[17] He returned to the United States, after this challenge, to fight acceptance of the award.

The award was announced on January 10, 1831, and was brought officially before the American government in mid-March. It had, in the meantime, informally reached the Maine government, which promptly declared that if the federal government were to accept the award it would violate the constitutional rights of Maine. Under these circumstances the federal government maintained a strict silence until President Jackson in his annual message to Congress, of December 6,

16. Moore, *International Arbitrations*, I, 119–138. Of the 12,027 square miles in dispute the award would have given the United States 7,908 square miles.
17. *Ibid.*, 137–138. For the terms of reference, see Miller (ed.), *Treaties*, III, 319–385.

1831, made known that the papers relating to the subject would be sent by a special message "to the proper branch of the Government with the perfect confidence that its wisdom will adopt such measures as will secure an amicable settlement of the controversy without infringing any constitutional right of the States immediately interested."[18]

These very general words and the preceding silence of the government were reflections of divergences within the cabinet. Jackson would have liked to accept the award provided the Maine legislature could be brought to approve it. He was persuaded by the cabinet, however, to submit, not the award itself, but a request merely for previous advice from the Senate as to whether he should submit the award. In a special message he did suggest that the British government was disposed to find the compromise in the award acceptable.

In the ensuing Senate debate Peleg Sprague of Maine vehemently opposed giving the requested advice. He brought before the Senate resolutions of the Maine legislature declaring that any cession of the state's territory without its consent was unconstitutional.[19] The Senate, in turn, overwhelmingly adopted a resolution to the effect that it considered the award not binding and that the President should open a new negotiation with Great Britain to ascertain the boundary "according to the treaty of 1783." This vote was reached on June 23, 1832, fifteen months after the award had come to the American government.[20]

In the meantime a commission consisting of three members of Jackson's cabinet, headed by Secretary of State Edward Livingston, had

18. Richardson (comp.), *Messages and Papers*, II, 547.
19. *Register of Debates in Congress*, 22 Cong., 1 sess. (1831–1832), VIII, Pt. 1, 1399–1417 (July 10, 1832). Sprague's speech was a powerful presentation of Maine's case. It contained the assertion that the highlands provision of the Treaty of 1783 was objected to in the British Parliament at the time, on precisely the ground that it would cut off communication between the cities of Halifax and Quebec. The Senator pointed out that while the arbitration was proceeding the King of the Netherlands had lost the better half of his dominions by rebellion and had become dependent on Great Britain. The constitutional rights of Maine were vigorously set forth in the speech. Sprague's assertion that the treaty had been under fire in England in 1783, on the ground of severing communications, is borne out by a complaint of the Earl of Carlisle that the treaty makers had "through inaccuracy, or egregious folly, drawn such a line of boundary as delivered Canada and Nova Scotia, fettered into the hands of the American congress." J. Bew [ed.,] *Political Magazine and Literary Journal*, IV (1783), 131. See also Lord North in *Hansard's Parliamentary Debates*, vol. 23, 451 (Feb. 17, 1783). For the resolutions of Maine, see *Register of Debates in Congress*, 22 Cong., 1 sess. (1831–1832), VIII, Pt. 1, 1387–1388 (Jan. 24, 1832).
20. *Journal of the Executive Proceedings of the Senate*, IV, 263.

entered into an agreement of a quasi-diplomatic character with three representatives of Maine—Preble, Reuel Williams, and Nicholas Emery. The agreement was that Maine provisionally yield to the United States all its claim to soil and jurisdiction in the region north of the St. John and east of the St. Francis. It would receive as indemnity a million acres of unappropriated federal land in the territory of Michigan, the land to be sold as part of the public domain by the federal authorities, with all proceeds to be paid to Maine. The proceeds could have amounted to $1,250,000. The indemnity was, however, to be proportionately reduced if, in the anticipated new negotiation with Great Britain, Maine's territorial loss should be less than it would have been under the arbiter's award. Also, the indemnity was to be reduced if, in the new negotiation, British territory contiguous to Maine were won for the state. This bargain was approved in secret session by the Maine legislature on March 3, 1832, an important step toward its consummation.[21]

In view of the Senate's recommendation that a new negotiation directed to ascertaining the treaty line be opened, Secretary Livingston proposed this to the British Foreign Office. He suggested Washington as the seat of the negotiation. He held out the possibility that if the treaty line were not attainable in such a negotiation "more ample powers" might come to the federal government than it had hitherto possessed, as a result of an arrangement made with Maine. He suggested further that an item of importance in a negotiation would be a concession by Britain of a right to navigate the lower St. John which would be of benefit to both countries. This could have been construed as an intimation that a negotiation for a conventional line—a line of convenience—might be in the offing.[22]

Palmerston was uninterested. He replied on February 25, 1833, that the navigation of the St. John and a boundary negotiation were not necessarily connected with each other and that he could not consent to "mixing up" the two issues.[23]

---

21. *Resolves of the State of Maine* (Augusta, 1832–1835), 465–467; see also Henry S. Burrage, *Maine in the Northeastern Boundary Controversy* (Portland, Me., n.p., 1919), 195–216.

22. Livingston to Charles Bankhead, July 21, 1832, *Senate Docs.*, 24 Cong., 1 sess. (Ser. 284), No. 414, 8.

23. Palmerston to C. R. Vaughan, Feb. 25, 1833, *British and Foreign State Papers*, XXII (1833–1834), 793–796.

Maine proved even less cooperative. It withdrew on March 4, 1833, from the bargain its legislature had approved in secret on March 3, 1832. In doing so the legislature voted that no settlement reached by the federal government in a future negotiation "shall have any binding force, effect, or operation, until the same shall have been submitted to the people of this State in their primary assemblies [town meetings], and approved by a majority of their votes."[24] Maine thus clothed itself in the shining armor of states' rights as protection against whatever compromise the federal government might be tempted to approve in a future negotiation.

Jackson had clearly wished to accept the arbiter's line if Maine could somehow be satisfied. He believed the treaty line could not be implemented. He is reported to have said later that this, "the only occasion of importance in his life in which he had allowed himself to be overruled by his friends, was [the] one of all others in which he ought to have adhered to his own opinions."[25] He was reluctant to offend Jacksonians in Maine and yielded to their states' rights demands. In a few months he was to take stronger measures against the states' rights elements led by Calhoun in South Carolina.

Rebuffed by Palmerston and by Maine, and regretting that everything was now as it had been before the arbiter's award, Livingston still sought to implement the Senate's recommendation of a new negotiation to determine the treaty line. He proposed to the British minister on April 30, 1833, to do this by means of joint commissioners attended by an umpire selected by some friendly sovereign, who would be empowered to decide disputes, or alternatively, a commission composed of European experts, chosen by a friendly sovereign, and attended by agents selected by the British and American governments. In a further endeavor to convert the British to an agreement of this sort he suggested that the principle be adopted of drawing a line from the head of the St. Croix to the highlands, not necessarily due north

24. *Resolves of the State of Maine* (Augusta, 1832–1835), 580–581.
25. Jesse S. Reeves, *American Diplomacy under Tyler and Polk* (Baltimore, Johns Hopkins Press, 1907), 10–11. Jackson wrote Francis P. Blair ten years later: "I had determined to accept the award made by the King of Holland regardless of the remonstrances of Judge Preble, but my whole cabinet remonstrated against my decision . . . to lay it before them [the Senate]. I yielded to this recommendation, but sincerely have I regretted it since." John S. Bassett (ed.), *Correspondence of Andrew Jackson* (7 vols., Washington, Carnegie Institution, 1929), VI, 162.

but northeast or northwest, whichever was shorter, to the highlands designated in the Treaty of 1783. He confessed that the agreement that had been contemplated with Maine had failed and that therefore the treaty line was all the federal government could contemplate.[26]

This wavering on the part of Livingston between a treaty line negotiation and one for a conventional line was no mere indecision on his part. It reflected a clash between Maine, which was determined to have the treaty line, and those outside of Maine, who had become persuaded by a long history that a treaty line was unattainable. Livingston's proposal to seek a treaty line with the understanding that a joint commission might be authorized to abandon the prescription of a line due north from the source of the St. Croix, and to take instead a line deflected—a line obliquely drawn—to meet the highlands of the treaty, was virtually an offer to modify the treaty. He continued to press this proposal.

It was not well received by the British. The British minister in Washington discouraged any new attempt, either by commissions or by negotiations, to find the treaty line. He thought it would be "perfectly useless," and so did Palmerston; they were sure a search for a conventional line was all that was feasible.[27] For more than a year the governments made no progress, therefore, toward a compromise of their differences.

In the autumn of 1834 Palmerston did indicate a willingness to accept, since no hope remained of overcoming Maine's objections to a conventional line, a new joint commission of survey as proposed by the United States. He attached conditions, however, in addition to the concession already made by the Americans of a "western deviation from the due north line." The commissioners must be governed by principles settled in advance. Those principles were seven, as laid down by the Dutch arbiter. The two most important were that the American government admit as a fact that no highlands existed either north or south of the St. John which could be identified as those of the treaty, and that neither the Restigouche River nor the St. John River

26. Livingston to Vaughan, Apr. 30, 1833, *Senate Docs.*, 24 Cong., 1 sess. (Ser. 284), No. 414, 8.

27. Vaughan to Livingston, May 11, 1833, *ibid.*, 10; Vaughan to Palmerston, May 13, June 4, 1833, *British and Foreign State Papers*, XXII (1833–1834), 799, 809; Palmerston to Vaughan, Dec. 21, 1833, *ibid.*, 826.

was to be regarded as an Atlantic river in the sense of the Treaty of 1783.[28] These principles were not acceptable to the Americans.[29]

In the final years of Jackson's presidency American diplomats shifted a little from adamant insistence on a treaty line. They allowed the British to know that while the President must adhere to the treaty line, yet he would be happy to receive any definite proposition the British might wish to make for a conventional line and take the sense of Maine on it.[30] The initial British response was that a negotiation for a conventional line must be preceded by a clear definition of the term "Atlantic rivers" and also that Maine's consent to such a negotiation must be obtained. But by the end of 1835 the British minister in Washington relented enough to agree to a negotiation if it were to be based on the fair principle of division of the disputed area in equal parts; he suggested a line drawn due north from the source of the St. Croix until it intersected the St. John, then went up the St. John to its southernmost source, and on, from that point, to the head of the Connecticut River.[31] The American Secretary of State. John Forsyth, felt obliged to decline this proposal, but offered instead to seek consent from Maine for a line that would follow the St. John from its source to its mouth in New Brunswick.[32]

The British minister promptly rejected this proposal, described in the note of rejection as an offer of "utter inadmissability." An offer was made, however, to appoint joint commissioners with the understanding that they report the results of their labors to their governments, though they were without power to decide upon points of difference.[33] This in turn brought a request from the President to be informed how a commission empowered merely to report the results of its labors could lead to a settlement of the boundary dispute.[34] On this querulous note the correspondence in the Jackson period ended.

28. Palmerston to Vaughan, Oct. 30, 1834, *British and Foreign State Papers,* XXII (1833–1834), 857; Vaughan to John Forsyth, Dec. 8, 1834, *Senate Docs.,* 24 Cong., 1 sess. (Ser. 284), No. 414, 42.
29. Forsyth to Vaughan, Apr. 28, 1835, *Senate Docs.,* 24 Cong., 1 sess. (Ser. 284), No. 414, 46.
30. *Ibid.*
31. Bankhead to Forsyth, Dec. 28, 1835, *Senate Docs.,* 24 Cong., 1 sess. (Ser. 284), No. 414, 56.
32. Forsyth to Bankhead, Feb. 29, 1836, *ibid.,* 60.
33. Bankhead to Forsyth, Mar. 4, 1836, *ibid.,* 60.
34. Forsyth to Bankhead, Mar. 5, 1836, *ibid.,* 63.

The British government showed disinclination to continue the correspondence at the opening of the Van Buren administration. Palmerston seemed weary of it, considered it futile, and may have been annoyed by it. In the summer of 1837 he was jogged by the United States minister in London to reply to Forsyth's last proposal of February 29, 1836, but he paid no attention to it. Forsyth presently complained to the British minister in Washington that he had received no reply. The President in his annual message to Congress of December 5, 1837, indicated anxiety concerning the absence of an answer.[35]

The answer, when it came, twenty months late, was hardly calculated to assuage ruffled feelings. It opened with a lordly explanation, sent to the British minister in Washington, that "various circumstances" had prevented giving earlier instructions with regard to the boundary. Then it again ruled out the St. John line and set forth in detail all the objections to joint commissions: the treaty line was impossible to find, and, besides, there were constitutional objections from Maine to a conventional line. If the two governments were to appoint a joint commission, previous agreement would be necessary, and it would be indispensable that Maine assent to it.[36]

A new and more dangerous stage in the controversy now opened. Maine, Massachusetts, and New Brunswick all had made grants of land in the contested area. Settlers had come to exploit the grants. Timber thieves from New Brunswick swarmed over the area. Ejections and arrests on the ground of trespass followed. Early ejections were made under the authority of Maine; arrests were made under the authority of New Brunswick. An armed posse was sent by Maine, accompanied by a land agent, to discourage timber thieving and assert authority. British troops were summoned by New Brunswick. Maine summoned its militia. Van Buren reported the crisis to Congress in a special message (February 26, 1839), in which he mentioned an urgent request of the Maine governor for military aid. He tactfully reminded Maine of the nation's solicitude for the preservation of peace and of his

35. For American efforts to extract an answer from Palmerston, see *House Exec. Docs.*, 25 Cong., 1 sess. (Ser. 311), No. 31; *British and Foreign State Papers*, XXV (1836–1837), 909; Richardson (comp.), *Messages and Papers*, III, 374.

36. Palmerston to H. S. Fox, Nov. 19, 1837, *British and Foreign State Papers*, XXV (1836–1837), 910. The dispatch apparently arrived just after Van Buren's message went to Congress.

reluctance to use the military power of the federal government to aid in a state attempt to take possession of territory that was still a subject of negotiation. Yet Congress voted a war credit of ten million dollars and empowered the President to enroll fifty thousand volunteers. The drift to war was clear.[37] Only the moderation of Van Buren, the tactful mediation of General Winfield Scott, whom the President sent to the troubled area, and the cooperation of the Lieutenant Governor of New Brunswick restored an uneasy truce. It became the fashion in some quarters to ridicule the "Aroostook War" as a war without bloodshed, but to the sober-minded in the United States it seemed alarming enough.

In the course of these troubles the Maine legislature had confirmed its earlier reputation for being difficult to deal with. It stubbornly adhered to the view that the treaty line could be ascertained and that the federal government was obligated to resist British invasion of the disputed area. The legislature had gone so far as to resolve in the spring of 1838 under the promptings of its Whig governor, Edward Kent, that it would not accept any negotiation by the federal government for a conventional line. Also, it stated that it had never agreed to the appointment of an arbiter. It requested the state delegation in Congress to press for a new survey. If a new commission of survey were not appointed before September 1, 1838, the imperative duty of the Governor would be to appoint a state commission for

37. For a detailed account of the drift toward war and its halt under the *modus vivendi* of March 1839, arranged by Scott, see the congressional documents of the period, especially:
House Exec. Docs., 25 Cong., 1 sess. (Ser. 311), No. 31;
House Exec. Docs., 25 Cong., 2 sess. (Ser. 326), No. 126;
House Exec. Docs., 25 Cong., 2 sess. (Ser. 330), No. 380;
Senate Docs., 25 Cong., 3 sess. (Ser. 339), No. 35;
House Exec. Docs., 25 Cong., 3 sess. (Ser. 347), No. 181; (Ser. 348), No. 222;
Senate Docs., 26 Cong., 1 sess. (Ser. 356), No. 107;
House Exec. Docs., 26 Cong., 1 sess. (Ser. 357), No. 129; (Ser. 366), No. 169;
and Richardson (comp.), *Messages and Papers*, III, 404–412, 516–520. The more important of these documents are gathered in W. R. Manning (ed.), *Diplomatic Correspondence of the United States, Canadian Relations, 1784–1860* (3 vols., Washington, Carnegie Endowment, 1940–1943), III, 3–189. For a summary, see John F. Sprague, *The Northeastern Boundary Controversy and the Aroostook War* (Dover, Observer Press, 1910). The British correspondence for 1838–1839 is gathered in *Parliamentary Papers, 1840*, XXXII, "North American Boundary, Part 1," 1–168, and for 1842–1843, *ibid., 1843*, LXI, 9–267. Good surveys by Canadian scholars are A. B. Corey, *The Crisis of 1830–42* (New Haven, Yale University Press, 1941); and J. Mackay Hitsman, *Safeguarding Canada, 1763–1871* (Toronto, University of Toronto Press, 1968), Chaps. 6, 7.

locating the boundary and to cause the same to be carried into operation. These resolutions were sent to the President and were published in the congressional documents. Their meaning was that the state would survey the boundary and, with the aid of the federal government, would enforce it.[38]

On March 18, 1840, Governor Kent's Democratic successor, John Fairfield, approved a belligerent set of resolutions by the legislature declaring that unless the British government should make a distinct and satisfactory proposition during the present session of Congress for the immediate adjustment of the boundary, the duty of the federal government would be to take possession of the disputed territory, and, if the federal government should flinch, it would become the imperative duty of Maine to assume the defense of the honor of the state and nation and expel from its limits whatever British troops were quartered there.[39] The resolutions reflected the fact that war feeling was again on the increase.

Such a temper contrasted sharply with that of Massachusetts, another of the parties to the dispute. Massachusetts had a half interest in the unappropriated lands in the disputed region, under an agreement made with Maine as part of the separation. Its authorities had exhibited for the most part a spirit of forbearance and restraint.

The intransigence of Maine was a reflection of local politics. Political parties in the state were closely divided between Democrats and

38. *Resolves of the State of Maine* (Augusta, 1836–1838), 343–344.

39. *Acts and Resolves of the State of Maine* (Augusta, 1840), 226–227. The response given by the peace-minded in the United States to such sentiments is indicated in an article appearing originally in the Washington *Madisonian* and reprinted in a number of the journals of Maine. The article, said to have been by the editor of the *Madisonian,* proposed three alternatives for the solution of the boundary controversy: let the American government propose to accept the Dutch award even at that late date; let the American government ask the consent of Maine to enter on a new discussion for settlement with full power to make a settlement; "In case of refusal on the part of Maine—let the Congress inform Maine that she must manage the matter in her own way, and if she chooses, fight Great Britain 'on her own hook,' without any aid from the 25 states of the Union." This article called forth from the aggressive Portland *Eastern Argus,* after reprinting it, the comment: "These suggestions are so mean-spirited and degrading that we can hardly imagine them to come from any former citizen of our own state . . . Either, according to this treasonable adviser, she must be forced into a sale of her territory for British gold, or else she must be totally abandoned by the Union and left to battle for her dearest rights alone! Heaven forbid that sentiments like this should actuate the new Administration." *Eastern Argus* (d), Feb. 16, 1841.

Whigs. Elections to the legislature and to the governorship were annual, and the voting was so even that the balance normally shifted back and forth. Anti-British feeling was strong throughout northern New England, and the temptation existed in both parties to escape embarrassing local problems by emphasizing the foreign ones. Twisting the lion's tail was a national sport, played not only in northern New England, but elsewhere in the nation. Expansionism was pressed increasingly by Democrats in other states, and in Maine any yielding to the grasping tactics of hated Albion was considered proof of lack of spirit.

Maine took a legally strong stand. It was a joint claimant with Massachusetts to the soil in dispute, no part of which had ever been ceded to the federal government, and it was the sole American claimant to the jurisdiction of the area. Under the Constitution each state was entitled to federal protection against invasion. On this ground Maine could confidently expect help from the other states in defending its claim. In any crisis over an adverse treaty it could look for support to the Senate, the fortress of states' rights. In the Senate a two-thirds majority was needed for the ratification of a treaty. A majority of that dimension for an agreement denounced by Maine as a dismemberment of its territory was most unlikely. This meant Maine held a veto power over any boundary agreement with Great Britain with which it was dissatisfied.

In 1841, as a result of changes of government in the United States and Great Britain, an opportunity opened to clear away this ancient tangle. In the United States a Whig government came into office, and Whigs traditionally were readier than Democrats to seek harmonious relations with the British. Daniel Webster was the new Secretary of State. In Great Britain the Conservative party took office in August 1841; Lord Aberdeen, a man of conciliatory temperament and friendliness to the United States, was Secretary for Foreign Affairs. He succeeded the truculent Palmerston, who for years had stood in the way of composing differences. For the first time since Federalist days the governments on both sides of the Atlantic were simultaneously eager to clear away their differences.

The eagerness of the British government for a settlement was indicated as soon as it received a hint from Webster that he was ready for a new negotiation. A special mission was named at once with Lord

Ashburton at its head. He had been a defender of American causes in England for almost a half century, was a conspicuous champion of Anglo-American reconciliation, had participated in business relations with Americans all his life as a member of the great international banking house of Baring Brothers & Company, and was a personal friend of Webster.[40]

The Peel government wished the earliest possible opening of a negotiation. Virtually the whole Anglo-American boundary was in need of pacification. Westward of the Maine-New Brunswick area were border frictions on the upper waters of the Connecticut, on the New York frontier, on the Grand Portage west of Lake Superior, and in the Oregon Country. The more heated of these frictions threatened to erupt into violence. Maritime problems, equally dangerous, needed attention—problems resulting from peacetime "visitation" by British cruisers of vessels on the high seas suspected of being slavers and from the old related problem of impressment. One cause of tension was the *Creole* case. The *Creole* was a coastwise vessel carrying slaves from Virginia to New Orleans. The slaves had risen in mutiny, had killed one of the ship's owners, and had taken refuge in a British port in the Bahamas, where all of them, except the one who had done the killing, were freed. The need for a prompt settlement of all these issues was intensified by the political situation in Washington. The split between Tyler and the Whigs after Harrison's death imperiled Whig control in national affairs and endangered ratification by the Senate of any compromise treaty on the boundary that might be concluded. Ashburton was hustled off to Washington in February 1842, even before his instructions on the issue had been completed.

In Maine, in the meantime, a quiet process of preparing the state for a compromise of the issue was under way. It had been initiated by Francis O. J. Smith, an influential Maine politician, as early as the spring of 1841. His collaborator, who remained out of sight, was the Whig Secretary of State, Webster. Smith was a native of New Hampshire, born there in 1806, and educated at Phillips Exeter Academy. He had gone to Maine, following graduation, in search of fortune. In 1826, after reading law with the notable Portland legal firm of Fessenden and Deblois, he was admitted to the bar at the youthful

40. Frederick Merk, *The Oregon Question* (Cambridge, Mass., Harvard University Press, 1967), 189–215.

age of nineteen and soon built up a lucrative practice. He had political ambitions and by 1829 was already in public service. He won election in 1832 to the Maine House of Representatives. By 1833 he had risen to the state Senate, where he was honored by being chosen its President. He won a seat soon after in the lower house of Congress and remained there through the Twenty-third, Twenty-fourth, and Twenty-fifth Congresses. He early acquired sufficient capital to buy an interest in the Augusta *Age* and in the Augusta *Patriot*, and, in 1835, an interest in the influential Portland *Eastern Argus*. In 1838 he and the editor of the *Argus*, H. W. Green, became engaged in a heated political and personal controversy as a result of which the editor withdrew. Throughout the period of the boundary crisis, Smith remained part owner of the paper and as late as 1844 was corresponding with David Henshaw, the Boston Democratic leader, regarding its sale.[41] This newspaper connection was an important element of strength in his collaboration with Webster.

Smith had a record of freedom from dogmatic party regularity which was also an element of strength in the collaboration, though it was an element of weakness otherwise. He had been elected to Congress as a Democrat, but had early shown he was no emotional Jacksonian. He had parted company with Van Buren during the controversy over the Independent Treasury and the pet banks. His attitude was increasingly that of a prosperous lawyer and entrepreneur; he was interested in the growth of Portland's commerce, in the exploitation of the city's hinterland, in attracting railroads to his city, and in the spread of the magnetic telegraph of S. F. B. Morse through the Northeast. He held a substantial interest—a five-sixteenths share—in the Morse patent, which he had acquired in the course of financing Morse. In 1838 as chairman of the Commerce Committee of the House of Representatives he had brought a bill into the House for federal aid to the telegraph and in the same year had paid the costs of a voyage to Europe of himself and Morse to win European government support for the enterprise. He later was a contractor for building the experimental line from Washington to Baltimore in 1843–1844. He and Morse became alienated ultimately, but each won a fortune in the enterprise. The

41. Smith to Henshaw, Dec. 16, 1844, F. O. J. Smith Papers, Maine Historical Society. Early in 1842 Smith founded and became editor of the *Eastern Farmer*, a semimonthly, nonpolitical journal.

entrepreneurial interests of Smith were a factor in his desire for preservation of peace with Great Britain.

In the summer of 1838 Smith failed to win renomination as the Democratic candidate from his district for Congress. Instead, he was irregularly nominated for the governorship by a dissident faction of conservatives in the party. He was in Europe at the time and took no part in the campaign with the result that he won no substantial vote. In 1839, entirely at variance now with his former political associates, Smith founded the *Argus Revived,* a paper upholding the principles of the earlier and "better days" of the Democracy, and he supported the candidacy of Harrison and Tyler in the campaign of 1840. He helped to carry the state for the Whigs in that year and established standing as a man "between parties."

A venture into the banking field in April 1836 was a source of embarrassment to him in politics. In that era of speculation he and others established a "country bank" just outside Portland, at Westbrook, with a capital of fifty thousand dollars and an authorization to issue paper currency. The bank was in need of specie to satisfy state paper currency requirements and turned for aid to the Franklin Bank of Boston, which was a bank of deposit for federal funds. Smith obtained from it a loan of specie to the amount of fourteen thousand dollars and held it briefly until banking inspections required by Maine law had been satisfied. Then the specie was returned, and in its place a loan to the same amount in the form of a "blue book" was obtained. A "blue book" was a type of loan of doubtful legality under Massachusetts law. It rested on recourse to a broker or capitalist by a bank whose own credit was overextended. Such procedures were far from conservative banking, but were resorted to in an era of inflation, when bank morality was low.

The bank that had given these accommodations to Smith, the Franklin Bank, had once been in good standing. But it had fallen on evil days under a new set of directors and officers. In its quest of high interest and high profits it had made reckless loans. It permitted the specie deposited with it by the federal government to be loaned out for short terms to a succession of banks for meeting inspection requirements. It became the subject of an investigation by a committee of the Massachusetts legislature; the committee cited the loans to Smith in its report. The report appeared in the press of Massachusetts, Washington, and Maine by February 1838.[42] Though the Westbrook bank proved substantial enough to weather the financial storm following the Panic of 1837, the publicity given Smith's activities and his opposition to Van Buren's proposal of an Independent Treasury were factors in his lack of success at the polls in 1838.[43]

Webster, like Smith, suffered from unpopular bank relationships and from failure to obey party orders. As senator he had been an outstanding champion of the Bank of the United States and at the same time had been its paid counsel. He was a Whig, but not a thoroughgoing one. After the Clay-Tyler break over the issue of a "fiscal corporation," he braved the wrath of his party colleagues by remaining at his post in the cabinet until the Northeastern boundary issue should have been brought to a peaceful conclusion.

In the spring of 1841 Smith had been in Washington in search of appointment to office. His search was characteristically nonpartisan. He sought appointment to the office of clerk of the House. He desired appointment at the same time to the office of secretary of the Senate. He solicited Clay's help in that quest. Also, he sought appointment as a commissioner on the boundary survey in the highlands that Congress had authorized by an act of July 20, 1840, a survey that was already in progress.[44]

42. The report is No. 25 in *Mass. Senate Docs., 1838*. See also *ibid., 1834*, Report No. 50. For press accounts, see Washington *Globe*, Feb. 10, 1838; *Boston Daily Advertiser*, Feb. 3, 1838; Portland *Eastern Argus* (tw), Feb. 16, 1838. For the banking practices under discussion, see Fritz Redlich, "On the Origin of Created Deposits," *Business History Review*, XLIII (No. 2, 1969); also Wilfred S. Lake, "History of Banking Regulation in Massachusetts, 1784–1860" (Ph.D. diss., Harvard University, 1932).

43. Smith is a neglected figure in the history of Maine and in the history of the Northeastern boundary dispute. No critical biography of him has appeared as yet, though the basic materials for one are available in the voluminous Smith Papers. Extended obituary notices appeared in Maine papers after his death on October 14, 1876. Two in the Portland papers are especially useful: *Portland Daily Press*, Oct. 16; and *Weekly Eastern Argus*, Oct. 19. In the *Lewiston Journal Magazine*, Mar. 27, 1943, appears a valuable, somewhat jaundiced, sketch by Alice Frost Lord. For an account of Smith's relations with Morse, see Carleton Mabee, *The American Leonardo* (New York, Alfred A. Knopf, 1943), *passim*. The account is hostile to Smith.

44. U.S., *Statutes at Large*, V, 402, Chap. LII. Congress approved this survey in response partly to insistence by Maine, and partly as an answer to a British survey of 1839 by R. Z. Mudge and G. W. Featherstonhaugh that had been ordered by Palmerston. The printed report of the British survey is "North American Boundary, Part 2," in *Parliamentary Papers, 1840*, XXXII. Palmerston had sent the report, immediately on publication, to the American State Department where it was read with scorn. It had placed the northwest angle of Nova Scotia, in

He had a conference in Webster's home in May 1841 during which he outlined to his host a means of winning the adherence of Maine to the principle of a conventional boundary. He had earlier proposed this in a letter to President Van Buren, written on December 7, 1837, at the onset of the Aroostook disturbances.[45] He proposed to Webster that he quietly win key figures in Maine politics and in the press to the view that the state would find more advantage in a negotiation for a conventional line than in the stubborn insistence on the treaty line, which had hitherto brought only costs, delays, and disappointments.

The outcome of the meeting was that Smith was taken into Webster's confidence and into employment as a secret agent of the State Department for the Northeastern boundary. An advance payment of $500 was made him out of the President's secret, or contingent, fund, and he was invited to submit a plan of action for Maine. The plan was sent to Webster on June 7, 1841,[46] and was approved. Smith was to circulate quietly among Maine politicians and editors and convert them to the view that it would be to the state's advantage to consent to negotiate for a conventional line. Such a negotiation would be based on the principle of an exchange of equivalents in territory, with the understanding that any losses to Maine would be compensated by a pecuniary indemnity and, more important still, a cession by Great Britain to the United States of free navigation of the lower St. John. The compensation Smith suggested for his labors was $3,500 a year, plus ex-

---

reliance on "barometric observations," about halfway between Mars Hill and the St. John River. It added little in the way of argument or documentation to Barclay's report. Its chief author, Featherstonhaugh, had been a resident of the United States for thirty-five years, busying himself for a brief period as editor of a monthly journal of geology and afterward as a writer of popular works of travel on the West. He had been for a time employed as a geologist by the United States government. On his return to England in 1839 he was given an assignment by Palmerston as general agent for the Northeastern question in the Foreign Office. He was aware of the presence of the red line map of George III in the Foreign Office and withheld this crucial information from Aberdeen and Peel when they came into power. He reported it to Peel after the Webster-Ashburton Treaty had been ratified. For a contemporary comment on him by Edward Everett, see Miller (ed.), *Treaties*, IV, 408. For a devastating attack on his report, see Albert Gallatin, *The Right of the United States to the Northeastern Boundary Claimed by Them* (New York, 1840), 137–179; also "Report of the Commissioners for the Boundary, 1842," in Richardson (comp.), *Messages and Papers*, IV, 124–150.

45. See Documents, under date here given.
46. See Documents, under date here given.

penses, with authorization to employ assistants. The group was to circulate unobtrusively among the political leaders of the state and among editors of newspapers, spreading the word of the advantages to be gained in a negotiation for a conventional line. It was understood that full compensation would be paid from the President's secret fund on completion of the work. All this was approved readily by the Secretary of State and by Tyler.

A major consideration in Smith's mind was an endeavor "to adjust the tone and direction of the party presses, and through them, of public sentiment, to the purpose so desirable of accomplishment."[47] Personal conferences with editors were relied on for this. But Smith advanced the cause, also, by writing a series of three articles, bearing the general title "Northeastern Boundary—Why not settle it?" over the pseudonym "Agricola," and persuading the editor of an influential religious journal, the *Christian Mirror* of Portland, to publish them. The first appeared on November 18, 1841; the others followed at varying intervals.[48] They were repeated in text or in sentiment in other journals.

This well-integrated program went forward for ten months. It was climaxed by a letter that Webster sent Governor Fairfield on April 11, 1842, of which he had informed Smith the preceding day.[49] Webster's letter was sent a week after Ashburton's arrival in Washington. It gave the Governor notice that a new, direct negotiation with the British was about to open. An agreement on a conventional settlement favorable to the United States had thus become possible. If the negotiation should fail, the next step would have to be submission of the issue once again to arbitration. The federal government was obligated by treaty to resort to arbitration if other means failed, and the President believed that this obligation must be honored. But another arbitration would be time consuming, expensive, and uncertain of result. It would probably entail more surveys, more hearings, and more reports. Seven or eight years might be consumed in these labors, perhaps again without result. The letter was a skillful play upon Maine's aversion to, almost horror of, another arbitration. A direct negotiation would offer escape from this quagmire. The state was invited to take part in the negotiation in the persons of commissioners whom it would appoint.

47. See Documents, under date Aug. 12, 1842.
48. See Documents, under dates Nov. 18, Dec. 2, 1841, Feb. 3, 1842.
49. See Documents, under date here given.

It would be understood that the goal of the negotiation would be a conventional line and that the commissioners would be empowered by their signatures to commit the state. The Governor was asked to call a special session of the legislature to consider the new mode of procedure.[50] A similar letter was sent to the Governor of Massachusetts.

The Governor of Maine was easily persuaded of the force and truth of Webster's argument. Indeed, he hardly needed to be persuaded. He had heard such views for months from the people of Maine, Democrats and Whigs alike. Editors and politicians of both parties had abandoned their intransigence on the boundary issue. A consensus seemed to have been reached in favor of a negotiation for a conventional line. On April 29, 1842, a fortnight after the receipt of Webster's letter, the Governor issued a proclamation calling a special session of the legislature to meet on May 18.

In anticipation of the session Webster sent to Augusta an expert who had scholarly knowledge of the peace negotiations of 1782–1783—Jared Sparks, internationally known historian and distinguished professor, soon to be President of Harvard, and editor of a twelve-volume series, *Diplomatic Correspondence of the American Revolution*. In 1841 he had found in the archives of the French Foreign Office a map on which the boundaries of the United States were marked by a strong red line. He believed the map could have been one that Benjamin Franklin had mentioned as having been marked by him in December 1782. On his return to Cambridge he wrote Webster of the map and enclosed with his letter a recently published map of Maine on which he had drawn "a strong black line" corresponding with the red line he had found on the French map. His letter, endorsed by Webster "Very confidential," was in the State Department files two months prior to Ashburton's arrival in Washington. It fully supported the claim of Great Britain in the northeast. Sparks bore this terror-inspiring map with him on his trip to Augusta.[51]

50. *Works of Daniel Webster* (6 vols., Boston, 1853), VI, 272–275.
51. The letter of Sparks (Feb. 15, 1842) and the map are to be found in the State Department file classified as "Miscellaneous Letters" in M-179, Roll No. 96, National Archives. Webster allowed Sparks $250 for the map and the trip to Maine from the President's secret fund. He would have allowed a larger compensation, but President Tyler, to whom the suggestion was referred by the disbursing agent of the fund, wrote "I can only say that I should regard $250 to Mr. Sparks for the map fully enough. I do not doubt but that it will satisfy

Another map, the so-called Steuben map, was also exhibited confidentially in Augusta. A Mitchell map of the 1775 edition with a red line of unknown origin supporting the British claim, it had been purchased by Webster in 1838 from an heir of Baron Steuben. Soon afterward Webster had sold it to C. S. Daveis, an agent of Maine in Washington defending the 1783 treaty line, who put the map under wraps. Later, when Webster wished to use it to influence the Maine leaders to accept a compromise, Daveis (by this time a convert to the idea of compromise) transferred it to Webster and the State Department, receiving for it a payment of two hundred dollars from the President's secret fund. One hundred dollars more was allowed to Daveis for his travels with the map on Webster's behalf.[52]

Neither of these maps is now considered to have had any value as evidence of the intentions of the negotiators in 1782–1783. Neither was considered by Webster or by Sparks to have been traceable clearly to any of the peace commissioners of 1782–1783. But the two maps did indicate the confusion that any attempt to establish a line would run into if the case were allowed again to go to an arbitration. The Sparks map, exhibited in Augusta by a scholar of world repute, who had been sent by his government for the purpose of warning, was well calculated to produce apprehension in the minds of politicians as to the outcome of any future arbitration.

In addition to Sparks and Daveis, Webster sent Peleg Sprague and Albert Smith to work on the Maine legislators. Sprague had become, since his days of extremism in upholding Maine's claims, a federal judge in Massachusetts. His views on the boundary issue had undergone moderation as his years advanced. The allowance made to him

---

him. If otherwise we can see more about it." The map had been found, also, by agents of the British Foreign Office in Paris. See speech by Sir Robert Peel in *Hansard's Parliamentary Debates,* 3d Ser., vol. 67, 1248–1249.

52. These payments are listed in "Select Committee on Charges against Mr. Daniel Webster made by Mr. C. J. Ingersoll," labeled H.R., 29, No. 684, A-D, 24.1, National Archives. This is a manuscript report, to be differentiated from the committee's published report, appearing in *House Reports,* 29 Cong., 1 sess. (Ser. 490), No. 684. For a full record of the acquisition by Webster of the Steuben map, its subsequent sale to Daveis, and resale to the State Department, see C. S. Daveis Papers, Maine Historical Society; Miller (ed.), *Treaties,* III, 338–339; Herbert B. Adams, *Life and Writings of Jared Sparks* (2 vols., Boston, 1893), II, 400–406. A copy of the Steuben map is in the back folder of Volume III of Miller. The original is in the National Archives. For the earlier activities of Daveis as agent for Maine, see Burrage, *Maine in the Northeastern Boundary Controversy,* 229, 231–235, 244–245.

for his trip to Augusta and his services there was $250; he had estimated his expenses modestly at $30.[53]

Albert Smith was a former federal marshal in Maine and congressman from 1839 to 1841. He was a person of wide influence at the Maine capital, partly by reason of his abilities and his standing as a Democrat, but also because of his rare and genial humor. His efforts in the cause included two journeys between Boston, Portland, and Augusta and ninety days' service. He was allowed six hundred dollars from the secret fund[54] and, later, appointment to the profitable post of American commissioner on the joint Anglo-American commission to survey the boundary.

To this concentration of political and academic influence Governor Fairfield responded when the legislature convened in joint session on May 18. Giving up his old insistence on the treaty line, he observed in his message to the legislature that, if Great Britain was now prepared to offer to Maine, in exchange for a portion of its territory, an equivalent in British territory and free navigation of the lower St. John, he did not see why the vexed question should not now be settled. He therefore recommended the appointment of commissioners by the legislature with such powers as the case might require.

The legislature also displayed the effects of the new climate of opinion. It voted on May 26, 1842, to accept the Governor's recommendations.[55] It agreed to name commissioners who would represent the state in the negotiation. The commissioners were empowered to accept a conventional line based on an exchange of equivalents and to commit the state to it by their signatures, provided they should unanimously find the line advantageous. The vote by which these resolutions were passed was overwhelming.[56]

53. These payments are listed in the manuscript report cited above. The details of such expenditures from the secret fund and a large part of the testimony of President Tyler before the investigating committee were suppressed in the published report. They are restored to the report in the Documents section of this volume. Also Sprague to Webster, July 17, 1842, Daniel Webster Papers, Library of Congress.

54. For Smith, see William Willis, *A History of the Law, the Courts, and the Lawyers of Maine* (Portland, 1863), index; see index also for Peleg Sprague and other Maine figures mentioned here.

55. *Acts and Resolves of the State of Maine, 1842* (Augusta, 1842), 110–111.

56. The resolutions, framed by a joint legislative committee, and reframed from amendments proposed by both houses, won House engrossment by a vote of 177–11, and Senate engrossment, 29–0. Maine House and Senate Journals, May 21–26, 1842, mss., State Library, Augusta, Maine.

The legislature in joint session at once elected the commissioners: two Democrats and two Whigs. It took care to select only stout defenders of the state's interests. The Democrats were William P. Preble and Edward Kavanagh; the Whigs were former Governor Kent and John Otis. Their choice won general public approval. All the newspapers of the state except one supported the decisions reached.[57]

The Governor and the legislature were aware of Webster's agency in the calling of the special session. They were not aware of F. O. J. Smith's collaboration with Webster in preparing Maine's public for it. Webster knew, however, how significant the preparation had been.[58]

It is not necessary to conclude that the remarkable climatic change in Maine in the ten months prior to the decisive vote of the legislature was wholly, or even principally, the work of F. O. J. Smith and his sponsor. Changes in the climate of public opinion are the work ordinarily of basic forces, and this was true in the case of Maine. One of the forces was the Whig sweep of national and state governments in the elections of November 1840, which brought into control elements traditionally favorable to reconciliation with the British and tended to isolate extremism among Maine Democrats. Another of the forces was the economic collapse marking the period of the early 1840s following the Panic of 1837, the distresses in agriculture and in foreign trade, and the paralysis of state and national finances and credit. This created a yearning for peace with Great Britain as a restorative of economic confidence. Another force was the universal approval by the American public of the appointment of Lord Ashburton as head of the British

57. The commissioners were elected by separate ballots. Of a possible vote of 210 Kavanagh received 201; Kent, 198; Preble, 195; Otis, 178. Maine House Journal, special session, 1842, mss., 101–102. For public approval of the action of the legislature, see Burrage, *Maine in the Northeastern Boundary Controversy*, 326–327.

58. Webster, in a letter to Jared Sparks of March 11, 1843, jubilantly described these preliminary stages of the negotiation: "As to the *conduct* of the negotiation, there is one point on which I wish to speak to you very freely, even at the hazard of a well founded imputation of some vanity. The grand stroke was to get the *previous* consent of Maine and Massachusetts. Nobody else had attempted this; it had occurred to nobody else; it was a movement of great delicacy, and of very doubtful result. But it was made, with how much skill and judgment in the manner, you must judge; and it succeeded, and to this success the fortunate result of the whole negotiation is to be attributed." Daniel Webster, *Writings and Speeches*, J. W. McIntyre (ed.) (18 vols., Boston, Little, Brown, 1903), XVI, 397–398. The original of the letter is in the Jared Sparks Papers, Harvard College Library. The Massachusetts governor had authority, with the consent of the Council, to appoint commissioners.

mission to the United States and the confidence that he carried generous instructions for the settlement of the boundary dispute. The service
of Smith was to turn such forces in Maine toward acceptance of an
untried mode of removing an old source of disorder and danger.[59]

Four years after the conversion had achieved its purpose a challenge
to the mode of achieving it was leveled at Webster and at Smith.
The challenge was issued by a Democrat more than normally partisan
in temper and in reputation—Charles J. Ingersoll of Pennsylvania,
chairman of the House Committee on Foreign Affairs. He asserted
in a series of emotion-laden speeches in the House of Representatives
during the spring of 1846 that Webster and Smith together had "corrupted" the party press of Maine prior to the negotiation and had
done so out of the President's secret fund. Ingersoll had been admitted
to the secret archives of the State Department by a subordinate
while Buchanan was Secretary of State. He had found there a letter
that Smith had written on August 12, 1842, to Webster describing
his activities and costs.[60] Ingersoll demanded an investigation to which
the House agreed; a committee of five respected members was appointed to conduct the investigation. It called former President Tyler,
who came voluntarily and fully defended Webster's use of the fund

---

59. Smith's unobtrusive activity is reflected in the course of the *Eastern Argus.*
Until the spring of 1841 the paper's editorials and articles were charged with
belligerence on the boundary. In issue after issue the line of the Treaty of 1783
was pugnaciously demanded; any thought of compromise with the British was
denounced. After the conclusion of Smith's arrangement with Webster the paper
maintained for a time an unaccustomed silence on the issue. On December 8,
1841, it accepted, for reprinting, from the *Christian Mirror,* the first of the "Agricola" letters and gave evidence of a relenting spirit by declaring editorially that
if England would formally acknowledge Maine's right to the disputed territory,
"the nation will doubtless not object to treat with her on fair terms for the
angle of territory which she needs." By April 18, 1842, the editor hoped that
if the legislature were summoned to deal with this perplexing question no party
considerations would mingle in its deliberations. The question was not one of
party; it was purely national. "Every true patriot, to whatever party he may
choose to belong, should be ready to aid both the General Government and
the Government of Maine in all honorable efforts to bring this great question
to a bloodless issue." By June 11, 1842, the editor was ready to abjure all squeam-
ishness. "We think that a strip of territory on the St. John's [the Eel River
proposal], together with its free navigation and certain islands, may well be taken
as an equivalent for any [Maine] rights of jurisdiction; any lands belonging to
the British Government to be offset for an equal amount within the line of 1783
belonging to the United States; and . . . money may be received for the remainder
of the land."

60. See Documents, under dates Aug. 12, 1842, Apr. 27, 1846.

during his presidency. The committee summoned Smith, who testified under oath that he had not corrupted the party press and had merely written for a Maine religious journal three articles relating to the boundary problem.[61]

The committee in its majority report exonerated Webster of any wrongdoing in the use of the secret fund. It found he had received seventeen thousand dollars from the President, of which he had spent twelve thousand and had returned the unused balance of five thousand.

One member of the committee was Jacob Brinkerhoff, an Ohio Democrat hostile to Webster and to the British. He was an expansionist who wished to take from the British the whole of the Oregon Country even at the risk of war, but he had qualms as to the extension of American dominion southward over territory that would be given over to slavery and had voted against the Joint Resolution annexing Texas. He was in a hopeless minority on the committee, the majority of which contained two Whigs and two Southern Democrats.

His minority report, in which he took both Webster and Smith to task, contained a full copy of the letter Smith had written Webster on August 12, 1842, which revealed the fact of the Maine collaboration. As was intended, the letter received wide publicity. It appeared in the *Congressional Globe* and later in the *House Reports*. It was defended in detail by Smith in his testimony and later in his life, as the documents published here show. The letter sends a shaft of light into Webster's undercover preparations in Maine for the boundary negotiation.

The letter opened with a compliment to Webster for having brought a forty-year dispute to a close by adopting a "new mode of approaching the subject . . . while another forty years of circuitous diplomacy would have availed nothing." Then the subject of compensation was tactfully broached: "Considering the matter settled, I presume you can feel justified in enabling me to fulfil certain assurances which I made to a few individuals at different points in this State, whose services and influence I had occasion to resort to, in order to adjust the tone and direction of the party presses and through them of public sentiment, to the purposes so desirable of accomplishment under your administration. For my own services you can also make such allowance

61. See Documents, under date June 9, 1846—Smith's Testimony.

from the contingent fund as you may deem proper, merely remarking that all that was contemplated in my original letters to you of May, 1841, on the subject, so far as Maine and the voice of the people are concerned, has been happily realized."[62]

Secret funds were employed by Ashburton as well as by Webster in the preparatory stages of the negotiations. They were employed shortly after Ashburton reached Washington. To someone, not named, he gave £2998 1s. (approximately $14,500) to be used secretly. He disclosed this to Aberdeen in a note that was apparently destroyed on arrival. But on August 9, 1842, he referred to it again in a letter marked "Private & Confidential": "The money I wrote about went to compensate Sparkes [sic] to send him, on my first arrival, to the Governors of Maine and Massachusetts. My informant thinks that without this stimulant Maine would never have yielded, and here it has removed many objections in other quarters . . . I have drawn on you a bill for £2998.1—70 days sight for the purpose mentioned in my former private letter and you will find this put into proper form. I am not likely to want anything more."[63]

The private correspondence of Sparks contains no reference to a sum as large as $14,500 having been used to finance his mission to Augusta. He entered in an expense account, which he was in the habit of keeping, an item of travel costs to and from Augusta to the amount of $20. He was paid by Webster from the President's fund $250 for his trip and for his map.[64]

Who actually handled the money Ashburton wrote about, who suggested that it be employed in Maine, who in Maine distributed the money and who accepted it are questions answered nowhere; they are probably unanswerable. Secret funds are designed for purposes that are to be kept secret. Those used by Ashburton, with Aberdeen's approval, were employed for the same purposes, apparently, as those

62. This letter was published first in *Cong. Globe*, 29 Cong., 1 sess., 947–948 (June 8, 1846). It is reprinted in Documents, under date Aug. 12, 1842.
63. Ashburton to Aberdeen, Aug. 9, 1842, Aberdeen Papers, British Museum [hereafter cited as BM]; see also J. R. Baldwin, "Ashburton-Webster Boundary Settlement," *Canadian Historical Association Reports*, XIX (1938), 120–133; Bemis, *John Quincy Adams and the Foundations of American Foreign Policy*, Chap. 23 and Appendix 4.
64. Sparks Papers, 142E, 1837–1840. The account includes expenses after 1840. See especially entry under date May 21, 1842; see also Documents section of this book under date Aug. 24, 1842.

used by Webster with Tyler's approval. They were employed to disarm Maine, which had resisted, as the British knew, every attempt to settle the boundary dispute except on its own terms. They were designed to subtract from Maine the states' rights veto power it had been holding over any compromise settlement of the boundary issue.

Both Webster and Ashburton were undoubtedly guilty of improper use of secret funds in this case. Such funds are used by democratic governments to shape the course of foreign events or negotiations. Webster was using them to shape the course of state events, in a state that had made itself a menace to the peace of the Union. Ashburton used funds to the same purpose but at even greater hazard, for the funds he was employing in an American state were those of a foreign government with interests of its own to serve in the settlement of a boundary problem.

Ashburton's instructions on the boundary problem changed from time to time.[65] Those he carried with him from London, of date February 8, 1842, had been flexible. He was directed merely to avoid a Northeastern settlement less favorable than the Dutch award had been. Under that award the line proposed had been the upper St. John to a junction with the St. Francis, then along the St. Francis to the highlands marking the watershed of the St. Lawrence, then the line of the highlands to the source of the mainstream of the Connecticut.

Instructions, much hardened, were sent out at the end of March. Ashburton was directed to obtain the whole area bounded on the northwest by the highlands and on the southeast by the St. John River, and extending from the St. Francis southward to the source of the St. John—a rectangle that, under the Dutch award, would have gone to the United States. He was given this order at the wish of the military experts and the Colonial Office. The order reflected the anxiety of military authorities, such as the Duke of Wellington, for the safety of Upper and Lower Canada. It was intended to provide full security for the road connecting the Maritime Provinces with Canada's interior.

British anxiety had taken on new dimensions as a result of popular movements against British authority led by L. J. Papineau and W. L.

65. Ashburton's successive instructions are summarized in E. D. Adams, "Lord Ashburton and the Treaty of Washington," *American Historical Review*, XVII (July 1912), 764–782.

Mackenzie in 1837–1838 and the eager response to them of Americans on the border. Preparations for reconstruction of the road were under way in 1841.[66] The instructions to Ashburton permitted compensations to the Americans for concessions in the area of the road. The compensations were to lie in the upper valley of the Connecticut River and along the forty-fifth parallel. Also they might include a money indemnity to Maine.

Ashburton vigorously protested this hardening of his instructions, and a month later Aberdeen retreated, returning to the requirement of a line not less favorable to Great Britain than the Dutch award.

In the negotiations Webster and Ashburton dealt with each other in informal conferences. Webster kept the Maine and Massachusetts commissioners informed and used his influence to restrain their demands.[67] On one occasion he asked Ashburton to face the Maine delegation. Ashburton found the group unyielding, and he found Webster weak in resisting them. He wrote Aberdeen in discouragement on July 13: "Preble has got the deputation in his hands and is as yet obstinate and unmanageable, but my real difficulty is with Webster who yields and promises everything, but when it comes to execution is so weak and timid and irresolute that he is frightened by everybody and at last does nothing."[68] Ashburton became so discouraged that he suggested abandoning the negotiation; only the tactful intervention of the President prevented such an ending.

At length, near the close of July, the negotiators arrived at an agreement regarding the crucial area between the upper St. John and the highlands. They divided the area the Dutch King would have allowed

66. The road, as mapped by Major J. D. Graham, one of the American commissioners for the survey under the Act of 1840, followed an old route: the west bank of the lower St. John, the north bank of the upper river, and the west bank of the Madawaska River and Lake Temiscouata to Temiscouata Portage. Then, crossing the highlands at the Portage, it followed the Du Loup River, a tributary of the St. Lawrence, to its outlet. It then ran up the St. Lawrence to Levis, opposite Quebec. See *Map of the Boundary Lines Between the United States and the Adjacent British Provinces* (Washington, 1843). For British preparations to reconstruct the road, see Richardson (comp.), *Messages and Papers*, IV, 96. For the influence of British military experts on the hardening of Ashburton's instructions, see Baldwin, cited in fn. 63.

67. The correspondence between Webster and the Maine commissioners and authorities is found in *House Exec. Docs.*, 27 Cong., 3 sess. (Ser. 418), No. 2; also in *Cong. Globe*, 27 Cong., 3 sess. (Dec. 3, 1842), 14–21.

68. Ashburton to Aberdeen, July 13, 1842, Aberdeen Papers.

the United States. They gave about half of this to the British, which was about half what Aberdeen, under pressure of the British military, had asked Ashburton to try for. Their line, after following the St. John and the St. Francis to Lake Pohenagamook, as the Dutch award had done, departed from it at the lake and turned southwest by straight lines to the highlands at Metjarmette Portage, and thence by the same highlands to the head of Hall's Stream. To obtain this line Ashburton gave up the portion of the Madawaska settlements on the south side of the St. John and made other territorial concessions of major extent noted below. He had earlier made a commercial concession that had seemed of highest value to the Maine legislature and to Webster: the use of the lower St. John for the export of American forest and farm products on the same terms as those enjoyed by British subjects. Access to a seaboard market was especially valuable to the Maine settlers as it was the only means they had of exporting their surplus from the interior.[69]

Among Ashburton's equivalents for territory yielded by the Americans west of the St. John, one of importance lay in New Hampshire on the upper waters of the Connecticut. The issue here was the meaning of the term "northwesternmost head" of the Connecticut River in the Treaty of 1783. Americans had maintained that this meant Hall's Stream; the British contended that it meant the main stream. At stake were more than 150 square miles of land.[70] The Dutch arbiter had accepted the British contention. Ashburton conceded the American.

West of New Hampshire Ashburton made concessions of even greater value. One of the most important, in the view of Webster, was in the region of Rouse's Point on Lake Champlain. Here the United States had a fort to keep watch on an old invasion route from Canada. A million dollars had been spent on the fort, and the expenditures were continuing. The fort had unknowingly been built on Canadian soil because of reliance on an inaccurate early survey of the forty-fifth

69. For the line of the Webster-Ashburton Treaty, see Charles O. Paullin, *Atlas of Historical Geography of the United States* (New York, Carnegie Institution, 1932), Plates 91, 93. For the Webster-Ashburton correspondence and the text of the treaty, see *Senate Docs.*, 27 Cong., 3 sess. (Ser. 413), No. 1; and Miller (ed.), *Treaties*, IV, 363–477.

70. For the backgrounds of this issue, see Roger H. Brown, *The Struggle for the Indian Stream Territory* (Cleveland, Press of Western Reserve University, 1955).

parallel. The arbiter's award would have conceded the site of the fort and a radius around it to the United States. Ashburton agreed to the validation of the entire line as surveyed.[71]

Concessions were made by Ashburton also in the Great Lakes country. In the water communication between Lakes Huron and Superior lay Sugar Island fronting the present Sault Sainte Marie canal. Both in position and in soil it was of high value. It was claimed by both countries, but was conceded by Ashburton to the United States.

In the area of present-day Minnesota an extensive region was conceded that had been brought into contention by differences as to the line of the water communication between Lake Superior and the Lake of the Woods. Both the Americans and the English believed the region contained mineral deposits, though no one dreamed that under its surface lay the vast iron ore riches found later. The greater part of the region, a tract estimated by Webster at 6,500 square miles, came to the United States in consequence of Ashburton's agreement to accept, as the "Long Lake" of the treaty, the Pigeon River, which on the Mitchell map appeared as an estuary in the water and portage connection between Lake Superior and the Lake of the Woods. The Vermilion iron range and part of the Mesabi range were later found to lie there. All these exchanges were incorporated in the treaty that Webster and Ashburton signed on August 9, 1842.

Under these arrangements the total loss to the United States on the Maine border from the area claimed under the Treaty of 1783 amounted to about 5,000 square miles, most of which lay north of the St. John and the St. Francis; 893 square miles of it lay west of these rivers.

A limited part of the total given up was rich land—alluvial soil along the north bank of the St. John and good land along the Madawaska and the west shore of Lake Temiscouata. This was already occupied by French-speaking British subjects. Included in the relinquished area was timberland of some worth on the northern tributaries of the St. John, but the best of the timber had already been logged off.

The greater part by far of the yielded area was of low value, and

71. Webster considered the cession of Rouse's Point more important to the United States than all the concessions he had made to England. *Cong. Globe,* 29 Cong., 1 sess., 617 (Apr. 7, 1846).

much of it was worthless. According to the census of 1941 most of it was being used for combinations of subsistence farming and sales of small timber for firewood and paper pulp.[72] In 1956 population densities in the greater part of it were no higher than ten to twenty-nine persons per square mile, and in a fourth to a third of it population was so sparse as to be unreported in the census. The bare areas lay in western Restigouche and northern Madawaska counties of New Brunswick and in Rimouski and Kamouraska counties of Quebec.[73]

As for the area of 893 square miles conceded by the United States over and above what the Dutch award would have taken, it was valuable for little more than the protection it gave to the British line of communication to the interior. Much of it in Kamouraska County was in 1956 without population, and the rest had a sparse population engaged in a farming-forest products economy. It was pessimistically described by Captain Andrew Talcott of the Corps of Engineers (who had traveled over it for two summers) in a letter to Webster of July 14, 1842: "The territory is barren and without timber of value; and I should estimate that nineteen parts out of twenty are unfit for cultivation . . . On some of the ridges . . . birch and maple are found . . . and in the swamps, spruce . . . ; but the wood, everywhere is insignificant, and of stinted growth. It will readily be seen, therefore, that, for cultivation, or as capable of furnishing the means of human subsistence, the lands are of no value."[74]

Inasmuch as the lands ceded by the United States were not its own but state lands belonging to Maine and Massachusetts, and inasmuch as the territorial equivalents conceded by Ashburton were elsewhere than contiguous to Maine, Webster had promised the Maine and Massachusetts commissioners that they would receive from the federal government, if they assented to the treaty, $250,000 to be equally divided

72. The 1941 census statistics on farming are summarized in a publication entitled "Types of Farming in Canada," issued by the Minister of Agriculture: Publication 825, Farmers Bulletin 157, Ottawa, Dec. 1949. A useful map appears in the map pocket.

73. *Census of Canada 1956* (6 vols., Ottawa, Dominion Bureau of Statistics 1957–1958). County and subdivision figures of population for Quebec and the Maritime Provinces are reported in Vol. I, Bulletins 2 and 3. Folded maps showing population density by subdivisions of counties appear in Vol. 1, Bulletin 1, following p. xvi.

74. *Cong. Globe*, 27 Cong., 3 sess. (1842–1843), Appendix, 1–30 (Aug. 1842). The letter was part of the documents that the President submitted to the Senate with the treaty.

between them plus compensation for expenses each had incurred in maintaining a civil posse to protect their lands. In addition he promised Maine compensation for a boundary survey made in 1838.[75] These promises were more than fulfilled. The indemnity payment for lands ceded was increased to $300,000, and the two states were repaid their expenditures for their civil posse. They were given shares in a "Disputed Territory Fund" (fines accumulated in New Brunswick over the years for timber depredations in the disputed area), and Maine was well recompensed for its 1838 survey.

An element in the indictment brought against Webster in some historical writing is that he accepted responsibility on the part of the United States for these payments. The British are held to have been relieved of the responsibility unnecessarily, and the thesis is advanced that they would have assumed it if they had been sufficiently pressed. This is cited to illustrate Webster's negligence, or worse, in the negotiation. The truth is Ashburton's instructions varied from time to time on this subject. In the earliest of them he was permitted to make pecuniary indemnities to Maine. But Peel was fearful that if offered they might be rejected and be thereafter regarded as a British admission of Maine's right to the territory.[76] On June 1, 1842, Peel was assured by Aberdeen that Ashburton had "been set right with respect to the dreams of sale and purchase of territory, entertained by the people of Maine."[77] As for Webster, he had given the Maine commissioners assurances at a beginning stage that they would receive compensation from the American government for losses of territory, a principle recognized as early as the Jackson administration.

During the negotiation, maps were kept in the background, though they could not be wholly dispensed with. They had been needed because of the intimate association of the Mitchell map with the framing of the Treaty of 1783. On June 16, 1842, Edward Everett wrote Webster from London that a map supporting the American claim was likely to be found in the archives of the British Foreign Office.[78] He seems to have obtained a hint somewhere to that effect. His letter reached Webster after the agreement to seek a conventional line had been

75. Webster to the Maine commissioners, July 15, 1842, printed *ibid.*, 16.
76. Peel to Aberdeen, Mar. 1, 1842, Aberdeen Papers.
77. Aberdeen to Peel, June 1, 1842, Robert Peel Papers, BM.
78. Everett to Webster, June 16, 1842, Edward Everett Papers, Massachusetts Historical Society.

made and was being implemented. Webster had already written Everett a letter, which crossed the latter's in the mails, asking him to forego further search for maps in England or elsewhere, a communication much misinterpreted later by historians.[79]

Webster returned, however, to the use of maps for tactical purposes following the close of the negotiation. He did so during the Senate debate over the ratification of the treaty. He sent to William C. Rives, chairman of the Senate Foreign Relations Committee, the Sparks map (probably also the Steuben) which he had found so effective in Augusta. Those maps became known to all the members of the committee and entered prominently into the secret debate on ratification. They were assailed by opponents of ratification, especially by Thomas Hart Benton. In his assault he described ironically "the solemn and mysterious humbuggery by which Dr. Franklin has been made to play a part in ravishing this ratification from our alarms, and screening the negotiator from responsibility for his gratuitous sacrifices;—the awful apparition of the disinterred map discovered by Mr. Jared Sparks in Paris, with red marks upon it, and which was showed about to Senators to alarm them into prompt action . . . The impressive invocation to secrecy and despatch, lest the British should get wind of the aforesaid map and letter, and thereupon renounce the treaty."[80] Buchanan made a like attack on the Sparks map.

But those maps were more respectfully referred to by Rives. He had doubts as to the line on the Sparks map and called attention to Sparks's own admission of doubts. But he believed the maps could not fail to influence an arbiter if the issue should unfortunately go again to an arbitration. He thought other maps and documents, even though apocryphal, might be found in European archives; these could throw doubt on our title in the eyes of a sovereign arbiter. Similar views were expressed by John C. Calhoun, who favored ratification of the treaty.[81]

On August 20, 1842, the Senate voted to ratify the treaty. Ten days later it voted to remove the injunction of secrecy on its debates. The knowledge that Webster had been aware of the Sparks map before

79. Webster to Everett, June 14, 1842, Webster, *Writings and Speeches,* XVI, 374–375.
80. *Cong. Globe,* 27 Cong., 3 sess. (1842–1843), Appendix, 1–27 (Aug. 1842).
81. *Ibid.,* 49–53, 59–67 (Aug. 1842).

the opening of the negotiation and had not revealed it to Ashburton until the end was thus spread to the American press. It passed promptly to the British press, where Webster's conduct was denounced by the opposition journals as dishonorable.

Parliament was out of session when the news of the treaty arrived. It reassembled early the next year. Then the ministry was laid under bombardment by Lord Palmerston in a speech as partisan and interminable as Benton's in the Senate. Palmerston charged incredible bungling on the part of the ministry, just as Benton had against Webster, and he pictured the treaty as a dishonorable surrender of Canadian territory, of British nationals, and of the honor of the Crown.[82] The speech was the opening of Palmerston's prolonged crusade in Parliament and in the press to brand the treaty as one of the most disgraceful of all British treaty surrenders. He proposed to write across it for all time, in red letters of shame, the word "capitulation."

Peel immediately answered the speech. The treaty had won for England, he pointed out, more than the territory Palmerston would have been satisfied to accept under the Dutch award, especially the strategic area north of the St. John through which the road to the city of Quebec ran. The treaty had closed a dispute dating back half a century that Palmerston had failed, during ten years in office, to resolve.

With regard to the issue of maps which Palmerston had injected into the debate, Peel called attention to published maps appearing in London while the Treaty of 1783 was under debate. First he mentioned a map published in that year by W. Faden. On it, Peel noted, was the inscription: "A map of the Boundary of the United States, as agreed to by the treaty of 1783; by Mr. Faden, Geographer to the King." Peel continued:

> Now, Sir, that map placed the boundary according to the American claim, yet it was a contemporary map, and it was published by the geographer to the British King. There was a work which I have here, a political periodical of the time, published in 1783, called *Bewe's Journal* [J. Bew, ed., *Political Magazine and Literary Journal*]. It gives a full report of the debate in Parliament upon the treaty then being concluded, and, in order to illustrate the report, it also gives a map of the boundaries between the countries

82. *Hansard's Parliamentary Debates*, 3d Ser., vol. 67, 1162–1218 (Mar. 21, 1843).

as then agreed to. That map, Sir, also adopts the line claimed by the United States. On subsequent inquiry, at Paris, we found a map, which must be the map referred to by Mr. Jared Sparkes [*sic*]. There is placed upon that map a broad red line, and that line marks out the boundary as claimed by the British . . . but we can trace no indication of connection between it and the despatch of Dr. Franklin. To say that they were connected is a mere unfounded inference. But there is still another map. Here—in this country. In the library of the late King, was deposited a map by Mitchell, of the date 1753 [1755]. The map was in the possession of the late King, and it was also in the possession of the noble Lord [Palmerston], but he did not communicate its contents to Mr. Webster. It is marked by a broad red line, and on that line is written, "Boundary as described by our negotiator, Mr. Oswald"; and that line follows the claim of the United States . . . On that map, I repeat, is placed the boundary line—that claimed by the United States, and on four different places on that line, "Boundary as described by Oswald." Now I do not say that that was the boundary ultimately settled by the negotiators; but nothing can be more fallacious than founding a claim upon contemporary maps, unless you can also prove that they were adopted by the negotiators.[83]

The King George III map, as already noted, had gone to the British Museum in 1828. Its presence there had been brought to Palmerston's notice in 1839, and he had at once arranged to have it removed to the privacy of the Foreign Office. He, and one of his creatures, G. W. Featherstonhaugh, a special agent for the Northeast boundary, alone in the government had known of it. No word of it had been allowed to reach Peel or Aberdeen on their coming into office, and Ashburton had known nothing of it. Only after the arrival of the signed treaty had Peel been told of it. His informant had been Featherstonhaugh, who was still in the Foreign Office.[84]

The red line marked on it coincided with the American claim. At the north the two were identical. Along the Mississippi the line was located along the east bank of the river, immediately to the east of earlier treaty lines, but this was no issue since the treaty provided

83. *Ibid.*, 1248–50 (Mar. 21, 1843).
84. Everett to Webster, Mar. 3, 1843, State Department Despatches, Great Britain, 50.

specifically that the line was to follow the middle of the river. At the south, the St. Mary's line was inaccurate; it appeared on the map as a sinuous line passing just north of Amelia Island into the Atlantic.[85]

Peel's comments on this map and on the others noted by him are valuable in appraising the role of maps as evidence in boundary disputes. Contemporary maps, marked with purported boundary lines, are reliable evidence only if carrying proof also of having been "adopted by the negotiators." Only then can they be taken as exhibiting the intentions of the treaty makers. If they lack such evidence they are inconclusive, whether their lines are inserted or are in engraved form. The best evidence of the negotiators' intentions becomes, then, the words of the treaty, and if they are themselves doubtful, the only recourse of a later generation is to negotiate a fresh treaty of accommodation.

The judgment of Peel as to the value of contemporary maps, or lines on maps, was readily accepted by Webster. In a letter to Everett, replying to one in which Peel's speech had been enclosed, Webster compared the King George III map with one recently discovered in the Jay Papers, on which a line had been marked by John Jay and accepted by the British negotiator at one stage in the peace negotiations. He thought neither map was conclusive as to the line agreed on finally by the treaty makers. "Both these last discovered maps are evidence, and important evidence; but in my judgment more weight attaches to the map published by Beers [Bew] under the circumstances of that publication, than to either or both of these."[86]

The question of an arbiter's response to less than definitive map testimony seemed to both Peel and Webster of importance. Peel observed in the course of his answer to Palmerston:

> When the noble Lord takes it for granted that if we had resorted to arbitration we should have been successful in obtaining our claims, I cannot help thinking that the matter would be open

85. For the King George III map and other Mitchell maps relied on in the controversy, see Miller (ed.), *Treaties*, III, 328–351; IV, 403–413. The Stevens transcription of the King George III map is now in the Map Collection of the Library of Congress.

86. Webster to Everett, Apr. 25, 1843, Webster, *Writings and Speeches,* XVI, 402–406. The spelling "Beers" in the printed letter is a misprint for Bew. For the original of the letter using Bew, see Everett Papers; see also an illuminating article by Jared Sparks, "Treaty of Washington," *North American Review,* LVI (Apr. 1843), 452–496, in which he describes the "labyrinth of conflicting maps."

to much discussion. Indeed, I do not believe that that claim of Great Britain [Featherstonhaugh line or Mars Hill line] was well founded; that it is a claim which the negotiators intended to ratify. I cannot say, either, that the inquiries which have been instituted since Mr. Sparkes's [sic] discovery have materially strengthened my conviction either way. I think they leave matters much as they were, and nothing, I think, can be more delusive than the expectation that, if the question were referred to arbitration—the decision would inevitably have been given in your favour, in consequence of the maps, which would not be regarded as maps recognized by the negotiators themselves.

The doubts of Peel as to the British line were shared by Aberdeen; at least Webster was so informed confidentially.[87] The Prime Minister and the Secretary for Foreign Affairs seemed to agree with the Dutch arbiter that the line described in the Treaty of 1783 could be found neither north nor south of the St. John River.

To Webster and even more to Gallatin it seemed clear that an arbiter would be unimpressed by map testimony that was short of being absolutely conclusive. Gallatin, in an address before the New-York Historical Society on April 15, 1843, which Webster heard and applauded, ruefully recalled the mass of map evidence he had submitted to the Dutch arbiter. He had listed ten maps of the years 1783–1784 published in London, including those of Faden and Bew, on all of which the boundary was depicted as claimed by the United States. In addition, he showed that no contrary map had been printed in London in that period. For good measure he listed also the nineteen British maps of the period 1763–1781 that he had submitted in 1829 to the arbiter, placing the northwest angle of Nova Scotia where the United States claimed it to be, and the absence of any British maps to the contrary. All that cartographic evidence had proved unconvincing to the arbiter.[88]

The problems that the treaty makers of 1783 laid in store for the

87. Webster to Sparks, Mar. 1843, Webster, *Writings and Speeches*, XVI, 402.
88. New-York Historical Society *Proceedings*, 1843, 46–47; [Gallatin and Preble,] *North Eastern Boundary Arbitration*, Introduction, 33. Notable historians of Canada and Great Britain were convinced by Gallatin's evidence and argument; see especially William F. Ganong, "Boundaries of New Brunswick," *Proceedings and Transactions of the Royal Society of Canada*, 2d Ser., VII (1901–1902); Dudley Mills, "British Diplomacy and Canada; the Ashburton Treaty," in *United Empire: Royal Colonial Institute Journal*, New Ser. II, No. 10 (Oct. 1911), 681–712.

future by failing to attach maps to their text bearing boundary lines confirmed by signatures were remembered six years after the troublesome Northeastern boundary was settled, in framing the Treaty of Guadalupe Hidalgo closing the Mexican War. To that treaty the American and Mexican negotiators attached maps and plans, bearing signatures, seals, and the date of signing, which underscored a common understanding of the line of the treaty.

After Peel disclosed in Parliament that the King George III map had been in the possession of the Foreign Office throughout the last years of the boundary dispute, Aberdeen felt it necessary to offer the American government an explanation. He invited Everett to the Foreign Office where he gave his word that neither he nor Peel nor Ashburton had known of the presence there of that map. He pulled down on a roller an old and battered Mitchell map of 1755 bearing a red line that more than upheld the British claim. Its line ran from the source of the St. Croix River [Kousaki Lake] in a westward direction to the Chenbesec [Sebec?] Lake, then southwestward to the headwaters of the Connecticut River. This was roughly the line on the terror-inspiring Sparks and Steuben maps, which Webster had used to good effect in Maine and in the Senate.[89] Had the King George III map come to the attention of the Peel ministry during the final negotiations over the boundary and had a choice become necessary between its red line and the line found on the map which had been long in service, preference would doubtless have been given the one which upheld the British claim rather than the one which cast doubt on it. While the provenance of the line on neither map could be fully established, the Peel ministry, if it had relied on any map, would have used the one which upheld the nation's basic interests.

The Parliamentary debate initiated by the exchange between Palmerston and Peel continued for weeks, with adherents of the one assailing the treaty and adherents of the other defending it. Notable speakers on the Whig side were Lord John Russell, the Whig leader, Thomas B. Macaulay, the historian, and Sir Charles Napier, the admiral. They were not as vitriolic as Palmerston and very soon left the Viscount to carry on alone, which he energetically did. On the ad-

89. Everett to Webster, Mar. 31, 1843, State Department Despatches, Great Britain, 50.

ministration side the chief spokesmen were Sir Howard Douglas, a former governor of New Brunswick, Benjamin Disraeli, and Lord Brougham, an independent. Douglas was an expert on military roads and had influenced the instructions to Ashburton. Brougham came nearest to actually charging Palmerston with having kept the embarrassing King George III map under wraps in the Foreign Office. That story was more fully documented later by historians.[90] All this hurling of charges and countercharges in England and across the Atlantic was later derisively described as "The Battle of the Maps."

By exchanges of notes valuable supplements were added to the boundary accord reached in the Webster-Ashburton Treaty. One exchange related to the *Caroline* and McLeod affairs, discussed in the Introduction. Webster's note, indicating that cases like McLeod's (where the subject of a foreign country was in the custody of a state court) would be a proper subject for congressional legislation, was a return for Ashburton's note admitting that his government had been dilatory in expressing regret for a hostile invasion of an American harbor by British forces. This exchange, together with Article 10 of the treaty defining Anglo-American extradition procedures, cleared the air on the New York frontier.

The device of an exchange of notes was used to draw the heat also from the *Creole* case, discussed earlier. Ashburton had no authority to agree to close British colonial ports to mutinous vessels such as the *Creole*, but, as a result of Webster's statement of the administration's position on this issue, reported by Ashburton to his government, instructions went to colonial governors not to "interfere" with crews of American vessels forced into British ports by weather or violence.

Webster and Ashburton dealt also with the still unresolved conflict over British impressment of seamen from American vessels in wartime. Impressment had never been renounced in principle by the British government, though it had ceased in practice since the War of 1812. Ashburton had no power to alter the British position on this issue, but he accepted for conveyance to his government an able statement by Webster. These exchanges of notes became by agreement part of the documents published with the treaty.

90. A brief account of the transfer of the map to the Foreign Office is found in Miller (ed.), *Treaties*, IV, 408–410.

On the issue of peacetime "visit and search" of merchant vessels on the high seas, a practice followed by British cruisers off the slave coast of Africa to discourage the slave trade, an article (Article 8), was incorporated in the treaty by which the two nations agreed to cooperate in maintaining adequate naval forces on the African coast, and their naval officers were permitted to consult with each other in "separately and respectively" enforcing the laws of each against the slave trade.

The reception of the treaty and the accompanying documents in the two countries forms a useful gauge of the contribution that the treaty made to peace. In both countries the reception in government circles was favorable, despite the clamors of opposition politicians. In the United States the treaty won an overwhelmingly favorable Senate vote of ratification (39–9). Calhoun warmly endorsed the treaty, despite the antislavery character of its cruising agreement, and felt that the exchange of notes on the *Creole* case was a step in the right direction. He helped to win the South's approval of the treaty by an admirable speech in the Senate.[91]

Even in Maine the reception given the treaty was favorable, though

91. In drafting the article of the treaty providing for joint cruising against ships engaged in the slave trade (Article 8), and in the exchange of notes on the *Creole* case Tyler participated actively. After the ratification of the treaty, Article 8 came under criticism from Lewis Cass, the American minister to France, who was hoping for the presidential nomination of his party in 1844. Cass objected to that article on the ground that it did not contain a British renunciation of peacetime visitation and search on the high seas. Webster rebuked him at the direction of the President. One lengthy letter (December 20, 1842) concluded with the words: "The President directs me to say . . . that, in the Treaty of Washington, no topics were omitted, and no topics introduced at the mere direction of the negotiator; that the negotiations proceeded from step to step, and from day to day, under his own immediate supervision and direction; that he himself takes the responsibility for what the treaty contains and what it omits." Webster was writing for publication with the intention of demonstrating that the President himself had taken the responsibility for the sections of the treaty relating to slavery issues. On January 9, 1843, Tyler informed the Senate that Article 8 had been proposed to the British minister "under my express sanction." Later, Tyler's son, Lyon Gardiner Tyler, in *Letters and Times of the Tylers* (3 vols., Richmond, 1884–1896), II, Chap. 8, chose Webster's words to prove that the President had been his own Secretary of State throughout the Webster-Ashburton negotiation. For Calhoun's defense of the treaty, see *Cong. Globe*, 27 Cong., 3 sess. (1842–1843), Appendix, 49–53 (Aug. 1842). For the letters of Cass to Webster, see W. L. G. Smith, *Life and Times of Lewis Cass* (New York, 1856), Chap. 28. For British peacetime visitation of vessels on the high seas, see Hugh G. Soulsby, *The Right of Search and the Slave Trade in Anglo-American Relations, 1814–1862* (Baltimore, Johns Hopkins Press, 1933).

one of its senators in Washington, Reuel Williams, in closing a speech against ratification, proposed a resolution directing the President to take immediate possession of the disputed territory, if ratification failed. The resolution was rejected by a vote of 31–8, and it had little support in Maine.[92]

From England, Everett reported that the treaty gave general satisfaction.[93] Aberdeen and Peel reported likewise. Palmerston's attacks on the treaty became, before long, a boomerang on himself and on his party. They produced division in the party and, ultimately, the failure of Lord John Russell to form a ministry when the Peel government dissolved during the Corn Law crisis at the end of 1845.[94]

A renewal of the "Battle of the Maps" occurred in the twentieth century. In 1933 a map was found in the map collection of the Spanish Foreign Office in Madrid. Its base was a French Mitchell map of the right vintage, and it bore a broad red line in the same location as that found on the King George III map. It had come to the Spanish Foreign Office from Count Aranda, the Spanish ambassador at Paris. Its line, Aranda reported, had been copied from a map marked for Vergennes by Franklin after the conclusion of the preliminary peace articles of November 30, 1782.[95] The map had been separated from its covering dispatch to the Foreign Office in the course of filing. It

---

92. The reception of the treaty in Maine after rumors of its content had leaked out is described below. The vote on the Williams resolution is recorded in *Cong. Globe*, 27 Cong., 3 sess. (1842–1843), 1–2 (Aug. 1842). A resolution resembling that of Williams, offered by Benton, was defeated by a vote of 37–2. On a later issue—appropriations to carry the treaty into effect—the vote in favor was 137–40 in the House and 36–4 in the Senate. *Ibid.*, 336, 370. Webster's comment on these majorities was: "You notice the great majorities with which, after all the high sounding notes of opposition, the appropriations for the Treaty passed both Houses. There is, probably, no instance of a similar approach to unanimity." Webster, *Writings and Speeches*, XVI, 398. An account of the reception of the treaty generally in the United States is in R. N. Current, "Webster's Propaganda and the Ashburton Treaty," *Mississippi Valley Historical Review*, XXXIV (Sept. 1947), 187–200. Current stresses the role that Webster personally took in preparing the way for the treaty before its terms became officially known. For the Canadian response to the treaty, see Mills, referred to in fn. 88.
93. Everett to Webster, Sept. 19, 1842, Everett Papers.
94. Merk, *Oregon Question*, 263–271.
95. Lawrence Martin and S. F. Bemis, "Franklin's Red-Line Map was a Mitchell," *New England Quarterly*, X (Mar. 1937), 105–111. A map bearing the line of the treaty was brought to America by Jay and was placed in the diplomatic files of the Continental Congress, but was subsequently lost.

had about the same value as had the King George III map, and it had the same weaknesses. It lacked the signatures of the negotiators and other evidences of having been "adopted by the negotiators." Had Peel known of it at the time of his speech in Parliament he doubtless would have given it approximately the weight he gave the King George III map.

Maps had become in truth an irrelevance in the Webster-Ashburton negotiation. Their relegation to the background was the meaning, the essence, of the agreement to seek a conventional line. Insofar as maps were afterward used by Webster they were to implement the results of the agreement. They had become mere propaganda devices for ratification of the treaty.

Acceptance by the American government of the principle of a conventional line was not solely a concession made to the British; it was a concession to domestic demands for tranquillity. Tranquillity was required for recovery from an utterly disorganized economy. It was requisite especially for the industrial and business sections of the North and for the cotton-raising regions of the South. It was reflected in the thinly veiled impatience at the obstinacy of Maine (in holding out for the treaty line) expressed by certain "sister states" in legislative resolutions addressed to Maine (reprinted here in the Documents). It was evident also in a growing understanding, North and South, of the complexities of the boundary problem and a general desire to bring to an end forty-four years of futile negotiation devoted to it. Equally basic to an understanding of the Webster-Ashburton negotiation is the synchronization of sentiments such as these with the advent of governments in the United States and in England eager for a settlement of their outstanding controversies.

With regard to tactics, Smith's recommendation to Webster of recourse to a conventional line was not as new as Smith imagined. It was as old as the Jackson administration. What was new in it was the method proposed for making it palatable to Maine: a sub-rosa program of propaganda, spread in Maine by local agents paid from secret funds of the federal government. This idea would not normally have commended itself to a states' rights man of the period, for it was subversive of existing federal-state relationships. That it was embraced by Webster is not remarkable. What is remarkable is that it was embraced and financed by Tyler, as revealed in his confidential testimony before the special House investigating committee in 1846.[96]

An open program of education in this case would have been preferable to a concealed one. It would have accorded with democratic process and with open diplomacy openly arrived at. But on the other hand it would have produced argument and differences, which would have become partisan. It would have called forth in Maine renewed demands for the 1783 treaty line and would have encouraged extremists to flag-waving of a demagogic sort. As Tyler described it later, "parties in Maine seemed to vie with each other as to which should be most extreme on the subject of the boundary. The public press there was but the exponent of this state of feeling. The administration had no press in Maine to enforce its views and wishes. It wanted merely to be heard and understood, and the only way which seemed to be open to it was by the employment of persons to make known its views by all proper means."[97]

The employment of persons to make known its views by "all proper means" raises the question of "proper means." The means Smith employed were described by him to the congressional committee of 1846 in terms that emphasized their legitimacy and minimized their sub-rosa character. Speaking of his aides Smith said, "their services consisted in obtaining interviews with leading and influential men of their party, to induce favorable action on the subject of the compromise of the boundary on the part of the legislature, and procuring a favorable expression thereto on the part of the press, by republishing the articles first published in the Christian Mirror, as stated above, or otherwise."[98] This statement also described his personal contribution.

A more critical statement of the means and program was made by Brinkerhoff, the dissenter in the congressional committee just mentioned. He observed, concerning Smith's tactics, that "from his [Smith's] testimony, it would appear that the object of his agency in Maine was to institute and prosecute a course of systematic electioneering; and, by correspondence and confidential communication with the leading and influential political characters of both political parties, so to

96. See Documents, under date June 9, 1846—Tyler's Testimony.
97. *Ibid.*, 193.
98. See Documents, under dates Nov. 18, Dec. 2, 1841; Feb. 3, 1842; and Smith's Testimony under date June 9, 1846.

influence the public mind, and 'adjust the tone and direction of the party presses,' as to secure a majority in the legislature of that State favorable to the appointment of commissioners with full powers to bind the state in the anticipated negotiations."[99]

This was the essence of the program, and also of its irregularity: the undermining of existing federal-state relations by the use of the President's secret fund. It meant federally subsidized underground electioneering to manage the sentiment of a state of the Union. Also, its leading agent was a politician of Maine whose political and business reputation was not impeccable.

Another means employed in the cause, which might seem to a later public not altogether "proper," was the enrollment and payment by the federal government of eminent persons to lobby with Maine legislators. The persons so employed, as has been seen, were a world-renowned Harvard scholar (Jared Sparks), a federal judge in Massachusetts (Peleg Sprague), a lame-duck Maine politician (Albert Smith), and a former Maine agent in Washington on the boundary issue (C. S. Daveis), most of whom had been identified with the cause of upholding the treaty line. The use of maps of dubious authenticity to alarm the Maine legislature might also be considered beyond "all proper means."

Ashburton's contribution to preparing opinion in Maine was likewise beyond "all proper means." It was the employment of secret government funds probably in the same cause as Webster's: the conversion of the public of Maine to an unrestricted negotiation. But the money used in this case was "British gold." A kind of Anglo-American partnership in propaganda was thus a prelude to the Webster-Ashburton negotiation. Fortunately it was all directed to a worthy end—the preservation of peace.

All this brings the historian face to face with the moral issue: whether a desirable end may be sought by questionable means. Certainly the Webster-Ashburton Treaty was a desirable end. It brought menacing controversies to a close with great advantages to both sides, as fair-minded persons agreed. It pleased even former intransigents in Maine.

The *Eastern Argus* had been one of the intransigents. Prior to 1841 its editor had been belligerent in his demands for the line of 1783

---

99. See Documents, under date June 9, 1846—Minority Report.

and nothing but that line. By the summer of 1842 his views had been transformed. He had acquired, by unknown means, advance knowledge of the treaty's boundary terms. In a leading editorial on July 29, 1842 (tw), he informed the Maine public that the boundary was substantially the one proposed by the King of the Netherlands, except for a small strip of barren territory in the extreme north. Maine had won the free navigation of the St. John River, a payment of $150,000 for lands relinquished, and $350,000 for the expenses of its civil posse. The treaty gave the United States disputed land in New Hampshire and a strip of land, including Rouse's Point, along the forty-fifth parallel in Vermont and New York.

The editor believed this settlement was a good one and that it was so considered in Maine. He had conversed with a great many men, and he had encountered only one opposed to confirming it. In Portland he had found opinion unanimously favorable. In York, Kennebec, and Lincoln counties all agreed that the treaty should not be rejected. Some thought the terms could have been better, but none denied that, so far as money was concerned, Maine had made a "good trade." He concluded: "We feel proud of the course the Democracy of Maine have pursued . . . And we are very much obliged to our political opponents for accepting, in so good spirit, and in so good faith, the full share of the honors and responsibilities tendered them by the majority, in the State and its Legislature." The editor became an actual champion of Webster and of his treaty, which was unusual in a Democratic paper.

On August 5 he observed: "Maine would be much better off under the present arrangement than with the award of the Dutch King, or even the line of '83. We consider the acknowledgment of our right to the whole territory, and yielding the free navigation of the St. John, and the *free trade* in the products of the fine forests of its tributaries, and the *agricultural* products of their rich vallies as a fair equivalent for the jurisdiction surrendered. There is no business man that would hesitate a moment to make the trade for himself."

In the same issue the editor was tormented by uncertainty as to whether the Senate would ratify the treaty. He expressed views that were a mixture of old and new attitudes. If the Senate should fail to ratify, he hoped Maine would "at once, without distinction of party, take possession and call on the general government to defend her from foreign aggression. Senators and Southern representatives opposed to ratifying will then have an opportunity to show their patriotism and courage."[100]

When the editor read in the New York *Journal of Commerce* a premature announcement that the Senate had confirmed the treaty he gave his readers, on August 15, 1842, the exciting word on his front page, headlined, "Glorious News!"[101]

Ashburton was less exuberant than the Maine editor regarding the treaty, but was clearly pleased that the dangerous dispute had finally been peacefully settled. After the boundary had been agreed to he wrote Aberdeen a private message worth quoting in part as an indication of the temper he had brought to the negotiation and also as evidence—important to keep steadily in mind—that the Maine commissioners who had been sent to Washington had received none of the British secret money he had written about to his government:

> You will see that I have at last made my important move, and that my Boundary is on the high road to the Senate. The men of Maine were most difficult to deal with, and I was obliged somewhat irregularly to undertake them, for the Sec'y of State has no influence with them, and for a day or two I was in doubt whether I might not fail altogether, but at last Preble yielded and after signing, he went off to his wilds in Maine as sulky as a Bear. You may rely that no better terms were obtainable, and that if obtained would be decidedly in danger in the Senate. For my own part you are aware that I have been fighting for details to which I do not attach the same importance as my masters. My great wish was that there should be *a* settlement, because I was sure that if this failed we should come very soon to collision, but I am well pleased that we end by driving the enemy off that crest of Highlands so much coveted at the War Office. There has been no demand of money by anybody during the whole discussion,[102] and I need not add that on this subject I have been cautiously silent. I am now fully occupied getting this treaty into shape and advancing other subjects.

> I am charmed with the prospect of getting away. The heat of this place is beyond all description and I am sitting with my pen

100. Portland *Eastern Argus* (tw), Aug. 5, 1842.
101. The *Journal of Commerce* announcement was dated Aug. 11, 1842.
102. This refers to indemnity payments to Maine and to Massachusetts.

in one hand and a fan in the other, but I shall make no improper haste. Webster does not look as if he would much outlive our treaty and I would not answer for myself if the work were to last long, but I am much more comfortable since Preble is gone back to Maine.[103]

The references to Preble in this letter are suggestive of the theme of this essay. Preble had been an intransigent for years in Maine on the issue of the treaty line of 1783. He had been included among Maine's commissioners by the legislature as a protection for the state's interests. Yet he did yield his personal views and, with the other commissioners, signed acceptance of the conventional line of the Webster-Ashburton Treaty before going off "to his wilds in Maine as sulky as a Bear." He could have held up acceptance of the treaty, for unanimity of the commissioners was required, but he and his colleagues signed without other conditions than that the treaty and its agreements be ratified by the Senate.

The overwhelmingly favorable vote of ratification, the equally favorable press reaction even in Maine, and the cordial approval of the treaty by the British government indicated a general feeling that the treaty was mutually advantageous. Opposition denunciation was discounted as normal politics in both countries and seemed to indicate that any losses resulting from the treaty had not been all on one side. In addition the treaty did prevent collision. All this may suggest that the proceedings described in this essay, which won freedom for the two governments to hold an untrammeled negotiation, were endurable even if they did include departures from "all proper means."

103. Ashburton to Aberdeen, July 28, 1842, Aberdeen Papers.

Part Two.
Propaganda for
Expanding
the Southwest

A Safety Valve Thesis and Texan Annexation*

In 1844 a nationwide debate took place in the United States. It was on the issue of the annexation of Texas to the Union. It turned on three theses relating to slavery, each of which was sponsored by an individual well known to American history. One was the conspiracy thesis, sponsored by John Quincy Adams. Another was the safety valve thesis, sponsored by Robert J. Walker, the "king maker" of that era. The third was the protection of slavery thesis, sponsored by John C. Calhoun. The three were given in the order listed here and will be presented in that order. They all had their origin in the Texan war for independence and its aftermath.

The war was ended in 1836 at the Battle of San Jacinto. It was not formally terminated, but neither was it seriously resumed. Texas became the Lone Star Republic as a result of the battle. Its people were eager to exchange their independence for union with the United States. They expressed a desire for this not long after the battle by an overwhelmingly favorable popular vote. But times were not auspicious. In the United States the slavery controversy was becoming acute again. Petitions from Northerners to prohibit slavery in the District of Columbia and to enjoin the interstate traffic in slaves were flooding Congress. They were being presented, despite Southern protests, on the floor of Congress by Northern congressmen, especially by Adams.

* This paper, presented at the annual dinner of the Massachusetts Historical Society in Boston on October 13, 1960, was published in the *Mississippi Valley Historical Review*, XLIX (Dec. 1962), 413–436. It is republished, somewhat revised, with permission of the Organization of American Historians.

Gag rules that infringed constitutional guarantees of the right of petition were used to silence them. Inherent in the controversy was the problem of the extension of slavery. A presidential canvass was under way. Encouragement by the Jackson government to Texas to enter the Union was likely to become a campaign issue and to impair the chances of Martin Van Buren for election. Andrew Jackson refused even to recognize Texan independence, persisting in this caution almost to the end of his presidency.

Objection to annexation was made in the United States before Texas had achieved independence. A Quaker abolitionist, Benjamin Lundy, opened a campaign against it in the Philadelphia press before news of the Battle of San Jacinto had arrived. He maintained that annexation had been the aim of Southern slaveholders from the time of the first migrations to Texas and that the entire process of migration, defiance of Mexican law, and revolution had been a Southern conspiracy to extend the area of slavery.[1] An eminent Northern preacher, William Ellery Channing, during the summer of 1837 in a letter to Henry Clay that appeared with the arrival of a formal Texan application for annexation, restated eloquently this conspiracy thesis.[2] The thesis was given its final and most extreme form by John Quincy Adams, who maintained in Congress that the conspiracy involved even the American government, especially that of Jackson. When a joint resolution of annexation came before the House in the summer of 1838, Adams talked it to death in a filibustering speech that consumed every morning hour devoted to it for three weeks from June 16 to the final adjournment of Congress.[3] Efforts subsequently made for five years by the Texans to achieve annexation were all fruitless.

In the meantime Texan leaders sought status in Europe. They won

1. Benjamin Lundy, *Origin and True Causes of the Texas Insurrection* (Philadelphia, 1836).
2. William Ellery Channing, *Works* (6 vols., Boston, 1866), II, 183–260.
3. *Speech of John Quincy Adams on Resolutions of Seven State Legislatures Relating to the Annexation of Texas, Delivered in Fragments of the Morning Hour, June 16 to July 7, 1838* (Washington, 1838). The most thoroughgoing statement of the conspiracy thesis is found in an address to the public drafted by Adams and signed by himself and twelve other congressmen on March 3, 1843, which appeared in the Washington *National Intelligencer*. It contained the statement that annexation would be identical with dissolution of the Union. It was reprinted in *Niles' Register*, LXIV (May 13, 1843), 173–175.

recognition, treaties of commerce, and British intercession with Mexico for an armistice. Some of these leaders considered retaining a separate existence and expanding their boundaries. Sam Houston predicted that Texas, before long, would absorb all the northern states of Mexico, including California, and would even possess itself of the Oregon Country. With broad frontage on two oceans it would be in a position to stand alone and to become a rival ultimately to the United States. When a precarious suspension of hostilities was finally arranged by the British in the summer of 1843, the Texan agent in Washington informed the American government that annexation was no longer a matter open for discussion.

This change of tone was alarming to President John Tyler. It led him to reverse the attitude of his predecessors and to begin pressing annexation on Texas. In the autumn of 1843 he opened discussions in Washington through his Secretary of State, Abel P. Upshur, looking to a treaty of annexation. Early in 1844 a formal negotiation was under way.

Yet Tyler was realistic enough to understand that the real problem would be ratification of a treaty and that attention should be given immediately to the creation of a climate of opinion favorable to that end. He turned for help to Robert J. Walker, a fervent annexationist and personal friend. Walker was just the man for giving help. He was well acquainted with attitudes in the several sections of the Union. Himself northern-born—in Pennsylvania—he had grown to political maturity there as a Jacksonian. He was by adoption a Southerner and was one of the senators from Mississippi. He reflected expansionist desires in the two sections. He was without any ingrown conscience regarding the morality of slavery; he considered it an economic problem, intrinsically, which would solve itself in due time in response to economic laws. Since it would do so, it should not be allowed to interfere with the creation of an American empire. The Negro as a slave and the Negro as a race he recognized to be two aspects merely of the same problem. Slavery basically was a race problem, and the final solution of both problems would be removal of the race altogether from the soil of the United States. That concept was common in the Union. It had been held by idealists of the past such as Thomas Jefferson and James Madison; it was held by the still active organization of the American Colonization Society; and it was held as late as the Civil War by Abraham Lincoln. Other Walker endowments for appraisal and manufacture of climate were traits of character. By temper he was sanguine and supremely self-confident. He was confident especially of his powers of persuasion and political management. He was enlisted by the President for the work of winning public opinion to the ratification of an annexation treaty.[4]

The scene of his labors was the North. Public opinion there on the Texas issue was deeply divided. So were political parties. They differed over it not only from each other but within their own ranks. The Democratic party was divided three ways: its expansionists desired immediate annexation even at the cost of extending the boundaries of slavery; its antislavery elements opposed immediate annexation; its neutrals, relatively indifferent to slavery, and eager for Texas, were hesitant to accept it for fear acceptance would break up the party and even the Union. Whigs were also divided: one element, the conscience Whigs, opposed any extension of slavery and energetically resisted annexation; another element, probably more numerous, disliked slavery, but hesitated to oppose annexation because of a desire to remain in harmony with Southern Whigs, who were prevailingly for annexation. In all this variety of sentiment the hesitating, the wavering, held the balance of votes. They held it likewise in the South, where the division over Texas tended to be over timing rather than over the issue itself. The uncommitted were the opportunity of Walker. By framing concepts agreeable to them, by presenting a thesis attractive to middle-of-the-roaders, he might line up enough of them to assure ratification. Should a program of education prove unavailing, however, and the treaty fail, the issue could still be thrown as a last resort into the presidential canvass of 1844. Early in 1844 Walker began preparation of a letter to the North intended for middle-of-the-roaders.

The letter was completed late in January 1844. It was lengthy, mea-

4. The only full-length biography of Walker is James P. Shenton, *Robert John Walker* (New York, Columbia University Press, 1961). Its account of the Walker letter is surprisingly brief. Somewhat fuller is James C. N. Paul, *Rift in the Democracy* (Philadelphia, University of Pennsylvania Press, 1951), 97–101. A good sketch of Walker is H. Donaldson Jordan, "A Politician of Expansion, Robert J. Walker," *Mississippi Valley Historical Review*, XIX (Dec. 1932), 362–381. The thesis that Walker was a free soiler at heart in his early years is not substantiated by sound evidence and conflicts with his own declarations. Actually Walker was of the school of Lewis Cass and Stephen A. Douglas.

suring thirty-two pages of fine print.[5] It was an appeal to all northern Democrats. For expansionists among them it combined the case for Texas with the case for the occupation of the whole of Oregon. It played on anti-British feelings and warned Democrats that, unless promptly annexed, Texas would become a British satellite, which would mean laying open the whole West, including the city of New Orleans, to a combined British and Indian attack. The Gulf coast would be similarly laid open. The nation would be encircled north, south, west, and at sea by British power. Andrew Jackson was cited as favoring annexation. He had already been called to the minds of Walker's readers by the simple device of dating the letter January 8, an anniversary dear to the heart of every good American—the anniversary of the Battle of New Orleans. Appeal was made to Northerners in terms also of the pocketbook. Texas was pictured as promising, if annexed, an open market for Northern agriculture, industry, commerce, lumbering, and mining. Pages of statistics were appended to support this argument.

The main feature of the letter, however, was the reassurance given to frightened Northerners—to Democrats and Whigs—regarding a bogey: that annexation would extend the boundaries of slavery. Annexation would not extend the boundaries of slavery; it would, on the contrary, contract them and ultimately would remove slavery altogether from the soil of the United States. It would do this simply by accelerating economic and sociological forces already at work undermining slavery.

Slavery, Walker maintained, is a self-destroying institution. It contains within itself the poisons of its ultimate death. It is self-destroying because of the ignorance and carelessness of workers of the Negro race. It entails inflicting the same soil-destroying crops on the same land year after year and generation after generation until the soil is lifeless. Slavery undermines the very basis of its support. It survives as a system only by reason of incessant movement, of repeated migrations, of flight by slaves and masters from soils it has worn out to soils that are virgin. The ruin it leaves behind is evident in whole sections of the border states and seaboard states. Already from four

5. *Letter of Mr. Walker of Mississippi, Relative to the Annexation of Texas.* It was first published in the Washington *Globe* on February 3, 1844, and later put into pamphlet form. For its many printings, see Thomas W. Streeter, *Bibliography of Texas 1795–1845* (5 vols., Cambridge, Mass., Harvard University Press, 1955–1960), Part III, vol. 2, 509–510.

states—Delaware, Maryland, Virginia, and Kentucky—slavery is in flight. From these a half-million slaves have withdrawn to the Gulf Plains, if it is permissible to include descendants with migrants. Delaware and Maryland have fewer slaves, as the last census shows, than they had at the census of 1790. If that rate of withdrawal were to be doubled, as it would be following the annexation of Texas, slavery would disappear from Delaware and Maryland in twenty years and would be in the process of doing so from Virginia and Kentucky. In a true sense migration of slaves westward had never been, according to Walker, an extension of slavery. It had been a mere relocation of the slaves. It had, moreover, been of benefit to the slaves. It had alleviated their condition, physical, moral, and spiritual. It had enabled masters to provide, from more productive acres, more food and better care. It had encouraged better care, also, because of the higher value of the slaves in an area of higher labor productivity.

Relocation had long since brought slaves from worn-out eastern areas to the country beyond the Mississippi. It had brought them to the rich cotton and sugar lands of Louisiana and Arkansas. If Texas were annexed the flow would turn, at an accelerated rate, to its virgin lands. Slaves would be drained off gradually from all exhausted eastern areas and would be concentrated in the rich Texan soils. This would be, as in the earlier cases, no extension of slavery. It would be mere relocation. The more slaves in Texas, the fewer in the worn-out areas of the East. But the relocation could occur only if Texas were annexed. If Texas were kept out of the Union it could not occur. An independent Texas would become a British satellite. As such it would be abolitionized, and the migration road to Texas for slaves would be permanently closed.

But if a slave concentration did occur in Texas, the inexorable laws of economics would operate there. Texan soils would become exhausted. They would no longer give sustenance to a large labor force. The imperative need of movement would again appear. Virgin lands to which slavery could move would, however, not appear. No other lands suitable to slave crops exist in that part of the world. On exhausted soils slaves would confront masters with the alternatives of liberation or bankruptcy. Liberation would be the choice. Slaves would become freed-men, and slavery would at last disappear from the confines of the United States.

But this would be only the beginning of the happy change. On exhausted soils freed Negroes would have no opportunities for employment. In search of employment they would flow southward, into Mexico, Central America, and, ultimately, South America. There they would find a blessed haven of refuge. The climate of these tropical lands is ideal for Negroes. It is the same genial climate as that of the African homeland and of the Southern states of the United States in which they have thrived. The land itself is fruitful—it would easily yield an abundant life to the tillers of the soil. The sparse population occupying that land would welcome the Negroes and treat them as equals. The people of Latin America are overwhelmingly persons of color. From Mexico southward to Central America and over South America 90 percent of all the people are of the colored and mixed races. They are either Indians, or Negroes, or mestizos, or sambos, the last a mixture of Indians and Negroes. These people cherish no race prejudices against Negroes. The barriers of color, which in the United States would exclude Negroes forever from the privileges of equality, would not operate there. The Negroes would be integrated as equals in a society of equals and not be always sullen inferiors in a despised caste.[6]

Such was the landscape set before the eyes of uncommitted Northern Democrats and Whigs. It was a landscape beautiful not only in itself but as lighted by the dawn of a new day. The road to Texas was the road to the future. At its terminus would be the safety valve, the outlet to Mexico, Central America, and South America.[7] There the whole of nature would conspire with man to make the Negro happy and secure. Through this outlet would disappear slavery, the

6. Spanish America was in 1801 considered by Thomas Jefferson as a colonization ground for emancipated American Negroes, but was dismissed in favor of Santo Domingo. Continental America was reserved for higher uses: "However, our present interests may restrain us within our own limits, it is impossible not to look forward to distant times, when our rapid multiplication will expand itself beyond those limits, and cover the whole northern, if not the southern continent with a people speaking the same language, governed in similar forms and by similar laws; nor can we contemplate with satisfaction either blot or mixture [of races] on that surface." Paul L. Ford (ed.), *Works of Thomas Jefferson* (12 vols., New York, G. P. Putnam, 1904–1905), IX, 317.

7. The concept that a safety valve would be found in the West for problems of the East was common in the nation before Walker's day. A good account of it is in Rush Welter, "The Frontier West as Image of American Society," *Mississippi Valley Historical Review*, XLVI (Mar. 1960), 593–614; Edward Everett, "Flint's Geography and History," *North American Review*, XXVIII (1829), 82.

Negro race, and the problem of race relations. All those explosive forces of American life would pass off quietly, automatically, and in the foreseeable future. The enslaved race, released from bondage, would distribute itself happily over the boundless latitudes of the tropics and would help the tropics to rise to maturity. The American republic and the continent would become, in fact as well as in name, the land of the free.

Walker gave warning, however, as well as hope to the hesitating in painting this glowing picture. The warning was of an unmeasured disaster that would befall the North if defeat of annexation were permitted to occur. Texas would become an abolitionized state. Its gates would be closed to slaves. The slaves would be left in the East to multiply. The time would come when the soil of all the East and the Southwest, as well, would be ravaged by the destructiveness of slave cultivation. Masters would be faced with bankruptcy. They would have no escape from it except by emancipation. Emancipation would come in the border states first, since slavery is already decaying there. Freed Negroes, bereft of the opportunity of a livelihood, would turn north and would inundate the Northern states. Already these states, especially the cities, are saddled with many of them. If the number of freed Negroes were doubled by border state emancipations and should become concentrated in the North they would total 800,000 by 1853; 1,600,000 by 1865; and 3,200,000 by 1890.

Freed Negroes resident in the North are in a deplorable state. They are reduced to it by such forces as climate, urbanization, and lack of self-discipline. Among Northern Negroes percentages of insanity, idiocy, blindness, deafness, and dumbness, and, also, pauperism and crime are higher by far than among slaves in the South. This is true also of European free Negroes. These high rates of defectivism and also of criminality are the result of vice and degeneracy.[8] Northern states already groan under the burden of maintaining even those Negroes now resident among them. What would they not endure when a horde of newly emancipated slaves overran them! The problems would become staggering, the costs of correctional and relief agencies beyond computation. Moreover, white workers, in competition with starving blacks, would be reduced to the lowest levels of survival.

8. Calhoun was even more specific on this point than Walker. *Senate Docs.*, 28 Cong., 1 sess. (Ser. 435), No. 341, 52.

This frightening prospect of cities overrun by emancipated Negroes Walker contrasted with the happy one of a flow southward by way of Texas over the balmy lands of Central and South America. The contrast was meant to give pause to any who thought of rejecting Texas on the score of welfare of the Negro.

The evidence cited by Walker to prove the sad effects of Northern urbanization on Negroes was drawn from neutral sources or, even more impartially, from Northern sources. It was drawn from the federal census of 1840 and from state and local documents of Maine, Massachusetts, and Pennsylvania. Speeches by Northern congressmen, delivered in response to petitions for the abolition of slavery in the District of Columbia, were also cited. One, cited with particular effect, was by an antislavery Democrat, Dr. Alexander Duncan of Cincinnati, delivered in the House on January 6, 1844. Duncan was quoted as saying that any general abolition of slavery in the South would inundate his own community with free blacks who would be "paupers, beggars, thieves, assassins, and desperadoes; all, or nearly all, penniless and destitute, without skill, means, industry, or perseverance to obtain a livelihood . . . No man's fireside, person, family, or property would be safe by day or night. It *now requires* the whole energies of the law and the whole vigilance of the police of all our principal cities to restrain and keep in subordination the few straggling *free Negroes* which now infest them." This vivid language was not precisely what Duncan was reported in the *Congressional Globe* as having used, but even the authorized version was devastating enough. It declared that the people of the North would have to treat the freed Negroes as "beasts of prey" and pronounced Negroes inferior to whites in mental and physical qualities—as inferior as the orangoutang is to them.[9]

A Northern source was cited, also, for the useful information concerning the racial composition of the population of Central America and South America. The source was Thomas Gamaliel Bradford, *Comprehensive Atlas, Geographical, Historical and Commercial,* published in Boston in 1835, the maps of which were accompanied by statistical information. The compiler was a much-respected Boston scholar and

---

9. *Cong. Globe,* 28 *Cong.,* 1 sess., 109 (Jan., 6, 1844). Richard D. Davis, a Democratic congressman from New York, was cited to the same effect. *Ibid.,* 84 (Dec. 29, 1843). In the Senate, William Allen (Ohio) expressed like views. *Ibid.,* 28 Cong., 2 sess., 343 (Feb. 25, 1845).

cartographer, descendant of the eminent governor and historian of Plymouth Plantation. He had earlier been an associate of Francis Lieber in the preparation of the monumental *Encyclopaedia Americana.* By citing such sources Walker gave authority to his thesis.

How well did this thesis serve Tyler's need of ratification of a treaty?[10] The question is difficult to answer. Tyler was himself a confusing element in the answer. He was known for having proslavery views; he was unpopular; and, what was worse, he was a President without a party. He had been elected as a Whig. He had broken with the Whigs, especially with Clay, and had moved toward the Democrats. Democrats would have none of him. Clay was the prospective presidential nominee of the Whigs; Van Buren, of the Democrats. Neither had yet declared his position on the Texas issue. Only one answer is certain: the thesis, in appealing to moderates, alienated extremists. It alienated abolitionists—the friends of the Negro, the immediatists regarding slavery—who resented the unflattering picture of the Negro painted in it. It alienated Southern extremists, who conceived of slavery as the very foundation of Southern life, as more precious, indeed, than the Union itself, and resented the doctrine that it was poisonous and destined to die of its poisons.

A series of accidents derailed the plans of Tyler. In February 1844 in an exhibition of firing potency, a cannon on the naval vessel *Princeton* exploded before a delegation of dignitaries and killed, among them, Tyler's Secretary of State, Upshur. Upshur had to be hurriedly replaced to complete the treaty. The man recommended as replacement was Calhoun. Tyler resisted the recommendation. The great South Carolinian was anathema to the Van Buren and Jackson wings of the Democratic party. He was, moreover, likely to overshadow the President in the cabinet. He was foisted on the President by a close friend and adviser, Henry A. Wise. At a conference Wise confessed to Tyler that he had already half committed him to Calhoun. Calhoun was ap-

---

10. Walker was charged by Whigs with having a pecuniary stake in the annexation of Texas. According to an anonymous correspondent of the New York *Weekly Express,* a Whig organ, he was rumored in Congress to have interests in Texas lands and scrip to the extent of $200,000. He categorically denied it. In a letter to the editor of the *Weekly Express,* written on April 8, 1844, he declared that he owned no lands, scrip, or stock in Texas whatsoever. He owned, he said, a body of valuable cotton lands in Mississippi, which he was being warned by opponents of annexation would depreciate in worth by not less than $100,000 if Texas were annexed. New York *Weekly Express,* Apr. 12, 1844.

pointed. It was he who brought the treaty with Texas to a conclusion and set the stage for presentation of it to the Senate.[11]

Calhoun was an extremist in his slavery views. He considered slavery not only no evil, but a positive good. It is good for the Negro whom it improves and lifts in the scale of civilization; it is good for the Southern states; it is a necessity for the nation. It is exposed to foreign dangers if Texas stays independent. Great Britain is resolved to abolitionize Texas. Its cotton and sugar interests in the West Indies and East Indies are suffering from the abolition of slavery there. Its competitive power in the markets of the world has declined. It will be restored only if American competitive power can be reduced to the same low level by the destruction of slavery in the United States. Such destruction will begin with the abolitionizing of Texas. Slavery cannot be preserved in the eastern states if a free society arises on the borders of the western. The only means of preserving slavery in the eastern states against such a calamity is to incorporate Texas into the Union. Ratification of the Texan treaty is thus an imperious duty of the federal government and especially of the Senate. Other more national grounds were used by Calhoun to make his case, but the slavery thesis was outstanding. It was embodied in the documents sent to the Senate with the treaty.[12]

Calhoun's was the third of the theses injected into the Texas fight. It was a thesis distorted by strong feeling, a missile fired by an extremist. It resembled the Adams thesis fired first in the exchange. The two were fired by fighters singularly alike in temper—aggressive, dogmatic, and uncompromising, especially on the slavery issue. Each fighter brought to battle the moral dignity and personal prestige of an unsullied private life and the respect felt for sincerity of convictions even by those who detested the convictions. Each represented the extremism of a section. In an opinion poll neither would have commanded the vote Walker would have commanded for his thesis.

11. St. George L. Sioussat, "John Caldwell Calhoun," in Samuel F. Bemis (ed.), *American Secretaries of State and Their Diplomacy* (10 vols., New York, Alfred A. Knopf, 1927–1929), V, 127–129. For light on Calhoun's appointment, see American Historical Association, *Annual Report, 1899* (2 vols., Washington, G.P.O., 1930), II, 934.

12. The documents appear in *Senate Docs.*, 28 Cong., 1 sess. (Ser. 435), No. 341, 52. The Calhoun thesis was foreshadowed in the Upshur portion of the correspondence.

The treaty and the correspondence came to the Senate under seal of secrecy on April 22. They came with a covering letter from Tyler containing a mixture of arguments for ratification, national and sectional, though with the proslavery ones muted. The message was such a combination of incompatibles as only a Tyler would have been capable of. It almost invited defeat.[13] Its accompanying documents were meant for reading only in executive session. Five days after they arrived they were flung to the public in the columns of the New York *Evening Post*. They had been betrayed to that paper, as was later revealed, by Senator Benjamin Tappan of Ohio, a Van Buren Democrat and a free soiler.[14]

This upset was but one of a series. On the same fateful day two momentous letters appeared in the press, one from Henry Clay, the other from Martin Van Buren, each announcing that its author was opposed to an immediate annexation of Texas. The authors clearly hoped by this maneuver to keep the disruptive issue out of the campaign. The combined effect of these overturnings was utter confusion. The confusion was heightened when in May, at the Democratic national convention, Van Buren was defeated for the presidential nomination, and James K. Polk, pledged to immediate annexation, was chosen instead. The defeat of Van Buren was accomplished largely by the convention activities of Walker; the nomination of Polk afterward was accomplished by a union of Walker and George Bancroft, the Boston intellectual. With Polk pledged to annexation and Clay opposed, Senate ratification of the treaty became a party matter. The strategy of winning a biparty vote large enough to ratify the treaty collapsed.[15] When the vote was finally taken in June 1844 two-thirds of the Senate voted

13. *Ibid.* See also *House Exec. Docs.*, 28 Cong., 2 sess. (Ser. 463), No. 2, 3–110. In 1850 Tyler disclaimed responsibility for the proslavery argument of Upshur's and Calhoun's correspondence. Tyler to Webster, Apr. 17, 1850, John Tyler Papers, Library of Congress.

14. Tappan was severely censured by the Senate. *Senate Jour.*, 28 Cong., 1 sess. (Ser. 430), 426–443. Tyler's reliance on the slavery protection thesis was attacked promptly by Francis P. Blair, editor of the Washington *Globe*, a close friend of Jackson and Van Buren. Calhoun was charged with a secret desire to effect a rejection of the treaty as a prelude to Southern secession and a union of the South with Texas. Washington *Globe* (sw), May 6, 16, 1844.

15. A Washington correspondent in the New York *Daily Tribune* (Mar. 19, 1844) reported that a count of Senate votes on ratification had been taken by Walker and that his figures were 38 pro, 13 con. Greeley questioned the figures. *Ibid.*, Mar. 20, 1844. Upshur had made an estimate of 40 pro, 12 con.

to reject the treaty. Every Whig, North and South, except one, so voted.[16] The issue was thrust into the oncoming campaign.

In the campaign the Walker letter formed a virtual arsenal for annexationists in the North. It provided a thesis—a valuable middle-of-the-road thesis. It also supplied arguments, facts, and statistics by which the thesis could be upheld on the hustings. As an arsenal it drew intense and continuous fire from the enemy, from unconvinced free soilers, Democratic and Whig. The intensity and continuity of the fire were indications of the importance of the thesis.

The fire was opened by Theodore Sedgwick even before the campaign formally began. Sedgwick was the grandson and namesake of the great Federalist who had given tone to national and Massachusetts politics in Alexander Hamilton's day. A Democrat of anti-slavery views, he considered slavery a curse to the South and to the nation. He selected the New York *Evening Post* to deliver his fire. Its editor, William Cullen Bryant, had views on slavery similar to his own and was a friend and former neighbor in western Massachusetts. The attack took the form of a series of articles, republished in April 1844 as a pamphlet.[17]

In these articles Sedgwick traversed the whole Walker letter with special attention to its slavery thesis. He pronounced the thesis one of the most extraordinary for boldness ever put forth. He was glad to concur in one of its positions—that slavery, if left to itself, would work its own cure, that it carried the seeds of its own destruction. But it would work that cure only if new lands were kept closed to it. New lands opened to it would extend its life, indeed, would rehabilitate it in old areas. New lands would afford slave breeders new markets. In Virginia, Sedgwick charged, slave breeding was a form of "rotation of crops." Worn-out lands were used for it and would continue so, as long as a profitable market for slaves remained in the West. Texas, if admitted, would, for the indefinite future, provide such a market.[18] The argument that migration of slaves did not extend the area of

16. A good contemporary analysis of the vote appears in *Niles' Register*, LXVI (June 15, 1844), 241. The best historical analysis is Arthur C. Cole, *Whig Party in the South* (Washington, American Historical Association, 1913), 109–116.

17. [Theodore Sedgwick,] *Thoughts on the Proposed Annexation of Texas to the United States* (New York, 1844). Two editions of the pamphlet appeared.

18. This view had been set forth by Channing in his letter of 1837. *Works*, II, 219.

slavery Sedgwick pronounced stale as well as bad. It had been employed at the time of the fight over the admission of Missouri. Its form then had been that slavery would be mitigated by dispersion of the slaves over new lands. The tragic fallacy of that argument had been demonstrated, Sedgwick believed, by history.

Dismissed by Sedgwick as unworthy of serious consideration was Walker's warning of disaster to Northern cities if slaves were prematurely emancipated. The emancipated Negroes would not move north. They were children of the torrid zone, and, if ever they won freedom, the inclement temperatures of the North would repel them and keep them in the South. Sedgwick challenged the statistics Walker had used in his warning. They were, he charged, vitiated by wholesale distortions. The figures cited from the census of 1840 as to Negro defectives in the North were not to be relied on. The census of that year was notoriously careless and inadequate. As for insanity among Northern Negroes, Sedgwick argued, insanity results from use of the mind, and among slaves the mind goes unused. Concerning pauperism, he said, if Northern rates are high, Southern are higher. Slaves are all paupers. As for the crime rate among Northern Negroes, it could not be compared with that of slaves because most plantation crimes are dealt with by overseers and go unrecorded.[19]

These blows were telling ones in exposing weaknesses and exaggerations in the Walker thesis, but they did not overturn its central concept. Indeed they somewhat strengthened the concept. The concept was that slavery was destructive of soil,[20] that it necessitated constant migration, that the slaves would flow to Texas if Texas were annexed. Sedgwick not only agreed to this; he adopted it for his own argument. He introduced, to be sure, the argument of slave breeding. But that

19. Some Northern states, Ohio, Indiana, and Illinois especially, prohibited or restricted by "Black Laws" the entrance or settlement of free Negroes or mulattoes. References to such legislation are given in Leslie H. Fishel, "The North and the Negro, 1865–1900" (2 vols., Ph.D. diss., Harvard University, 1954), I, 23. A free Negro, James McCune Smith, in letters to the New York *Daily Tribune* (Jan. 26, Feb. 1, 24, 1844), challenged the prevalent notion that free Negroes were in a worse state in point of defectives than slaves. A recent bibliography is in Richard Bardolph, *The Negro Vanguard* (New York, Rinehart, 1959), 343–369.

20. Agreement on this point was widespread in the North. A more balanced view is presented in Avery O. Craven, *Soil Exhaustion as a Factor in the Agricultural History of Virginia and Maryland, 1606–1860* (Urbana, University of Illinois Press, 1926); and Paul W. Gates, *The Farmer's Age* (New York, Holt, Rinehart, Winston, 1960).

was disputable and was not, in any case, altogether germane, for however slaves were created, the creating would stop if the markets for them were shut off. This was Sedgwick's argument, and it was precisely Walker's as applied to an exhausted future Texas, a Texas that would be the last refuge of slavery in the West. In the meantime Sedgwick had left unanswered Walker's thesis that Texas, by becoming annexed, would keep open the safety valve to adjacent Mexico.

Even as Sedgwick thundered, reinforcement came to Walker. It came from home ground, from a member of Tyler's cabinet, Secretary of War William Wilkins, a close friend and relative of Walker by marriage, a prominent Pennsylvanian, who had served the nation as senator, judge, and diplomat. A devoted Jacksonian and a warm expansionist, especially as to Texas, he was without strong convictions concerning slavery, though he did not approve it. In an address to his old Pennsylvania constituents, prepared in April 1844, he earnestly urged support for annexation. He urged it in Walker's terms. Annexation would be followed, he maintained, by emancipation of slaves in the border states, which would be a gratifying result. Slavery would finally become concentrated in Texas. There it would evaporate. The freed Negroes would disappear across the Rio Grande into Mexico and South America, where they would be among peoples who had no prejudices of caste or color and where they would attain a status of equality and elevation. Texas was the one real hope ever offered Negroes, in all the weary years since they had been forced upon the New World by British cupidity, of an ultimate free home of their own. This address was taken by the *National Intelligencer* for reprinting, which assured it a wide reading.[21]

Reinforcement to Walker came from another prominent Pennsylvanian, Charles J. Ingersoll. Ingersoll was a veteran of Congress, chairman of the Committee on Foreign Affairs of the House in 1844, and a litterateur of note. He was eager for annexation as an expansionist and as a Jacksonian. He prepared a report for his committee urging ratification in which he wholeheartedly accepted the Walker thesis. A hostile majority of his committee, consisting of three Clay Whigs and two Van Buren Democrats, relegated the report to a pigeonhole.

21. William Wilkins, *Address to the People of the 21st Congressional District of Pennsylvania* (Washington, 1844); reprinted in *National Intelligencer,* July 6, 1844. The address was replied to in the New York *Daily Tribune,* Apr. 17, 1844.

Ingersoll was determined that it should not stay there. He sent it to the Washington *Daily Globe,* where it was joyfully printed on May 1, 1844, with the author's explanation that circumstances beyond his control had required him to publish it on his own responsibility. A triumphant editor's note was appended that it was "an extensive presentment of all the titles, facts, dates, and circumstances involved in [the] great question." In truth it was a summarization of Walker, though in less guarded terms. If Texas is annexed, Ingersoll maintained, at least Maryland, Virginia, the two Carolinas, Kentucky, and Tennessee, if not all the slaveholding states, will have their slaves withdrawn to those fresh lands. Many slave states will become free; they will join that part of the Union where slavery is disliked. In Texas, itself, three-fourths of the land is upland, the soil and climate of which is suited only to grazing. This will be divided into free states. Only one-quarter of the land is suited to slave crops. That area, having drained off most of the slaves of the South, will itself ultimately become free by operation of economic laws. The freed Negroes will drift to Mexico and to its neighbors, where a society essentially African will develop. The dream of philanthropists, that a peaceful and "grateful" disappearance of slavery will occur, will thus take on reality. Every other dream of that sort—Liberia, Haiti, Canada—had ended in rude awakening. Ten thousand copies of this hopeful vision were purchased as offprints at once by private subscription for circulation to the nation.[22]

Another member of Tyler's cabinet entered the lists: David Henshaw from Boston, whom the President had named in 1843 as Secretary of the Navy and who had served as such until February 1844, when confirmation in the Senate failed. He was a Calhounist in political affiliation and ranked high with Southern Democrats. In a letter to the *Boston Post* of May 29, 1844, he maintained that slavery would not be extended by annexation, that it already existed in Texas, and that the only effect of annexation would be to transfer slaves to Texas from border states. The result would be that all the border states

22. The report occupied most of the front page of the *Daily Globe* and four more columns inside. It was reprinted immediately as a pamphlet at the *Globe* office in consultation with Calhoun and Tyler, and ten thousand copies, paid for by private subscription, were sent out. It heavily emphasized the theme of British interference in Texas. See *Mr. C. J. Ingersoll's View of the Texas Question* [1844]; also William M. Meigs, *Charles Jared Ingersoll* (Philadelphia, 1897), 265.

would soon become free. The chief preoccupation of the letter was the author's indignation at British interference in Texas, which annexation would foil.

George Bancroft took the same line. In August 1844 he became the Democratic nominee for the governorship of Massachusetts. On August 15 he wrote an acceptance letter in which he declared: "The extension of slavery is not involved in the [Texas] question. Slavery is already in Texas; its re-annexation, in that point of view, tends rather to set a territorial limit to slavery; and would exclude in perpetuity, and still more effectually than now, all increase of slavery from abroad. A variety of causes conspires with an impulse of their own nature to draw those of African descent towards the South; the boundary line of slavery would recede all along its present northern frontier, and as the spirit of emancipation increases, an avenue would be opened to them to pass to social and political equality in the central regions of America, where the prejudices of race do not exist."[23] Exceptional care was taken by Bancroft in framing this part of his letter. The manuscript copy of it among his papers in the Massachusetts Historical Society is so revised, rephrased, and rewritten as to be almost unreadable. It was much less specific, also, than Walker's letter. But it did not fall behind Walker in its denunciations of British interference, nor in its promises of economic benefits of annexation to Massachusetts. These occupied much of the space of the letter, and the anti-British line was the one emphasized on the hustings. In an address at Faneuil Hall, Bancroft assured a cheering audience that on the Texas question Polk, if elected, would not be found acting under the red cross of Britain; nor would he be "a lacquey taking his cue from the cabinet at St. James."[24]

23. The manuscript draft of the letter is in the George Bancroft Papers, 1843–1844, Massachusetts Historical Society. The printed form is in Boston *Weekly Bay State Democrat*, Aug. 23, 1844.
24. *Boston Post*, June 5, 1844. The same line was taken by Benjamin F. Hallett, Democratic candidate for Congress from Boston. In a speech to a Boston audience he declared that if Texas were annexed slavery would give way to free labor in the border states just as it had earlier in the Northern and Middle states, including Massachusetts. The slaves would pass off by diffusion into Texas and then by more diffusion into Mexico. Only Whigs, taking the British side of every issue, were opposed to annexation. *Ibid.*, Aug. 20, 1844. Other instances of the acceptance of Walker's safety valve thesis in editorial or pamphlet or broadside form are listed in Streeter, *Bibliography of Texas 1795–1845*, Part III, vol. 2, 480–481, 494, 534.

What attracted middle-of-the-road Democrats in the North to the Walker thesis repelled extremists in the South. They cited the thesis in demanding rejection of the treaty. One of them was Waddy Thompson of South Carolina, a large-scale cotton planter, owner of a hundred slaves, and an active Whig politician. He had once advocated the Texan cause in Congress. He had been a leader in obtaining a favorable vote in the House for a resolution recognizing Texas. In 1838 he had sponsored a measure looking to annexation by joint resolution, which Adams had defeated by his filibustering speech. No love was lost between the two men. In 1844 Thompson was a Clay supporter. He had long been a foe of Calhoun. On the slavery issue, however, he had Calhounist views. In July 1844 he sent a letter to the *National Intelligencer*, which constituted for him a complete reversal of former views regarding Texas.

He began the letter—a five-column affair—with the assurance that though he opposed annexation he was a warm friend to Texas. He opposed annexation because it would injure Southern agriculture. In Texas there are millions of acres of land that will produce cotton at an exceptionally high rate per acre. The cotton is of superior quality—better than that of the eastern states. The soil is rich, the climate ideal. Provisions are cheap. Cotton is raised profitably at three cents a pound. Planters are now moving to Texas from exhausted lands in the East in large numbers. An estimate, made by an advocate of annexation, is that two million Negroes will be taken there in a short time. Is it wise, Thompson asked, to stimulate such competition by annexation when "demand and supply" for cotton are trembling in the balance?[25] On old lands cotton is impossible to produce at three cents a pound. Slaves will become an encumbrance there. Little consolation will be found by a planter riding over lands, grown up in broomsedge and washed into gullies, in the reflection that slavery is prospering in Texas. Slavery deserves to prosper. The African is more contented and happy, and he is better cared for, more moral, religious, and virtuous in slavery than in any other condition. Slavery will be utterly destroyed in the old states by Texan competition. Slaves will flow

25. The year 1844 marked the lowest average annual price for cotton in all American history (5.6 cents per pound). This was a significant factor in southern attitudes toward annexation. U.S. Department of Commerce and Labor, *Census Bulletin 134* (Washington, G.P.O., 1916), 51.

in response to this competition to Texas by "a law as fixed and certain as that by which water finds its level." From all the border states they will flow, and in a short time those states will become nonslaveholding. Those states will no longer have, when this has happened, a common interest with the slaveholding states. They will soon partake of that fanatical spirit of a false philanthropy that now pervades the world. The slaveholding states will lose their most important allies, not only at the ballot box but on the battlefield if, alas, they should be driven to that extremity as a final defense.[26]

Here, in reverse, was Walker's thesis. Because Texas would, as a certainty, drain slaves from the East and convert border states into a zone of freedom, allied with the North, Texas must be denied admission to the Union. The arguments of Walker, Wilkins, and Ingersoll, all cited in the letter, had succeeded too well. Thompson was candid enough to admit that Texas, even if not admitted, would be a serious competitor to the eastern cotton grower. But he felt that it would compete less effectively as a foreign state than as part of the Union, for as a foreign state it would attract fewer of the planters of the Old South. Moreover, Thompson argued, Mexico would be alienated by the annexation of Texas. If a treaty of annexation were ratified, it would be the equivalent of a declaration of war on Mexico. The fairness of attacks made on England by Democrats, Thompson questioned. He thought England and all other commercial nations acted perfectly naturally in preferring that Texas remain an independent power with markets open to the world.

This letter was read by John Quincy Adams on the day it appeared. It was read with distrust and yet with grim satisfaction. The distrust was occasioned by Thompson's admission that he might be reconciled to the incorporation of Texas if it were divided into several slave states. Adams had long been suspicious of Thompson. He once described him in his diary as a snake,[27] which was a harsh judgment, for Thomp-

---

26. The letter appeared in the Washington *National Intelligencer,* July 6, 1844. It was republished in *Niles' Register,* LXVI (July 13, 1844), 316–319. An earlier letter from a Louisiana planter, Senator Alexander Barrow, setting forth the same doctrines, appeared in the *National Intelligencer* on May 25, 1844, and was copied in its entirety by the New York *Daily Tribune* on May 27, 1844. Barrow was a Whig.

27. Charles F. Adams (ed.), *Memoirs of John Quincy Adams* (12 vols., Philadelphia, 1874–1877), XII, 42, 68.

son was a man of honesty and political independence. On the day the letter appeared the two men chanced to meet, and they discussed it amicably. Afterward Adams entered in his diary the comment that Thompson was "as cunning as four Yankees, as sly as four Quakers, and just now admires the people of Massachusetts too much." But Adams was pleased that Thompson had knocked down "Walker, Wilkins and C. J. Ingersoll with their own maul," and he went on to say: "I hope his letter will be eminently useful at the present crisis, and devoutly pray that he and Benton and the 'Princeton' gun may be the instruments for the deliverance of my country."[28]

Before long a new appraisal of the safety valve thesis appeared. It came from the pen of John L. O'Sullivan, editor of the *Democratic Review* and of the New York *Morning News*. He was a fervent expansionist—the very embodiment of the Manifest Destiny doctrine of his day. He thought Texan annexation a stage in the evolution of the doctrine. In the July number of the *Democratic Review* he offered his readers Walker's thesis in essence though in a slightly different terminology and with a new dressing.[29] Slaves, he believed, would flow to Texas from all the border states. In Texas they would ultimately gain freedom. They would then flow southward into Mexico, and the problems of slavery and race would be solved together. But what especially interested O'Sullivan was the manner in which adjustment would be made in the border states to the loss of slaves on exhausted land. That was spelled out in detail. Those lands will be occupied by Northern whites. Whites are more intelligent, more enterprising, more industrious than slaves, and are actuated, as freemen, by incentives of self-interest. They will rehabilitate the lands and prosper. Their prosperity will demonstrate the superiority of freedom over slavery. The border states will be won to freedom. Already in parts of Virginia that process is under way, and it will be hastened if Texas is annexed.[30]

28. *Ibid.*, 68. Benton at this time was opposing immediate annexation.
29. *Democratic Review*, XV (July 1844), 11–16. The title of the article was: "The Re-annexation of Texas—in its Influence on the Duration of Slavery." The Philadelphia *Pennsylvanian* reprinted it as a pamphlet for distribution, under the same title.
30. *Ibid.* The Whig editor of the New York *Morning Express* used this argument in opposing annexation. What Thompson had done in the name of cotton growers of the East this editor did, after a visit to Virginia, in the name of tobacco growers. He believed Texas, if annexed, would drain the Old Dominion of slaves, land values would drop away, and Northerners would purchase the wasted areas

O'Sullivan described another boon that the flow of Negroes from exhausted land would bring. The Negroes would be removed from potential troublemaking. If they were left in the South in an emancipated state they would expect to have political and social equality. Friction with whites would develop that would be fanned by Northern zealots into a race war, the horrors of which would sicken humanity. Writers other than O'Sullivan had dwelt on this aspect of the problem. Upshur, as Secretary of State, had described it the year before in a letter to Edward Everett. "No man, who knows any thing of his own nature can suppose it to be possible that two races of men, distinguished by external and ineffaceable marks obvious to every eye, who have held towards each other, from time immemorial, the relation of master and slave, could ever live together as equals, in the same country, and under the same Government. If, therefore, slavery be abolished, the one or the other of the races must leave the country or be exterminated."[31] Texas would solve that problem, O'Sullivan believed, by drawing Negroes to its soil and later freeing them to go to Latin America, where generals, congressmen, and presidents were of mixed blood.

The Walker thesis scored again in the September issue of the *Democratic Review*, where Alexander H. Everett, the distinguished elder brother of Edward Everett, gave it his adherence. He was a graduate of Harvard, the youngest in his class and highest in rank. He had been secretary to John Quincy Adams at St. Petersburg and had later been appointed by Adams as minister to Spain. He had been editor of the *North American Review*. He had lost standing in Boston, and even in the household of his brother, by deserting the old standards in 1832 and joining the Democrats. He was a believer in the doctrine of Manifest Destiny and an ardent supporter of the annexation of

and rehabilitate them. He later reconciled himself to Texan annexation by the reflection that it would redeem the border states. New York *Morning Express*, Nov. 18, 1844; New York *Morning News*, Feb. 1, 1845.

31. *Senate Docs.*, 28 Cong., 1 sess. (Ser. 435), No. 341, 33. Jefferson was equally positive if less fierce. In 1779 he wrote in his autobiography: "Nothing is more certainly written in the book of fate than that these people [slaves] are to be free. Nor is it less certain that the two races, equally free, cannot live in the same government. Nature, habit, opinion has drawn indelible lines of distinction between them." Ford (ed.), *Works of Thomas Jefferson*, I, 77. Also, Senator George McDuffie in *Cong. Globe*, 28 Cong., 1 sess., Appendix, 532 (May 23, 1844). A revealing contrast between the United States and Latin America in the raising of Negro slaves to freedom is in Frank Tannenbaum, *Slave and Citizen* (New York, Alfred A. Knopf, 1947).

Texas. His article on Texas in the *Democratic Review* was in the form of a twenty-one-page letter. He canvassed in it every aspect of the question with much attention to British interference in Texas, which must have embarrassed his brother, then minister to England. He wholeheartedly accepted the Walker thesis; indeed, he stretched it. He thought the weight of the slaveholding states in Congress would diminish by reason of annexation even if Texas became three slave states. Six or eight or even ten states, now slave, would become free if Texas were annexed. Among the states making the change would be South Carolina and Georgia.[32]

A savage reply to this letter was made by Horace Greeley in the New York *Daily Tribune*. Greeley began calmly, with repetition of the slave breeding arguments of the Sedgwick letter. Then he descended to sheer personal vilification. He traced out Everett's apostasy of an earlier day—his turning from vehement opposition to Jackson to a hireling status after Jackson's second triumph in 1832. He had to admit the plausibility of Everett's writing; Everett had learned to write before he turned his coat. But the present letter was dishonest, deceptive, and knavish, intended to drug the conscience of those who wanted to believe they could give a vote for Texas without incurring the guilt of extending human slavery. Sad to relate Everett was a Boston boy who had sold himself to the South Carolina slave oligarchy for pap in the form of patronage expected from a Democratic administration.[33] Everett replied to this tirade in the pages of the New York *Morning News*.[34] But it only started another flow of bile from the pen of the aroused Greeley.[35] Altogether the exchange brought less light than heat to readers interested in the validity of the Walker thesis.

The campaign ended in balloting in November. In the balloting Polk carried the day. In the North he did it in a three-cornered contest

32. *Democratic Review*, XV (Sept. 1844), 250–270. In an early phase of the New York campaign of 1844 Silas Wright, Democratic candidate for the governorship and a key figure in the campaign, expressed views reflecting those of the Walker letter. *New Hampshire Patriot*, Aug. 8, 1844.

33. New York *Daily Tribune*, Nov. 27, 1844. Everett was appointed commissioner to China early in Polk's administration. He accepted and died in China after a brief service.

34. New York *Morning News*, Nov. 30, 1844. Everett pointed out that even Clay believed annexation of Texas would not extend slavery.

35. New York *Daily Tribune*, Dec. 2, 1844. Greeley admitted that he did not see eye to eye on slavery issues with Clay, especially with Clay's view that slavery would die of itself.

in which, by pluralities of popular votes, he won decisive electoral ballots. He held Democratic strength, whereas Whig strength strayed to the Liberty party. In New York and Michigan, in particular, Polk held his party sufficiently to win electoral decisions. His ability to do so revealed the potency of the Walker letter, which had satisfied the mind or drugged the conscience of enough Democrats, allergic to slavery, to permit them to remain in the fold. The editor of the *Democratic Review* thus happily accounted for the victory shortly after the election. He wrote that the letter had been the "text book" of the party in the campaign and had produced a more decided effect on the popular mind than any other publication of the day.[36] Tyler, in 1847, named prominently among those who had brought annexation to pass, Walker, "whose writings unveiled the true merits of the question, and, aided by the expositions of many editors of the newspaper press, brought the public mind to a just and sound decision."[37]

But the Texas issue came to a head before Polk was installed as President. In the lame-duck session of Congress, convened in December 1844, it was brought by Tyler's influence to the House in the form of a Joint Resolution of annexation. The resolution, amended to make it palatable, was adopted in the House by a vote of 120–98, a response to the recent election.[38] In the Senate it was expected to encounter resistance. To promote its passage Walker introduced an amendment whereby a choice was offered the President between annexation by invitation at once or by a new negotiation. The resolution in that form was acceptable to Benton and to several others. By a margin of 27–25 it was adopted. Those voting for it included the following Northern believers in the Walker gospel: Levi Woodbury of New Hampshire, Daniel S. Dickinson of New York, James Buchanan of Pennsylvania,

36. *Democratic Review*, XVI (Feb. 1845), 162. For further contemporary comment on the *Letter's* impact, see "Other Theses in the *Letter of Mr. Walker;* Its Mode of Distribution and Its Impact," which appears below.

37. *Niles' Register*, LXXIII (Sept. 11, 1847), 31. In December 1847 Lewis Cass said of the Walker *Letter* that it "everywhere produced so favorable an impression upon the public mind as to have conduced very materially to the accomplishment of that great measure." William T. Young, *General Lewis Cass* (Philadelphia, 1853), 326.

38. The original House resolution and the substitute of Milton Brown are in *Cong. Globe*, 28 Cong., 2 sess., 26 (Dec. 12, 1844), 193 (Jan. 25, 1845). The House vote on the Brown resolution is in *House Jour.*, 28 Cong., 2 sess. (Ser. 462), 264–265. Northern Democrats divided in the vote: 53 for, 28 against. Northern Whigs were solid against, to the number of 59.

William Allen of Ohio, and Sidney Breese of Illinois, to say nothing of Walker himself.[39] If Charles G. Atherton of New Hampshire, Edward Hannegan of Indiana, and James Semple of Indiana, who voted for annexation, had spoken they would probably have proclaimed their conversion to Walker also. These Democrats were all imbued with that zeal for expansionism and indifference to slavery which was the hallmark of the Walker school of politics.

The resolution received its final approval in the two houses in the waning hours of the Tyler administration. Congress expected that it would be left to the incoming administration to implement. The President was persuaded by Calhoun, however, to act on it himself. On the night of March 3 Tyler sent an invitation to the Texan government to enter the Union, which Texas presently accepted.

In retrospect, the Walker thesis was an appeal to the electorate to leave the slavery issue to the future in the interests of peace and of territorial gain. It was an appeal to reject extremism—extremism of those in the North who demanded that slavery be halted at once and of those in the South who demanded that it never be halted. It was defended by postulates and arguments that were not preposterous or fraudulent, as charged by extremists. Many of the postulates were widely accepted at the time: the self-destructiveness of slavery, the constant migration necessitated by slavery, the precarious state of the institution in the border states, the gradual concentration of it in the Southwest, and the feasibility of Negro colonization in Latin America. Some of the postulates were actually employed later in abolitionist programs, as for instance, the postulate of the redemption of

39. The Senate vote on the resolution as altered by the Walker amendment is in *Senate Jour.*, 28 Cong., 2 sess. (Ser. 448), 215–221. The concurring House vote is in *House Jour.*, 28 Cong., 2 sess. (Ser. 462), 527–529. Northern Democrats changed to the aye column in the concurring House vote to the number of 24 (14 from New York and Michigan). Northern Whigs remained solidly nay. House speeches of significance using the Walker thesis were made by the following Democrats: John W. Tibbatts (Kentucky), Charles J. Ingersoll (Pennsylvania), Robert D. Owen (Indiana), Ezra Dean (Ohio), Alfred P. Stone (Ohio), Andrew Johnson (Tennessee), Moses Norris (New Hampshire), Chesselden Ellis (New York). *Cong. Globe*, 28 Cong., 1 sess., Appendix 450 (May 7, 1844); 28 Cong., 2 sess., 86, 111, 123, 189 (Jan. 1845); Appendix, 105, 223, 189–190, 141–142 (Jan. 1845). Senate speeches relying on the thesis, by Woodbury, Dickinson, Buchanan, Allen, and Breese, are found scattered through *ibid.*, 28 Cong., 1 sess., Appendix, 543, 722, 767 (June 1844); 28 Cong., 2 sess., 343 (Feb. 25, 1845); Appendix, 324 (Feb. 22, 1845). Woodbury's views are most clearly set forth in Concord *New Hampshire Patriot*, Aug. 22, 1844.

Virginia by Northern freemen which Eli Thayer tested in his well-known Ceredo demonstration project of the late 1850s. The Latin American colonization idea seemed more promising by far than the Liberia project had ever been.[40] It avoided problems of organized transportation on a large scale, which had baffled the American Colonization Society. It depended on individual mobility, which planters seeking fortune in Texas would provide, and likewise the mobility of emancipated Negroes seeking the wide open spaces and free opportunities of the wilderness paradise of Latin America. It relied, as did the better-known frontier safety valve thesis of Frederick Jackson Turner, on individual enterprise as its motivating force.

The Walker thesis was a panacea to cure two problems—slavery and race—together. The time it would take for the cure was variously estimated at three-quarters of a century to a century. That much time was in the end denied it. The Civil War intervened to cure slavery by the sword. The sword did not cure the race problem, the more difficult one of the two. That problem is with us yet despite the urgent protests of antisegregationists, the offense it gives the colored races of the world, and the exploitation of the issue by the Soviet Union and its satellites. Its persistence is an indication of the magnitude of the problem which middle-of-the-roaders vaguely realized in the pre-Civil War era and stressed in the debate of 1844.

In the debate similar attitudes were taken in the two sections concerning the Negro. They were the common denominator sought by Walker and were exploited effectively by him. In the North, the attitude, taken by Democrats especially, was that the Negro for racial reasons is an afflicting problem; in the South, that the problem can be dealt with only by slavery, removal of the race, or race war. The concept of a society consisting of two races, each free, each possessed

---

40. A valuable brief account of projects financed by Congress (1862–1863) to colonize free Negroes in Central America is an essay by Frederic Bancroft, in Jacob E. Cooke, *Frederic Bancroft, Historian* (Norman, University of Oklahoma Press, 1957), 192–227. See also Francis P. Blair, Jr., *The Destiny of the Races of This Continent* (Washington, 1859); and Francis P. Blair, Jr., to James R. Doolittle, Oct. 18, Nov. 3, 1859, and Montgomery Blair to Doolittle, Nov. 11, 1859, Southern History Association, *Publications* (Washington), X (Sept. 1906), 283–288. Walker became, during the Mexican War, an ardent advocate of the absorption of all Mexico by the United States. If he had succeeded, the safety valve would have admitted freed Negroes into a Mexican province of the United States.

of equal rights under law, and entitled to equal opportunity and dignity, was, in the North, deemed contrary to sober reality; in the South, it was deemed unthinkable. For the historian a state of opinion such as this is a base line for registering progress made since 1844. Measured in this perspective, the progress made, though slow, halting, and painful indeed in both sections, is far from discouraging.

Other Theses in the Letter of Mr. Walker; Its Mode of Distribution and Impact

The *Letter of Mr. Walker, of Mississippi, Relative to the Annexation of Texas* advanced reasons for the annexation other than the central one of ridding the nation of slavery. An important reason was that annexation would correct a lamentable diplomatic error of the past. Texas, the reader is assured, had once belonged to the United States. It had been acquired with the Louisiana Purchase of 1803, but had been retroceded unwisely to Spain in the Monroe administration as part of the Adams-Onís Treaty. That cession had cut asunder the western half of the valley of the Mississippi. It had reconsigned to monarchy what had been gained for republicanism. The cession had been of doubtful constitutionality. Fortunately, patriotic American pioneers had settled in Texas, had reacquired it, and were offering it to the United States. If the United States were to accept the offer, the annexation would be merely a re-annexation. This was a palatable doctrine to American expansionists. But contemporary scholars who knew the facts, and historians of a later era scoffed at it.

To the demand for re-annexation of Texas Walker added the demand for re-occupation of the Oregon Country. The two were being joined by Northern expansionists. Walker believed that the Oregon Country, throughout its length and breadth, was the property of the United States. The British had no valid claim there. This thesis was in harmony with the anti-British feeling of the Old Northwest. The dual expansionist program of Oregon and Texas was incorporated, soon after the appearance of the *Letter*, in the Democratic platform of 1844 in a plank destined to dominate the ensuing presidential election. It reflected a doctrine coming into increasing vogue among American expansionists—the doctrine of Manifest Destiny, of which Walker was a conspicuous apostle.

Walker hoped that Northern elements other than land-hungry expansionists would respond to his call. He had in mind particularly the merchant and capitalist elements of the Northeast. He described in glowing terms to them the profits they could win from the expanding trade of Texas and the development of its resources. He cited history in this connection once more—the history of the rich commerce of the Mississippi Valley with New Orleans which had brought attractive gains to merchant and "navigating" interests in the Northeast and to the agricultural classes of the Northwest ever since the acquisition of the Louisiana province. The *Letter* concluded with an impressive array of statistics to prove this point.

Contrasted with these alluring visions was the depressing, indeed, the frightening one, of what would happen, both to the Northeast and to the Northwest, if annexation were to fail. The cities of both sections would be inundated by a flood of freed Negroes coming from the Southern states. Those states, especially in the border area, where exhaustion of soil was evident, were already releasing their slaves as freedmen northward. If the slave migration to Texas were to cease, the Northern cities would be overrun by freedmen and be obliged to carry for all future time a staggering burden of Negro pauperism, criminality, and insanity.

If annexation failed, the older South would be in equal trouble. It would be confronted by competition in cotton-growing from an alienated Texas, a land rich in virgin soils, its growers abundantly provided with capital by the British and aided in marketing their exports by the imperialist-minded capitalists of England. Texas would drift from a satellite status to that of colony of England. The South, suffering from declining soil fertility, from a high protective tariff imposed by the North, and from restricted access to the British market, would ultimately seek release from its bondage by joining Texas and seceding from the Union. The Union would be disrupted.

As terrifying as these internal perils would be external ones if re-annexation failed. The British would entrench themselves in Texas along the Gulf of Mexico. Inland they would adjoin American territory on the banks of the Sabine, the Red, and the Arkansas. Their control would be extended over the hostile Indians of the Southwest. New Orleans and the entire western half of the United States would be imperiled. In time of war the Northwest and the Southwest would be cut off from all access to the sea. Dangers from the British were woven into the very fabric of the *Letter*.

The *Letter* had an enormous distribution, estimated at the time in terms of millions of copies. It was published in full in three widely circulated expansionist newspapers, the Washington *Globe,* the Phila-delphia *Pennsylvanian,* and the *New York Herald.*[1] Other expansionist newspapers throughout the nation offered its facts and arguments in summarized form. Five pamphlet editions were published, two by the Washington *Globe,* and one each by the Philadelphia *Pennsylvanian,* the Bangor *Democrat,* and the St. Louis *Missourian.*[2] Whig journals gave the *Letter* coverage, normally hostile, but two, of expansionist inclination (the New York *Courier and Inquirer* and the New Orleans *Bulletin*), endorsed it. The publication of the *Letter* was subsidized, according to the New York *Tribune,* by a "Texas fund" established in Washington by wealthy Southerners and speculators in Texas lands.[3] To encourage distribution in quantity the *Globe* office set the low price of three dollars per hundred for its pamphlets.

In the distribution of the *Letter* in pamphlet form Walker relied heavily on the use of his franking privilege. The scale of this use is suggested in a letter he wrote Polk in July 1844 when the political campaigns had just got well under way: "I finished a few days since

1. Washington *Globe* (d), Feb. 3, 1844; Philadelphia *Pennsylvanian* (w), Feb. 9, 1844; *New York Herald* (d), Mar. 7, 1844.
2. For a listing of the pamphlet editions, see Thomas W. Streeter, *Bibliography of Texas 1795–1845* (5 vols., Cambridge, Mass., Harvard University Press, 1955–1960), Part III, vol. 2, 509–510.
3. A letter from the Washington correspondent of the *Tribune,* published March 18, 1844, reported: "A society has been formed here of Southern men for that purpose [the annexation of Texas] . . . who act in concert with Congress; the head and front and leader of this party is Mr. Senator Walker—a fund has been raised by rich Southern men to defray all the expenses of printing, publishing documents, speeches on the subject; and no feasible means is to be left untried to effect their object." In an editorial on the same subject on the following day the *Tribune* included speculators in Texas lands among those pressing annexation.

sending 14,000 copies of my Texas letter & Texas speech to N. Carolina & Indiana & the demand is unabated."[4] Candidates in state elections cooperated in the franking labors of Walker. One successful gubernatorial candidate, at the close of his September campaign, brought to Washington a batch of eighteen hundred unused *Letters* with a list of names and asked the Senator to "distribute" them in the remaining weeks of the national campaign.[5] Later a prominent Whig congressman from Kentucky, Willis Green, drew an intriguing picture of Walker in the folding room of the Senate, supervising the preparation for the mail of the pamphlet *The South in Danger* (see fn. 20 of the Introduction).

The *Letter* in its salutation, referred to a mass meeting that had been held on November 25, 1843, in Carroll County, Kentucky, for the purpose of sounding out presidential and vice-presidential candidates on the issue of the immediate annexation of Texas. The meeting had been called by George N. Sanders, an enthusiast for annexation and an exponent of Manifest Destiny. A fiery set of resolutions, drafted by Sanders, in which the Texas and Oregon issues were joined (with the British belabored in each), was brought before the meeting and was unanimously approved. A committee was formed with Sanders as chairman to dispatch the resolutions to aspirants for the presidency and vice-presidency in both parties to draw out their views. Some of the replies were noncommittal,[6] but not Walker's, which was the historic *Letter* of February 1844.

Walker made use of the same epistolary device in advancing other expansionist causes in the closing years of his life. He did so in a

4. Walker to Polk, July 10, 1844, James K. Polk Papers, LVIII, 3440, Library of Congress. For the franking privilege, see *Laws and Regulations for the Government of the Post Office Department* (Washington, 1843), especially Chaps. 43–49 of the "Regulations." A letter to Walker from Charles Drake, a resident of Ulster County, New York, on April 24, 1844, is meaningful enough to quote: [Your pamphlet] "came to hand a few days ago under your frank, and allow me, though a stranger to thank you for it. I am a Northerner, and of course have views and feelings upon the subject of domestic slavery." Robert J. Walker Letters, III (1815–1846), Library of Congress.

5. Hugh J. Anderson to Walker, Sept. 12, 1844, Walker Letters, III. The copies of the *Letter* to be franked from Washington were evidently of the Bangor *Democrat* edition.

6. For a printed copy of the Sanders resolutions, see Walker Letters, III, under date Nov. 25, 1843. The copy is accompanied by a Sanders letter of the same date to Levi Woodbury. For the noncommital reply of Woodbury, see *ibid.*, under date Dec. 16, 1843.

Letter of Hon. R. J. Walker, on the Purchase of Alaska, St. Thomas and St. John, which were then in the purview of American expansionists. And finally, he used it in 1869, in a *Letter of Hon. Robert J. Walker on the Annexation of Nova Scotia and British North America to the United States.*

The Texas *Letter* made an impact on American public opinion that was little exaggerated in a laudatory article on Walker, which appeared in February 1845 in the expansionist *Democratic Review:*

That letter has been more extensively read and circulated, and produced a more powerful and decided effect upon the popular mind, than any publication of any American statesman of the present day. It may be said to have laid the basis of the Texas party in the United States, and especially in the north and northwest. Although only designed as an argument in favor of the annexation of Texas, and addressed as such to all parties and all sections, from the unexpected events which followed, it may be said to have been the principal cause of the revolution in public sentiment, which resulted in the nomination and election of James K. Polk to the Presidency as the avowed advocate of immediate annexation. This letter of Mr. Walker's, together with his subsequent speech on the Texas question in the Senate,[7] were circulated by millions throughout the Union, and were the text-books of the Democratic party in the late victorious campaign.

An elder statesman of the Democratic party, Richard Rush, of Sydenham, Pennsylvania, wrote Walker several months after the *Letter* appeared:

7. The speech on the Texas question referred to here was delivered in the Senate on May 20 and 21, 1844, during the secret debate on the annexation treaty. It was given a wide circulation as soon as the veil of secrecy was lifted. It repeated the arguments and also the anti-British appeal of the *Letter.* Its peroration was: "Now, ere another year has closed upon us, I wish to see British intrigues and British influence forever expelled from the republic of Texas, and the ever glorious ensign of my beloved country unfolded throughout its borders. Such a result would indeed be great and glorious; it would be hailed with rejoicing from the St. Croix to the Del Norte; the swelling heart of every unprejudiced and true American would beat with joy, and England would feel as she did when her armies surrendered at Yorktown, and the forces of Pakenham retired discomfited from the plains of Orleans. But should it be otherwise—should the treaty fail and Texas be lost to the Union—great will be the joy of England; for it will be a British triumph, achieved in the American Capitol, and by the votes of American senators." *Cong. Globe,* 28 Cong., 1 sess., pt. 2, Appendix, 548–557 (May 20, 21, 1844).

Truly you have placed yourself on a Rock. You have swept so broadly over the whole ground, maintained your positions step by step with so much care and force, and such an insight into the most expanded interests of the future, as well as existing interests, that, as yet, none of the pieces on the other side which I have happened to see, touch your arguments in their great strongholds. The question, as you handled it, presents the highest considerations belonging to our foreign policy now and hereafter, in combination with all that is most urgent and permanent in our home system; and deeply to be lamented is it, that a question so bound up with the destiny of ages and millions unborn, shall be at all viewed as if it were a mere question of the day, or of a party.[8]

After Polk's victory in the 1844 election the Vice-President-elect, George M. Dallas, in recommending Walker (who was his relative) for appointment as Secretary of State, wrote: "Mr. Walker of Mississippi is obnoxious to none of the objections that might be raised against others, and his merits are conceded by every section of the Republican party. His letter on Texas flew like wild-fire through the whole country, and created for him a solid national reputation. Perhaps no one of our Statesmen is entitled to a larger share of merit and honor, as connected with the moving impulse or active progress of the late canvass."[9]

After learning of the almost unanimous vote of the Texan convention on July 4, 1845, to accept the congressional Joint Resolution on annexation, James Buchanan wrote Walker: "I have not had time to congratulate you on the *great measure of the age* until this moment. No man in the nation did more than you did to reunite kindred with kindred and person with person. The Annexation of Texas and the name of Robert J. Walker will, I prophesy, be sounded together in times *that are coming* on many glorious occasions."[10]

Buchanan hinted broadly that one glorious occasion might be Walker's election to the presidency. He ruled out himself as a future competitor.

8. Richard Rush to Walker, Apr. 20, 1844, Robert J. Walker Papers, New York-Historical Society.
9. Dallas to Polk, Dec. 15, 1844, George M. Dallas Papers, Pennsylvania Historical Society.
10. Buchanan to Walker, July 8, 1845, Walker Letters, III.

Other communications received by Walker from less eminent Northerners, while the campaign was still on, were even more illuminating. One was from Lewis Coryell of New Hope, Pennsylvania, a lumber dealer and local politician. Written on April 5, 1844, it went straight to the mark: "This is the most infected region[11] in our country with abolitionists. I have distributed your letter among them—new views to them, is the result, and I am convinced that the more intelligent are becoming converts to the annexation of Texas and from reasons of Philanthropy, as they know that they cannot ameliorate slavery in any other way so well and so surely."[12] A message of April 8, 1844, from A. R. Johnson of Utica, New York, who had recently read the *Letter*, ran: "I am happy to assure you that its effect on the public mind in this region has been great in removing the mountains of prejudice under which the real merits of the question have long been smothered."[13]

A Natchez friend of Walker's described (September 11, 1844) the travels of an acquaintance from Cincinnati to Cleveland and from Chicago to St. Louis, in the course of which that person had met many moderate abolitionists and others looking to the gradual liberation of slaves. He had explained to them the operation of the safety valve, and they had been delighted. Walker's correspondent suggested further reprinting of the *Letter* and sending it out "to every editor in the North with a request to insert." He believed it would reap a harvest of thousands of votes on the Texas question.[14]

On September 12, 1844, Hugh J. Anderson, who had just been elected to Maine's governorship, wrote Walker that the Texas issue had been partly responsible for his triumph. He added: "You have summoned up a mighty spirit in this great nation, and it stirs deeper and deeper as time advances. I rejoice at the honor and the glory that will cover the democracy and the honor and the glory that has been well and ably won by the master spirit in this conflict."[15]

The impact on public opinion of the Walker *Letter* is to be measured not only by the praise of the author's correspondents, but by the

11. New Hope, in Bucks County, was within the radius of the Philadelphia antislavery sentiment. Quakers were not normally aggressive abolitionists.
12. Coryell to Walker, Apr. 5, 1844, Walker Letters, III.
13. Johnson to Walker, Apr. 8, 1844, *ibid.*
14. Fred Woodson [illegible] to Walker, Sept. 11, 1844, *ibid.*
15. Anderson to Walker, Sept. 12, 1844, *ibid.*

ubiquity and persistence of public discussion of it, from the time of its appearance to the close of the debate on the Joint Resolution of annexation. In Congress, in the press, and on the hustings, its concepts were evaluated by friend and foe, by spokesmen of the East and the West, by abolitionists and middle-of-the-roaders on the slavery issue, by expansionists and those cautious of expansion, by the literate and the less literate. In the light of this great interest, the high estimates of its effectiveness ventured by the *Democratic Review* in 1845 and by former President Tyler in 1847 were not far from the truth.

One of the anomalies of the expansionist era and its propaganda is that the Walker *Letter,* having won such high praise and having so effectively served its purpose, passed so quickly out of notice after the need for it was gone. It moved into the archives of libraries and even there has been relatively little used by historians. It has never been reprinted. Well worth inspecting, as an example of the reasoning and emotionalism employed by expansionists in their causes in the 1840s, it is reproduced in facsimile at the end of this volume. The copy chosen is of the first *Globe* edition.[16]

16. On the title page of the later editions of the pamphlet the pallid term "Annexation" gave way to the more vigorous one, "Re-annexation."

Part Three.
Documents

Francis O. J. Smith
and the Maine Boundary

The letters published here, unless otherwise noted, are from the extensive Francis Ormond Jonathan Smith Papers in the Maine Historical Society, Portland, Maine, and from a smaller file there entitled "Miscellaneous Letters of F. O. J. Smith on the Northeastern Boundary." Smith's letters are copies in his own handwriting made at the time; those to Smith are originals. The rendition of all letters is verbatim. Idiosyncrasies in spelling, punctuation, and grammatical construction are preserved without the interruption of *sic*.

Other types of documents published here are from many locations. For these the location is given in a footnote with each entry. They are chiefly printed documents. In the case of the House of Representatives special report on charges against Daniel Webster, one part, available only in manuscript form, has characteristics in capitalization and spelling not found in the printed parts of the same report. Again the reader will not be interrupted by *sic* where these minor inconsistencies and errors occur.

The arrangement throughout is chronological.

F. O. J. Smith to His Excellency Martin Van Buren,
President of the United States.[1]

Washington, December 7, 1837.

SIR: According to the promise of my interview with you on yesterday morning, and without other preface, I will proceed to give you the

1. From the Martin Van Buren Papers, Library of Congress. These papers may now be consulted in a Library of Congress microfilm.

suggestions that have occurred to me, relative to the most efficient mode of adjusting the disputed boundary on the Northeastern frontier of Maine.

I take it for granted that there is a like sincere desire on the part of the Government of the United States and the Government of Great Britain, to adjust this dispute in a spirit and upon terms of amity and reciprocal justice.

I presume it to be equally certain and obvious that each government would cheerfully accede to any terms of settlement that could be known to be satisfactory and acceptable to the people of its local government immediately interested in the matter.

As a further corollary from the past history of this dispute, I presume that it has advanced already to that stage where neither party can hope to adduce any new matter of either fact or abstract right, and where, consequently an adjustment can be looked for in only one of two ways—viz, in resort to *force*, or to compromise.

The latter mode is most consonant with the habits and interests of our people and ought not to be sacrificed for the sake of a scrupulous adherence to the dilatory forms of diplomacy.

The delay that has been incident to the adjustment by compromise as already attempted has mainly arisen, if I am not mistaken, from a want of directness in the movements of the two primary governments concerned in it, to the acquirement of requisite knowledge respecting the specific terms of compromise that would, if submitted, be accepted and ratified by the people of the local governments of Maine and New Brunswick. And while directness in this particular shall be wanting, delay will be inevitable; and although both parties may act in the true spirit of compromise towards each other, each will be acting without such information as will be regarded satisfactory, and neither will readily decide when, or what offers can be either safely made or accepted. The little that is yet known of the history and fate of the proposition for compromise submitted on this subject some years since by your predecessor in office, and still unanswered, illustrates well what must be the history and fate of every other offer that is to be made on either side under the circuitous process of negotiation to which the two governments have heretofore confined themselves. The error lies in seeking for compromise at the wrong end of the governments interested.

To obviate this difficulty and further delay from such a course, and proceeding upon the supposition already stated, that the two primary governments will be satisfied with whatever shall be satisfactory in the premises to the two adverse local governments, my proposition is to have an agent, commissioner, or officer of any other designation, appointed by the President, and make it his business at once to visit Maine and New Brunswick, and the adjacent provinces if need be, and learn and decide there, by intercourse, consultation, advice and persuasion with the influential and intelligent citizens, both in and out of office, the terms and nature of such a compromise of the disputed boundary as would, in all probability, obtain the assent and support of their respective local governments and of their fellow citizens generally. Let this agent be entrusted with the power and means requisite to enlist such aid of counsel and personal influence as he might deem expedient to the accomplishment of his object, and adopt all necessary means to consolidate the views and feelings of those citizens, whose influence in each local government might be relied upon to give a controlling tone to the proceedings of their governments upon the subject, until the bases of a compromise shall have been secured in the shape, at least, of an informal mutual understanding. This much having been once accomplished it would doubtless be a very acceptable matter with each local government to reduce their assent to a conventional boundary line into the shape of advisory resolutions, for the ratification of their respective constituents, which ratification would in turn serve as conclusive authority with the two superintending governments for their final acquiescence therein.

In this manner, by the exercise of prudence, perseverance, and conciliatory address on the part of the agent of the United States in his intercourse with the citizens of the two before named local governments, the boundary in dispute may be speedily settled, the friendly relations of the two nations may be preserved, the galled and irritated feelings of the people in and contiguous to the disputed territory will be satisfied, party politics in Maine will be divested of that quality which threatens to become at the opening of the next political year in that State the most inflammable and pervading of all elements, and great expense of money if not of bloodshed will moreover be avoided.

After much and mature reflection upon the subject, and a careful consideration of the character and interests of the people immediately affected, I feel most sanguine in both the importance and feasibility of the proceeding I have suggested, and am also firmly persuaded of its expediency. I think that the pending popular commotions, amounting probably to civil war,[2] in one or more of the neighboring Provinces will have a favorable influence upon such an effort by way of inducing the citizens of New Brunswick to indulge greater anxiety to cultivate friendly relations with the people of Maine particularly, and with the United States generally. And this, together with the rapid approach of the period for the annual meeting of the Provincial Legislature of New Brunswick, and also for the meeting of the Legislature of Maine, furnish considerations for immediate proceeding on the part of him to whom the business shall be committed, should the opinion of the President concur with my own in this matter.

The expense of such an agency cannot at most exceed a few thousand dollars. And I cannot perceive that it is open to any objections of a national character. It would not be inconsistent with any existing relations of the Government of the United States with the British Government, for it would not have in view the consummation of any obligatory compact with the Provincial Government, or other purpose tending to forestall any wish of the British Government upon the subject of the boundary. On the contrary, its sole aim would be to aid and facilitate the designs, and promote the welfare and harmony of all interests, and people affected by the pending dispute. Energy, prudence, despatch and a correct knowledge of the character of the people of Maine, and of New Brunswick who are to be dealt with, and of their respective interests and probable inclinations, are requisite to the successful issue of such an enterprise. By the aid of these qualifications I am most sanguine of its success, and that its accomplishment may be so far effected before the close of the approaching sessions of the Legislatures of the two local governments interested as to leave nothing to be done hereafter except the formal acquiescence therein of the two national governments. To place my views of the authority proposed to be vested in the agent beyond mistake and to place the motives of the appointment (if made) above suspicion of wrong, I take the liberty to enclose herein a draft of the written instructions that might be appropriately given to the agent as the guide of his proceeding.

2. Refers to the Papineau and Mackenzie rebellions in Quebec and in Upper Canada in 1837–1838.

The President may be assured that the anxiety of the people of Maine upon this subject of dispute is intense, though thus far it has been suppressed to the extent that an honest and sincere regard for the success and honor of the last and present administration of national affairs (arising from great confidence in their ruling motives) could suppress it.

But when the delays that have attended this adjustment through many years past are reviewed, and a rehearsal is made of the indignities that have in the meantime at intervals been practiced upon the sovereignty of Maine, by the arrest and transportation of the citizens of that state to be tried by foreign tribunals and foreign jurors, under charge of offences against laws and authority not emanating from the government of either the United States or Maine; when the repeated imprisonment of their fellow citizens by the same arbitrary authority is recalled, and with a knowledge of the fact that one of those citizens is at this moment undergoing imprisonment in a foreign gaol for no other offence than that arising from a faithful execution of a law enacted by the Constitutional authorities of Maine, the indignation of the people of that state will be most easily aroused, and it will be most difficult to restrain them longer from taking into their own hands at every hazard of life, peace and property that defense of themselves which their relations to the federal government may warrant them in expecting from that quarter and which their honor as a people demands.

I look forward to the commencing of the next Legislature of Maine as a period when motives of patriotism and the narrow interests of party will combine to employ every impulse I have named, and others that I have not named, in arousing the sensibilities of the people of Maine and in irritating to action their already wounded pride upon this subject, and in concentrating whatever of prejudice that the unfortunate position of this matter is calculated to impart to their minds against those to whom it has been, and now is entrusted, as a national concern.

It is therefore most important, in view of our domestic politics, as well as to preserve harmony in our foreign relations, that no effort be spared to place the subject in the utmost state of progression towards an adjustment and to the full extent that a spirit of honorable compromise can carry it, and to deprive those (if such there be) who may be disposed to seek political power, either in Maine or in the federal government, at the expense of the peace of the nation, of an engine of discord and complaint so effectual as this subject will certainly become, if not disposed of. Or, if the peaceful genius of our institutions is to be foiled, and such a compromise as will be both honorable to the nation and just to the people of Maine cannot be obtained, it is most desirable that your administration should be as prompt to discover it as its opponents are to proclaim it, and as ready to meet the crisis as they themselves may be.

In conclusion let me add that in submitting these considerations to the President I will leave the spirit of them alone to vouch for their sincerity, and to prove that they have nothing in view which does not look to the peace of the nation, the welfare of that State with which I am proud to be in any measure identified, and the honor and success of your Executive administration.

> With sentiments of great esteem,
> I have the honor to be,
> Your obedient servant,

[Enclosure in above letter]
Instructions Proposed to be given
to an Agent on the N.E. Boundary, etc.

The President of the United States, reposing confidence in your ability and discretion upon the subject, has directed me to request your services in a manner hereinafter pointed out, in an effort which he is about to make to effect such an adjustment of the disputed boundary on the Northeastern position of the United States and State of Maine as will be satisfactory and honorable to all parties interested.

The President is fully persuaded that it is alike the interest and inclination of the people of Maine and of the people of the adjacent Provincial Government to adjust their divisional boundary line upon principles of amity and reciprocal justice and, moreover, that it is alike the disposition of the Government of the United States and of the Government of Great Britain to accede to any terms of adjustment in the matter that shall be mutually satisfactory to the two local governments immediately interested.

With a view to ascertain with every possible degree of certainty and despatch the nearest feasible approach to an adjustment of this boundary that would be satisfactory to the local governments interested you are requested to visit and consult, as the agent of the United States, such citizens of Maine and of the Province of New Brunswick, and also of the adjacent provinces if need be, as may be supposed best to understand the interests, wishes and welfare of their respective governments in this matter, and who may be relied upon as most influential in giving hereafter a tone to the feelings and views of the people of their respective governments in relation to it, and to report in detail such information as you may in this way acquire as the basis of future proceedings in the premises on the part of this government.

It is the desire of the President that you should not confine your intercourse to those persons who hold official stations, nor to those who are not thus situated, but to seek from influential citizens indiscriminately, and without regard to any merely personal or political considerations, their opinions relative to the specific terms of compromise and of a final settlement of the conflicting claims adverted to, that would be most likely successfully to enlist the support of their fellow citizens generally, and obtain the approbation of their respective local governments. He leaves it entirely to your discretion to make known, or not, as occasion may require, to those with whom you may hold intercourse, the character and purpose of your mission. He is particularly desirous that all your proceedings upon the subject may be characterized by an uniform regard for the friendly relations which exist between the Governments of the United States and Great Britain, and that while nothing shall be advanced or represented inconsistent with the fixed resolution of the former government to surrender nothing of the ascertained rights of the people of Maine, except in a spirit of adjustment and with the approbation and assent of that people, the utmost frankness with regard to the anxious desire of the government of the United States to effect a speedy and final determination of the pending dispute may be at all times indulged as being alike compatible with the truth of the case and with the best interests of all parties concerned.

You are authorized to employ the aid, counsel and influence of any other person you may deem useful to the purpose of your mission at the expense of the government of the United States, and in that event it will be proper for you to report the fact to the President. And the President also confides to your judgment and discretion the adoption of any and all other proceedings you may deem expedient and coming within the general scope of these instructions. The funds requisite to your purposes will be committed to you as may be needed; an account of the expenditures will be kept by you for the information of the President. You will bear in mind that the utmost despatch and diligence is desirable in whatever you may do, that every advantage may be taken of the favorable opportunities that the approaching sessions of the State and Provincial Legislatures will afford to your purposes. Frequent communications of your doings to the Department of State for the information of the President will also be desirable.

Alabama Resolutions.[3]

Executive Department, ⎱
Tuscaloosa, Jan. 15th, 1841. ⎰

SIR,—I have the honor to enclose you Joint Resolutions of the General Assembly of the State of Alabama, responsive to certain resolutions of the State over which you preside, in relation to the North-Eastern Boundary. With perfect respect, I am, your ob't serv't,

A. P. BAGLEY.

To his Excellency, the Governor of Maine.

JOINT RESOLUTIONS

OF THE GENERAL ASSEMBLY OF THE STATE OF ALABAMA IN RESPONSE TO CERTAIN RESOLUTIONS OF THE STATE OF MAINE, IN RELATION TO THE NORTH-EASTERN BOUNDARY QUESTION.

Be it resolved, by the Senate and House of Representatives of the State of Alabama, in General Assembly convened, 1st. That we hold

3. The Alabama Resolutions and the Maryland Resolutions which follow are reprints from Maine Senate Doc. No. 19, *Report of Committee on Northeast Boundary* (Augusta, 1841), 85–86. They show the uneasiness of these Southern states over the intransigent attitude of Maine. Resolutions were also sent to Maine by the legislatures of two northwestern states: Ohio and Indiana. These were less pacific than those from the South. The Ohio Resolutions, adopted on March 18, 1839, close to the period of the Aroostook War, declared that while Ohio approved the President's efforts to avert the calamities of war, yet, if a collision should take place, the state would tender "her whole means and resources to the authorities of this Union in sustaining our rights and honor." The Indiana legislature, on February 24, 1840, endorsed those resolutions. It cherished the hope that the integrity of our soil and the national honor could be preserved without an appeal to arms, but, should a collision occur, it undertook to sustain "our rights and honor." *Ibid.,* 83–84.

it to be the solemn and imperative duty of the Federal Government, faithfully to maintain toward the State of Maine, every obligation she is under, touching the establishment of the North-Eastern Boundary line of said State.

2d. That said Government is further bound in defence of her own honor, to not concede to Great Britain any claim not strictly founded in right and justice in the matter aforesaid.

3d. That we sincerely deprecate a resort to force, until every honorable, peaceful expedient has been exhausted, in this and in every other like controversy.

4th. That the question of the North-Eastern Boundary concerns the whole Union, and is not one local in its character to the State of Maine, although she is confessedly more interested than any other in its adjustment; and that, for the reason here set forth, it is the duty of the State of Maine to trust the decision of the matter to the councils of the Union, and abide thereby, whatever it may finally be whether exactly consistent with her own wishes or not. If Congress says go to war, we will cheerfully obey the mandate, but we should deeply regret to see the State of Maine take any rash step, which might tend to plunge her sister States into war, more through mere feeling and sympathy than from deliberate choice and determination on their part.

5th. That the Governor of this State be requested to forward to the Governor of Maine a copy of the foregoing Resolutions as the response of this General Assembly to her Resolutions of the 18th May [March] last, communicated to us by the Governor of this State, agreeably to a request contained in her said Resolutions.

(Signed,)   J. L. F. Cottrell, President Senate.
R. A. Baker, Speaker of the House
of Representatives.

Maryland Resolutions

To the Senate and House of Representatives:

I herewith present, for your consideration, a Report and Resolutions, from the State of Maryland, in relation to the North-Eastern Boundary.

Edward Kent.

COUNCIL CHAMBER,
  March 23d. 1841.

Resolved, That the Legislature of Maryland entertains a perfect conviction of the justice and validity of the title of the United States, and State of Maine, to the full extent of all the territory in dispute between Great Britain and the United States.

Resolved, That the Legislature of Maryland, looks to the Federal Government with an entire reliance upon its disposition to bring the controversy to an amicable and speedy settlement; but if these efforts should fail, the State of Maryland will cheerfully place herself in the support of the Federal Government, in what will then become its duty to itself and the State of Maine.

Resolved, That after expressing the above opinions, the State of Maryland feels that it has a right to request the State of Maine to contribute, by all the means in its power, towards an amicable settlement of the dispute upon honorable terms.

Resolved, That if the British Government would acknowledge the title of the State of Maine to the territory in dispute, and offer a fair equivalent for the passage through it of a military road, it would be a reasonable mode of adjusting the dispute and ought to be satisfactory to the State of Maine.

Resolved, That the Governor be and is hereby requested to transmit a copy of this Report and these Resolutions to each of the Governors of the several States, and to each of the Senators and Representatives in Congress from the State of Maryland.

Daniel Webster to F. C. Gray.[4]

Private and Confidential   Boston, May 11, 1841.

MY DEAR SIR,—I wrote you from New York, on the 3d inst., the day of your departure from Boston, expressing the wish that you would not leave London, until you should hear from me again.

---

4. Francis C. Gray, to whom this letter was addressed, was a friend of Webster, a lawyer resident normally in Boston. He had been a state senator in the Massachusetts legislature. The text is taken from Daniel Webster, *Writings and Speeches,* J. W. McIntyre (ed.) (18 vols., Boston, Little, Brown, 1903), XVIII, 102–103.

I avail myself of the opportunity of the return of The Britannia to inform you of the purposes of that request.

You are well acquainted with the history and the merits of the question respecting our Northeastern boundary, and advised, probably, of the state of the pending negotiation between the United States and England on that subject. In this last respect, nothing important has occurred since Mr. Van Buren's message to Congress, of last December.

It is much to be desired that this negotiation should be so hastened, as that the convention, in which it is expected to result, may be laid before the Senate, at the ensuing session of Congress. My purpose is, on my return to Washington, to address Mr. Fox officially, on this part of the subject.

But supposing this to be accomplished, and a joint exploration and survey provided for, with power in the commissioners to decide the question, and establish the line, or, in case of disagreement, an umpire to be resorted to, whose decision shall be final, it is obvious that much time must be consumed, and great expense incurred by such a proceeding, with perhaps a doubtful result at last.

It is therefore perhaps worth inquiry whether a shorter way to an amicable and satisfactory adjustment may not be found. Before suggesting my notions on this point, I wish to say that I write now, not only unofficially, but, if I may so express myself, merely experimentally, not intending to bind even myself by any thing I may suggest, and much less others. Indeed, I could not bind others, if I would. The substance of what I wish to say is this: You will, of course, be more or less in the court circles of London, and no doubt this question of the boundary will often be brought into conversation; and I should like that you should lead these conversations, if you can, so as to bring out suggestions from the gentlemen connected with the government.

I have some reason to think Lord Palmerston would be glad if this matter could be settled without the delay and expense of exploration, etc., etc. Possibly there may be some idea of an exchange of territory suggested. If you find it convenient, lead those you may meet with to this idea. You know we always thought the monument does not stand on the line of the St. Croix. How would England like to let us go down to the Madawaska, and in return, let them have the Dutch line, further up, Or, what perhaps is still more practicable, let us

141

run from the monument to Eel River,[5] and by that river to the St. John's, and let England go by the Madawaska, and the lakes at its head, and so reach the St. Lawrence at the mouth of the Trois Pistolles?

You know, also, we think Grand Menan should have been assigned to us. Does England attach great value to that island, or Campo Bello?

In these conversations you will, of course, not mention my name, or intimate any thing as being a proposition from this side of the water, official or unofficial; but get what suggestions you can from them.

If they wish nothing but a proper connection between their provinces, it is obvious that the line of the Madawaska gives them that.

You will see Mr. Senior, doubtless, and he is a man of intelligence and life. He will readily create accidents, which shall bring you and Mr. Backhouse together, and perhaps throw you in the way of Lord Palmerston. You will doubtless also see Mr. Francis T. Baring and Mr. Labouchere, and though they hold very high official stations, they are very likely to talk freely upon this subject of the boundary.[6] If you find Mr. Jaudon still in London, I wish you to show him this letter. He will understand the reason of this request, and explain it to you. But I apprehend he will have sailed for the United States.

I shall hope to hear from you so soon as you may have any thing to communicate.

Yours, with much true regard,

5. Eel River is a minor stream flowing into the St. John from the west. It runs near the St. Croix monument in its upper waters. If the suggestion of a line via the Eel River and the St. John had been agreed to by the British a long, thin wedge of New Brunswick territory lying east of the line drawn north from the monument would have come to the United States. It would have constituted a British equivalent for territory Maine would surrender at the north. It would have fulfilled the needs of an "exchange" of equivalents in territory. The idea was apparently discussed by Webster and Smith at their first conference, and it became an important item in Smith's campaign of propaganda.

6. Webster's list of Englishmen, whom Gray was to try to meet, consisted, for the most part, of Whig leaders of prominence, who, except for Palmerston, were considered friendly to the United States. Nassau W. Senior was a world-famous economist of liberal views; John Backhouse was the veteran permanent Undersecretary for Foreign Affairs. Francis T. Baring was Chancellor of the Exchequer and a kinsman of Lord Ashburton; Henry Labouchere was a member of the cabinet. Samuel Jaudon had been cashier of the Second Bank of the United States and was a financial adviser to Webster.

Francis O. J. Smith to Daniel Webster.

Washington, June 7, 1841.

Mr. Webster: I have revolved the boundary question still further in my own mind, with reference to my devoting my services to it, and I am yet of opinion, that an agency instituted upon the plan, and conducted in the spirit I have hinted at in our conversation, will bring the two people immediately interested in it to an agreement upon it, rendering other modes of negotiation between the two primary governments of those people unnecessary, except to execute the agreement of the former—though not designed to supercede its progress in the meantime.

The mistake and inefficiency of all past efforts upon this subject has laid in directing negotiation *at the wrong end of the dispute.* The dispute, in reality, and the interest in reality, has not been so much with the federal government and the British gov't. as with the people of Maine and the people of the British provinces. Consequently, semi-official intercourse among the latter parties might have been made long since altogether effectual, as well as direct; while official intercourse, through the studied and shy forms of diplomacy between the former, could hardly fail to be otherwise than indirect and ineffectual, from the very nature of the subject.

Now my plan is to prepare public sentiment in Maine for a compromise of the matter through a conventional line, *founded partly in consideration of an exchange of territory, and partly in a pecuniary indemnity to Maine and Massachusetts for the difference in the exchange of territory thus made.*

The process of exchange of territory and pecuniary indemnity would be a sufficient recognition of the rights of Maine to satisfy her honor & pride, while the latter would appeal to her *interests* and be just towards her *rights;* and her present pecuniary condition[7] will predispose her people towards it, if it can be made to seem to have its origin with themselves. This, however, is the most delicate part of the enterprise.

7. Refers to the intense economic depression in the nation following the Panic of 1837.

But public sentiment upon this matter can be brought into right shape in Maine by enlisting certain leading men *of both political parties* (yet not politically) and through them, at a proper time hereafter, guiding aright the public press.

Having obtained the favorable opinion of the leading political men of Maine, through regular and successive approaches, towards a conventional line (all of which is feasible by a few months of steady and well-directed correspondence, and the active agency of a very select few) and drawing after this an appropriate expression of the public press, the same work could be accomplished in a much less time among the citizens of the interested provinces; and the whole may be combined into corresponding and reciprocal resolutions of the Legislative Assemblies of the two local governments at their next winter sessions, in ample season for Congress to confirm all at its next regular session.

A few thousand dollars expended upon such an agency will accomplish *more than hundreds of thousands expended through the formalities and delays of ordinary diplomatic negotiations and surveys,* and more than millions would if the parties shall be brought into belligerent attitudes on the subject; and, what is more, it would avert all occasion for such a national calamity as the latter event would certainly be, however "thrice armed" in justice our quarrel might be.

The process must be conducted with system and prudence. I would favor commencing with the proper enlistment of the services of a few judicious co-operators at different points in Maine, extending their circle gradually, without display or the betrayal of official authority, as opportunity might be created, and drawing in silently *the voluntary and patriotic aid of men of influence of both political parties,* carefully ripening the whole into a compact before the supposed interests or prejudices of any class should be excited in relation to it on account of the credit it might reflect upon the administration which had accomplished it.

So confident am I that this proceeding would prove effectual and most honorable to all concerned, that I am extremely solicitous, for the honor of your own and President Tyler's administration, and for the interest and quiet of Maine, that it should be attempted.

In the worst view, the hazard will be of comparatively small amount in expenses before some developments will be made to you of its progress—such as would enable you and the President to judge of the propriety of pursuing it.

But the persons immediately engaged in it should feel as if it was a subject worthy of their whole time and effort to accomplish it, both in a personal, political, and national point of view; and, regarding it in this aspect, I have concluded, upon reflection, to say, that if you do not think of one more likely to render the desired service with more efficiency than myself, and I can be furnished with the requisite means to set such co-agencies at work as I may think essential, subject at all times to your cognizance, and accountable at all times for the use of the means wanted and furnished, I will enter upon it without delay.

My own compensation I should expect to be definitely fixed upon at the rate of $3500 per annum, and my necessary travelling expenses, postage, and incidental expenses (all subjected to your revision and approval) paid by the government. And, in case of a successful arrangement, it would not be unreasonable to expect the allowance of a liberal commission as disbursing agent on whatever sums the negotiation might ultimately involve. Success would warrant almost any expenditure.

In case you adopt these views, and decide to make the trial, the sooner I can be informed of it the more it will be to my accommodation; and, in that event there is a paper or two, signed by a former delegation from Maine in Congress, in your department, of which I should desire a copy.

With the most friendly consideration,

I have the honor to be
Your obedient servant,

F. O. J. Smith to John Hodgdon (of Bangor).[8]

Private   Washington, June 12, 1841.

DEAR SIR: The position of our Boundary question is such that Maine ought to improve the opportunity of effecting an adjustment of it by devising such a compromise of the dispute as will save her honor and secure her recompense for any territorial cession she may make.

8. John Hodgdon was a former Land Agent of Maine and later President of the State Senate.

It will take from six to ten years to settle it, under the most rapid progress which it is in the nature of the new arrangements for its settlement to admit of. For instance, it will take all this season and part of next for our *ex parte* surveyors to complete the survey now in progress.[9] The Commissioners must wait for that. Then there will be such a conflict between that survey and the *ex parte* survey of the British Government as will render it indispensably necessary for the Joint Commissioners to order, as they will have authority to do, a new joint survey. This will take two years more. Then it will take another year for discussion. Then they will not probably agree—and then they will be required to select an umpire, who, in turn, must take an indefinite period to make up his decision.

In the meantime our State will be under constant exposure to aggression and insult—our public debt, if not enlarged, will continue to press heavily upon our people, and not be paid off—the territory will be unproductive and worthless to us—and in the end our Sister States will unite in influencing our submission to a decision that will secure to Great Britain, with or without indemnity, the particular section of territory at which they aim. See already the resolutions of Maryland Legislature inclining to this result.[10]

Reasoning from these premises, which I believe to be all correct, and with a view to the honor of the present national administration, to the quiet and welfare of our State, and to the payment of our public debt, I am confident that an honorable compromise of the dispute is both feasible and expedient, and I *know* that whoever shall be instrumental in bringing it about, will reap a rich reward in the merit of the act and in the partialities of the President and his supporters.

Why would not this do for our State, in case Great Britain will concede to us the title we claim, to authorize the federal government to adopt as the boundary, a line commencing at the point where Eel River[11] in its most eastern source touches the present acknowledged

9. Refers to the survey ordered by Congress in 1840, the commissioners for which were James Renwick, James D. Graham, and Andrew Talcott. The ex parte survey of the British government, mentioned in the next sentence, was that of Mudge and Featherstonhaugh, initiated in 1839. For references to these surveys see above, p. 62, fn. 44.

10. For these resolutions, see above, p. 140. Note especially paragraphs 3 and 4.

11. This is the Eel River line suggested in Webster to Francis Gray, in Documents, under date May 11, 1841.

boundary—extending thence as the thread of that river directs to the St. Johns River—thence by the thread of the St. Johns to the mouth of the Madawaska River, thence by the thread of the latter river, and the centre of Temiscouata Lake to the point known as the Temiscouata Portage, and thence due south until it strikes the boundary now claimed by the United States. Provided, further, that Great Britain will concede to Massachusetts and Maine the title to the land acquired by them thereby on the south side of the St. Johns, and pay an indemnity of one and a half millions of dollars to Massachusetts and Maine, and provided the United States government will in addition thereto refund to Maine her just claim for her expenditures in defending said territory since the same has been in dispute. Provided, also, that Great Britain will stipulate to allow the citizens of Maine and of the United States the free navigation of the River St. John for conducting all lumbering operations for the period of fifty years from the date of the adjustment.

I cannot doubt that if the subject can be fairly brought before our people for their decision they would cheerfully agree to such an adjustment. Sure I am it would be most advantageous to them—would save their honor—promote the peace of themselves and the whole country, and redound immeasurably to the credit of all concerned in bringing it about.

I have reason for believing that our Government, as now organized in the Cabinet, could bring about these, or nearly these results, and would see those who should be instrumental in effecting this object, *amply recompensed* for their efforts in the matter, if they could feel authorized to go ahead by Maine.

What think you of it? If you think favorably of such an exchange of territory, or such an indemnifying adjustment, please to write me early on the receipt of this, and also any mode that may suggest itself to you for bringing our people to act upon it, and I will communicate further with you as to ulterior movements.

The pride, in reality, and not so much the true interest of the State otherwise, is now involved in the matter. If we can have our title *acknowledged,* and acquire territory while we cede territory, every honorable impulse must be satisfied, and becomes then a matter of mere national comity and convenience.

As I write not merely from speculative suggestions, but under a conviction that we may render the subject one of great personal and political merit for ourselves and friends, I want you to give it your sober thought, and write me the earliest answer you can. I shall be at Portland after Tuesday next, or, if you can meet me at Portland or Augusta at a given day in the latter part of the month to settle definitively upon a mode of proceeding in relation to it, I will explain to you how much it may be made an object worthy of our efforts.

Yours truly, in haste,

John Hodgdon to F. O. J. Smith.
(Copy in Smith's handwriting)

Bangor, June 17, 1841.

Dear Sir:—Your letter in reference to the N.E. Boundary was handed me by Mr. H[aines] this forenoon. As it was marked private, I showed it no one, and have given no one any intimation of its contents.

You take a common sense view of this subject, and if your project could be carried out, it would doubtless be for the interest of the State. I have long been of opinion that something of the kind should be done, but your details might be inconvenient to carry out.

Firstly, the British Government might be unwilling to acknowledge the right of Maine to the territory and trust to a promise from the General Government that Maine would consent to any given arrangement.

Secondly, in obtaining the consent of Maine to your proposition the idea of relinquishing territory to the *British* would be a subject for a minority to harp upon.

Thirdly, the British Government might not yield assent to any *precise* terms the State of Maine might agree to, although they might be satisfied with something substantially the same.

Would it not be well to modify your project thus:—The State of Maine to cede to the Genl. Government such portion of the disputed territory as the Genl. Government suppose is desirable to Gt. Britain. The Genl. Government as a consideration to pay the expenses of Maine in protecting said territory, both of the militia and of the people, and pay Maine & Massachusetts $1,500,000 & obtain for them the free navigation of the river St. Johns within five years for the period of fifty years for the purpose of carrying lumber from the tributary rivers of the St. Johns, or pay an additional sum of $500,000.

A bill can be carried through Congress authorizing the General Government to receive a cession on these terms. Maine and Massachusetts can then, through their Legislatures, the coming winter, authorize the cession, and the question, so far as Maine is concerned, is all settled.

To Maine this territory is not of any great value; but it is of importance to have the question put at rest, so far as regards the territory south of the St. Johns, that the settlements may go on unmolested. It strikes me that the subject would thus be disencumbered of its principal difficulties. There would be presented to Maine the naked question of cession to the United States Gov't. for a given sum. It would be a "selling out," but not "to the British." I have given my views in a hasty manner, but not without long previous consideration. I have long been satisfied that the question would never be settled in any other way. The U. States acknowledges our title to the territory. The honor of the State is not, therefore, compromised by ceding to the U. States for a suitable indemnity. As to the payment of the expenses attending the protection of this territory, it is but proper they should be paid before we begin to divide with Massachusetts. We, too, have a greater interest than Massachusetts. The sovereignty is ours. The payment of all the Aroostook expenses would soften down the Locos a great deal. If a move is desirable in the premises, I can get the leading Locos in Aroostook County committed to the measure in advance. By-the-By-I forgot one part of your plan—that the Gen'l. Gov't. should guarantee the quiet possession of the balance of the territory to Maine. Perhaps this might be desirable, or the business might be so altered that Maine might make the obtaining the use of the St. Johns for carrying lumber to market a part of the consideration of the cession, if the Gov't are certain that Great Britain will not object.

The inhabitants of the Aroostook County, and a good many of the inhabitants of Penobscot are extremely desirous of extending their enterprise to the territory south of the St. Johns. They are, as a preliminary, desirous of getting the free use of the St. Johns for carrying their timber out. Such a body can be obtained here in favor of the measure that no political advantage can be taken of it. And several Loco votes in the Legislature can be secured. I can so manage it with certain leading men of the opposition that they will stand as Godfathers to the project, and must fight it through. Their interest, their honor, and last, though not least, their *vanity* will unite in pressing them on.

My engagements are such I cannot well leave—except on business. To tell the truth, I got so involved in 1835 and 1836 by endorsing & buying goose pastures in the shape of house lots, I find it necessary, as John Q. Adams said in his administration, to put myself upon "a system of the most rigid economy." Aside from this I shall be detained in ———— by business until, say 20th July, and then must go to ————. On my return shall probably be in Portland. *Still, if necessary, I will meet you in Augusta or Portland sooner.*

Yours truly,

F. O. J. Smith to Daniel Webster.

Private   Portland, July 2, 1841.

DEAR SIR:—I have by correspondence and personal intercourse, communicated with leading and influential gentlemen of both political parties in five of our principal counties, on the subject of adjusting our N.E. Boundary, upon the basis contemplated in our late interviews; and the result is, that I am no less sanguine than heretofore that the proposition can be made to come before our next legislature *from our own people*, in the shape of which I now enclose a copy, unless you discover something objectionable therein.

I learn that the inhabitants of the Aroostook county (immediately interested) can be brought very unanimously into it, provided a stipulation can be secured for a limited navigation of the St. John, and hence I present *that* point. Can there be any grave doubt of Gt. Britain's acceding to it in that shape?

To our *maritime* towns and counties the worth of national peace, for the sake of commerce, is the inducement suggested.

To our *interior* counties, the payment of our public debt and riddance of taxation is the moving consideration which the proposition is intended to put forth.

To the partisans of Fairfield's late administration,[12] and the defenders of the late military fooleries on the lines, the payment of the expenses incurred by the State, is "a consummation devoutly to be wished," and it is here held out.

12. Refers to Fairfield's governorship, 1839–1840.

After I shall have procured the signatures[13] of certain leading men of both parties in this county I shall employ the necessary persons to visit every town in the county, and obtain the principal men in each to co-operate, and at once proceed to the execution of a similar operation in each of the other counties.

One friend of great sagacity and influence in Penobscot county,[14] and one intimately acquainted with the people and interests of Aroostook County, writes me thus:

"If a move is desirable in the premises, I can get the leading Locos in Aroostook County committed to the measure in advance . . . The inhabitants of the Aroostook County, and a good many of the inhabitants of Penobscot, are extremely desirous of extending their enterprise to the territory south of the St. Johns. They are, as a preliminary, desirous of getting the free use of the St. Johns for carrying their timber out. Such a body can be obtained here in favor of the measure, that no political advantage can be taken of it; and several Loco votes in the Legislature can be secured for it. I can so manage it with certain leading men of the opposition that they will stand as Godfathers to the project, and must fight it through. Their interest, their honor, and last though not least, their *vanity* will unite in pressing them on."

Such is the character of my encouragements, thus far, in confirmation of my original convictions.

I shall write as matters progress—that you may be minutely informed on it. With great regard,

Your obedient servant.

[Enclosure in the above letter. A printed petition to be circulated, July, 1841]

SETTLEMENT OF THE NORTHEASTERN BOUNDARY

To the governor, council, and legislature of Maine:

The undersigned, citizens of Maine, uniting without distinction of party, view with regret the protracted delay of the settlement of the northeastern boundary of this State.

13. Smith enclosed with his letter a sample of a printed memorial, which was to be circulated for signatures to prominent Maine public figures and editors and to be presented to the governor, council, and legislature of Maine. The memorial is the next document published here.
14. Refers to John Hodgdon.

From the best information we can obtain respecting the negotiation, it must be subjected to years of further delay, if not result in a war, unless the people themselves interpose their voice to direct its adjustment.

While unadjusted the sovereignty of the State is exposed to insult, the treasury of the State, though already burdened with a debt of a million and a half of dollars, is subject to constant expenditures for the protection of the territory in dispute, and the peace of the Union is in no less constant jeopardy from it.

That the claim of the State in all its extent is just and defensible, we cannot entertain a doubt. That any portion of it can ever be surrendered to an adverse claim, is what we never should assent to. The government of the Union stands pledged, and many of the States, acting in their local capacities, have generously pledged themselves as States, to stand by and defend to the last the claim of Maine, if force ever becomes the alternative. And our cause, therefore, is not only just, but "thrice armed" against opponents.

The people are, however, for peace, and the preservation of amicable relations with all the world. And in the event that Great Britain *shall abandon her unjust claim,* and the United States government shall deem it expedient, for a suitable indemnity to Maine and Massachusetts, *besides refunding all the expenses of Maine in the defence of the territory,* to negotiate with Great Britain for a new boundary, making, for instance, the St. John river, from the outlet of Eel river up to the Madawaska river, thence through the last river and the lake Temiscouata to the highlands, the boundary of the two nations, we believe the same may be done with honor to both the State of Maine and to the United States, and all future alienation of feeling between the United States and Great Britain on the subject be avoided: provided, in such exchange of territory the free navigation of the St. John were secured to the citizens of Maine and of the United States for a limited period, say fifty years, to enable them to carry to market the lumber of their territory.

We are of opinion that, while to the State of Maine said territory might be made of very great value, to the British provinces it may be of even greater value; and that, as this State does not need it for any specific uses, the cession of it to the government of the United States, upon the terms indicated herein, would enable the State to discharge its large public debt, and have a fund of considerable amount beyond to appropriate to useful purposes; and thus at once to relieve the people from heavy taxation, place the public treasury upon an independent footing with all the world, and quiet forever the evils of a border dispute.

Entertaining these views, we recommend to the executive and legislative authorities of the State to adopt the necessary measures for bringing such an adjustment of the boundary dispute to the consideration of the government of the United States, to the end that the same may be made the basis of its future intercourse with the British government in relation thereto.

Respectfully, your fellow-citizens,

July, 1841.

Reuel Williams[15] to Hon. John Fairfield.

Senate Chamber, July 19, 1841.

DEAR SIR: I went this morning to State Department and saw the Sec'y. He is a good deal fretted and says Fox[16] is cross, that Kent[17] has complained that Baker[18] is again arrested and claims protection for him. He don't know what to do. As well as I could understand, it seems to have been settled to order one Company of U.S. troops to Fort Fairfield and another to Fort Jarvis, but the order is not yet given.

Mr. Webster read to me his letter to Fox, not yet delivered, stating this arrangement and the reasons for it, one of which was that by placing the borders under the charge of national troops collisions would be less likely to occur, and trespasses could be prevented. Another

15. Reuel Williams was a power in Maine politics. He was a Democrat of considerable wealth residing in Augusta. He had been largely responsible for the shifting of the state capital from Portland to Augusta. In his earlier years he had served for long periods in the state legislature. He was United States senator from Maine at the time of the debate over the ratification of the Webster-Ashburton Treaty. He strenuously opposed ratification. The letter reproduced here is in the John Fairfield Papers, Maine Historical Society.

16. Henry S. Fox, British minister at Washington.

17. Edward Kent, a Whig, elected as governor of Maine by a slight plurality in 1840.

18. John Baker, a restless American who occupied a claim in the Madawaska settlements on the north side of the St. John.

was to relieve Maine from the expense of keeping up a posse and further that pending the negotiation the territory south of St. John would remain in custody of U. States and that north of it, in custody of G. Britain, each denying the other's right so to do. This has been seen by Mr. Fox and he has placed in Mr. Webster's hands his contemplated reply, in which he states that in his opinion G. Britain will not assent to it, because it would throw that portion of Madawaska S[outh] of St. Johns, under the jurisdiction of U.S. and that in his belief nothing short of giving the *valley* of St. Johns to the custody of G. Britain will answer.

Mr. W. says this will not be agreed to, but he shall see Mr. Fox and try to get him to yield, and should he not succeed, he sees no other way but to leave things as they are.

Fox thinks he shall soon get despatches about the commission and arbitration.

I wanted to see Kent's letter, but it was not convenient to find it. I would like to know for what cause Baker is again arrested. We have little reason to expect any bold action from the powers that be.

Yours respectfully

Reuel Williams to Hon. John Fairfield.

Washington, August 22, 1841.[19]

DEAR SIR: Genl Scott told me a few days ago that the order had gone for one company to be stationed at Fort Fairfield, and another at Fish river, Fort Jarvis.

By Clay's speech upon the veto message and Wise's[20] yesterday upon the Fiscal Corporation, the country will see that the breach between the President and the Dictator[21] is complete and irreconcileable. Clay relies upon his Bank and tariff friends, and Tyler must take the democratic road or be left without strength. There is good reason to expect that he will do the right thing and that democratic measures if not democratic men will be in the ascendent before we leave and other things will follow.

19. From the Fairfield Papers.
20. Henry A. Wise, congressman from Virginia.
21. Refers to Henry Clay.

There is no unwillingness among *any* of our friends to support Tyler so long as he will support our measures, and that must be soon and forever.

Your election is looked for with great interest and no effort should be spared to give Maine her proper standing.

Yours truly

Allen Haines to F. O. J. Smith.

Bangor, October, 1841.

DEAR SIR: I acknowledge the justness of all the views of State and National politics as expressed in yours of the 26th ult. It is really astonishing that a set of men so intelligent as are the leaders of the Whig party; so well read in political economy, and so sound in judgment as to what measures are best calculated to promote the prosperity of the whole country, and to secure the happiness of the whole people, should want the knowledge of human nature and the consequent moral power necessary to enable them to establish those measures in the policy of the Union, and that too, when the mistakes of their adversaries have given them the Administration and both branches of the National Legislature by decided majorities. But so it is; ever has been, and, for ought we now know, ever will be. They never appear to profit by defeat, or to get wisdom by experience. Seemingly because of their neglect or unwillingness to consider the rocks upon which they split. Instance their recent overwhelming defeat in Maine. This is charged upon the President's vetoes. But they cannot mark a single man who will acknowledge that his vote was in any way influenced by the action of the President upon the Bank question. On the other hand, there are many who did not go to the polls, because they did not wish to vote against the State administration, which they had helped to select, and they would not vote for it, lest they should find themselves voting for Mr. Clay in opposition to Mr. Tyler, as the leading supporters of Mr. Kent are the acknowledged champions of the former and openly sustain him in his warfare against the latter. There are others of a more mercenary character, who voted for Fairfield for the first time this fall,[22] because the conduct of leading Whigs shows a division in the Whig ranks, and like other equally valuable plunderers, wisely

22. Fairfield won the election in 1841.

deserted a falling house. On the whole I regard the result of the recent election in Maine, not as an indication of hostility to the National administration but as an assurance of unalterable opposition to the elevation of Henry Clay to the Presidency. Our people must be indeed much and radically changed before they can be brought to sanction by their votes his latitudinarian construction of the constitution upon the subject of the National Bank. Whether right or wrong, the fact is evident, and politicians should act accordingly.

With regard to the boundary question I hardly know what to say. Not that I am at this late day unable to make up my own mind upon a subject so important and one which has so long embarrassed both the State and National administrations. For I have given that much attention, and have been forced to the conclusion, that if it be ever arranged without a war, it must be by compromise—each party yielding something. And what are to be the concessions on either side, is clearly indicated by the character of the parties, and their respective relations to the territory in dispute. But the question arises from whom shall come the proposition for compromise? Shall the first step be taken and a basis be proposed by Maine, by the American or British government? This query involves not merely a point of honor, but a question of policy. Should Maine or the U.S. first move in the matter, would not England seize upon and hold our movement as vantage ground? I put these questions to you as one who has knowledge of what is going on at headquarters, which I have not. Meanwhile I assure you of my readiness to cooperate in any feasible plan of adjustment that may be deemed expedient. I deem an immediate settlement of the question upon terms less favorable, more, for our interest than a more distant one upon more favorable terms. Let me have your ideas of a basis of adjustment drawn out in detail and I shall be prepared to act when the proper season is indicated.

Yours truly

F. O. J. Smith to Daniel Webster.

Portland, November 20, 1841.

DEAR SIR: Since I had the honor to write you last on the subject of our boundary dispute, I have visited different parts of the State and had extensive personal and epistolary intercourse with the leading men of both parties, and I am persuaded the way is now prepared for a vigorous movement among our people towards the necessary preliminaries of a satisfactory compromise of the dispute.

I have commenced publishing the outline of them in a politically neutral, but extensively circulated religious paper, from which I have so arranged, I think, as to secure their reprint in the party newspapers of this State, on both sides.[23] And if in this I shall succeed, I feel confident all that was desired will be accomplished through the Legislature.

Now, what is most wanting is the means of employing a few persons in different parts of the State in whom I can repose confidence, to devote their time for a month or two next coming in getting memorials circulated among, and signed by the people, as a basis and inducement for the action of the legislature. One or two such men in each county, if I could indemnify them for their time and services, would give an effective concentration of the public sense upon the points desired for Legislative action. The truth is, divest a subject of *party* interest and *party* excitement, and it becomes that sort of "everybody's business which nobody attends to"—and from that moment it becomes necessary to make it, in some special manner, the business of some, or it will expire from stagnation.

If two or three thousand dollars could be rightfully employed in forwarding this matter at this juncture, it will accomplish *more* than armies can do after the subject shall be revived in a belligerent spirit.

Herewith I send the first article published, already adverted to, and will forward its successor shortly. If you were to consult Gov. Parris, of the Comptroller's Office, he would cause its republication by the *Globe*,[24] without connecting any name with the request, and the effect would be good here.

I have the honor to be, with great respect,

Your obedient servant

23. The religious paper referred to is the *Christian Mirror* of Portland. For the articles sent by Smith to it, see Documents, under dates Nov. 18, Dec. 2, 1841, Feb. 3, 1842.

24. Albion K. Parris, Governor of Maine from 1821 to 1826, had been concerned with the boundary dispute. He became Comptroller of the U.S. Treasury in 1836. The newspaper referred to is the Washington *Globe*.

[From the Portland *Christian Mirror,* November 18, 1841.][25]

NORTHEASTERN BOUNDARY—WHY NOT SETTLE IT?

MR. EDITOR: Some weeks since I forwarded you two articles, on the above subject, in anticipation of an event which has since happened, *in* the acquittal of *McLeod;* but it seems they miscarried, and so I propose to recur to it, re-stating the views which those articles imbodied.

I regarded, and still regard, the acquittal of McLeod as removing the only troublesome and really difficult matter of difference that ought to endanger the peace, or disturb the profitable intercourse of our own government and that of Great Britain. That involved a question of national law, about which, if pushed to extremes, two nations might differ, and about which no measure of value could be instituted for its adjustment. Our Disputed Boundary is of a different nature, involving a mere matter of fact, and such a difference as may be adjusted by the contending parties without the concession of any disputed *principle* on either side. It is undoubtedly true, that Great Britain wanted only a small part of the territory to which she advances a claim. It is no less true and obvious, that the actual, practical value of that portion which she really wants is to her very much greater than it is, or ever can be, to either Maine, as a State, or to the United States. To Maine it is valuable for its timber, and for settling purposes. It is, except in reference to a condition of peace, and for the support of quiet industry, of comparatively no value to Maine. But for this, it is of great value, and cannot, and ought not to be parted with by Maine, except for a corresponding benefit.

On the other hand, to Great Britain it is, for mere peace purposes,

25. The *Christian Mirror,* a weekly, established in Portland in 1822, was the organ of a Maine missionary society. Its editor and proprietor from 1826 to 1855 was the Reverend Asa Cummings. Cummings was a Harvard graduate and a tutor at the College for a time. He was a Congregationalist, widely known as a peacemaker. During the excitement over the boundary clash he maintained the peace view as against that of the fire-eaters. Thus he was easily persuaded to accept the peace views of the Smith articles and to endorse them editorially. The paper had a wide circulation in Maine and in other states of New England. The editor appears to have cooperated with Smith in obtaining transfer of the articles to political journals. Webster is said to have acknowledged his service in making possible a peaceful solution of the boundary controversy. A file of the *Christian Mirror* may be found in the Congregational Library in Boston.

for mere industrial ends, of only secondary or very trifling worth. But in reference to a state of war, it is of very great value and convenience to her. It consists of the angle that divides her upper and lower Provinces; and, without the free use of it, the connexion between those Provinces, over land, is necessarily exceedingly circuitous and remote. For a military *depot*, to accommodate the necessities of the upper and lower Provinces, it is invaluable. And yet, as a point from which to invade our country, or from which we could invade her, it is manifestly of very little account to either.

I have heard it urged, that, if it be of consequence to Great Britain in a military point of view, it must be of proportional worth to the United States, upon the principle of weakening the former by our withholding it. But, let this suggestion be looked at boldly, and weighed wisely. Suppose we were at war with Great Britain; would the Madawaska territory be the seat of war? None are so silly as to think it. If it were a *scrub*-fight between Maine and the British Provinces, respecting only this disputed territory, why then, while the quarrel should last, there, upon it, would be the undoubted theatre of it. But, it must be obvious to any mind, that as soon as the war had assumed a national aspect and bearing, the seaboard, and the ocean, and the interior lakes, would be exclusively the scenes of action and conflict. The woods of Madawaska would be deserted; or, if not deserted, they would be the quiet abode of domestic pursuits, or the mere pathway of unresisted troops, to and fro, between the Provinces.

Is any so credulous as to think the interruption of this pathway of British troops would be worth to the United States the expense of support? What would it accomplish for us, at last? Only this: compelling those troops to march *round* the angle that intersects the upper and lower provinces, *instead of crossing it!* To separate those provinces wholly from inter-communication would be impracticable. Were it not so, this disputed territory might be invaluable to us. But what practical benefit would the occupation of that angle by the United States be in time of war? Certainly very little at best. Yet what enormous expense, and diversion of troops would it not require for the United States thus to occupy that angle, and only to lengthen out the line of march between the British Provinces to an additional day, or two days at most! To me it is obvious, that while that territory is of very great convenience and value to the British government in a military point of view, it is of but little value to the United States, or Maine, in a like point of view. And then, again, while in a civil point of view it is of very little or no value to Great Britain, *to Maine it is of very great value.*

Now, as to title. That it is in Maine, beyond all doubt, every State, and every citizen who has given the subject any attention, of every State in the Union, is abundantly—yes, *unalterably satisfied.* That this point ever ought to be conceded by Maine or the United States, no public man will dare, and no private citizen ought to assert or believe. Nor do I believe it ever will be conceded by Maine, or by the federal government, while either has a spare cartridge to discharge in its defence. Honor, more imperiously, by far, than any pecuniary or industrial interest, forbids it; for, any nation or people that is incapable of asking by force what is notoriously wrong for them to have, is as incapable of yielding to force what is notoriously right for them to retain. Such is precisely the character of the American people, and they will certainly live up to it; and the administrators of their government, by whatever party name known, dare not depart from it, and never will depart from it.

Yet war, in its best aspect, is a deplorable calamity to any people; and, between two nations like the United States and Great Britain, it would be of unprecedented and incalculable horror, in the sacrifice of lives and of property on both sides. It must, and would terminate, after all, in negotiation and compromise; for neither would hope to exterminate, and neither, in fact, to conquer, the other. And in this case of boundary, it would also be, after all, only respecting that which one does need, and which the other does not need. Truly, such a subject furnishes no apology for recourse to arms; but it is exactly the subject for amicable negotiation.

But why has negotiation proved so long unsuccessful between the two countries? I will tell the reader why it has been thus, and will so continue, until an altered course of proceeding in the matter shall be instituted.

In the first place, it is a dispute having relation to local rights and local convenience, on both sides. The British Provinces are the parties immediately interested, and not the British nation at large, on the one side—and the people of Maine, not the people of the whole Union, are the parties immediately interested on the other side. Notwithstanding this, *not* the government of Maine, reflecting directly the interests and inclinations of its people, on one side, and *not* the government of the British Provinces, reflecting, in like manner, the interests and inclinations of their people, on the other, have had the adjustment of this dispute in their keeping and under their guidance. Had it been so, they would have come to an understanding and agreement concerning it nearly half a century since. But the Home Government, three thousand miles distant, have had the whole management of the dispute for the Provinces, and the federal government has had the whole management of it for Maine; and neither has made any movement to bring into compromise *the two subordinate parties* to furnish a basis and data that the two primary governments might adopt for their negotiation. It is most obvious, that whatever the two antagonist, local governments would assent to, the two upper governments would gladly adopt.—But while the whole negotiation is conducted three thousand miles distant from the real parties interested, and neither of the negotiators precisely understands what the distant party it represents would, in fact, be satisfied to give and take, how could negotiation be expected to advance?

The truth is, the people of Maine must take up this matter and proclaim what they will do, and what they will not do; and then the people of the Provinces, in like manner, will make known what they would like to have done, and what they would not like to have done, *for the sake of a final settlement of this perplexing and unprofitable dispute.* Let each act with reference to mutual honor, and mutual interests, and mutual peace; and the governments that are above them will readily listen, and cheerfully obey the dictates thus emanating from the parties immediately interested. Maine surely may speak on the subject, and ask the federal government to act up to her voice. What her people say, will not be gainsaid by their rulers, neither at home nor at Washington.

In another paper I will resume the subject, and submit other views, and the terms which Maine may well propose to the federal administration for bringing this dispute to an end.

AGRICOLA.

The above statement of the relations of the Boundary Question, is commended to the unprejudiced consideration of our readers. It should be looked at with minds unbiassed—with a heart of philanthropy. It is time the settlement were made on peaceable terms. The evils attending suspense are great; they need not be much longer endured. The difficulties may be adjusted without war, and without a greatly protracted delay, if there be a willingness to adjust them. We shall wait with interest the other views of our correspondent and the "terms which Maine may propose for bringing the dispute to an end."—*Mirror.*

Dr. Asa Cummings to F. O. J. Smith.

Portland, November 24, 1841.

DEAR SIR: A second number from "Agricola" on the N.E. Boundary I took from the P.O. yesterday morning. I am compelled to defer it a week. Our printers in their zeal to gain playtime for Thanksgiving, had not only got the inside of the paper full, but had so used up their type with matter for the outside of next week's paper that there was not an angle left of any [illegible word] fount to set up "Agricola." But for this I would gladly have put by any other matter to receive yours. As a citizen I feel under obligations for your labor. As a Christian, I am glad to give currency to a peaceful proposition.

[From the Portland *Christian Mirror,* December 2, 1841.]

NORTHEASTERN BOUNDARY—WHY NOT SETTLE IT?

MR. EDITOR: Before proceeding to state "the terms which Maine may well propose to the federal administration for bringing this dispute to an end," as promised in my former article, allow me to advert to the party bearings of the subject; for it must not be overlooked, that whatever movement men in power, or out of power, propose to make in relation to a matter of deep public concern, immediately suggests to them the inquiry, how will it affect, or be affected by, the party politics of the day? Will it benefit, or will it prejudice, politically, those who enter into it?

To remove all queries and doubts in relation to this aspect of the subject, it becomes the reader to reflect, and frankly admit, that to the party for the time being in power the care and management of this boundary dispute has been invariably an embarrassing and perplexing matter—one of deep responsibility. It has been one which the party out of power for the same period, when so disposed, has always been able to handle more to the prejudice of the party in power, than the latter could handle to benefit itself. And it is true, that as between themselves, and in conflict with each other, each party has alternately sought, as opportunity for it offered, to make political capital out of it for use against the other.

But, notwithstanding this disposition and practice, to the honor of both parties be it in this connexion spoken, whenever the subject has assumed the shape of a hostile issue between the State or nation on one side, and Great Britain or its provinces on the other side, State and national party lines have been obliterated, and wholly lost amid the higher, and nobler, and more patriotic impulses of the occasion; and their common adversary has consequently never been able, and never will be able, in respect to herself, to see *here* but *one* people, *one* government, *one* united country, rising to the conflict. This is a proud feature in the history of the American side of this dispute. Witness it in the State legislature under Governor Fairfield's former administration, and in the national legislature under Mr. Van Buren's administration. In the council and in the field, the same manifestation of unity of resolution and feeling has been made at every juncture.

A few weeks more will witness the administration of the State government in the hands of one party exclusively, and the national government in the hands of the opposite party exclusively. And so in proportion as this boundary dispute is in its nature perplexing and embarrassing to the one party in one of these governments, it must be so to the other party in the other government. Perhaps it is most happily and providentially so, that party interests in relation to it, if any have existed or could be excited, may be neutralized and harmonized, and brought to act in vigorous concert for its settlement. It is, indeed, true—

> "There's a divinity that shapes our ends,
> Rough hew them how we will."

Who can doubt, under the divided care and responsibility of this subject, both political parties in the State and nation would gladly see it adjusted, alike for their own comfort, and for the quiet and honor of both State and nation? It would be unpatriotic in either to entertain a different feeling. Then I assert, that a more propitious state of things than the present could not occur for bringing about an adjustment of it, *freed from, and uncontaminated by, the influences of party politics.*

The true way undoubtedly is, for the people themselves to move, one and all, and make known to their governor, and senators and representatives in the State legislature, about to assemble at the capitol of the State, "the terms" upon which *Maine* would be content to bring the dispute to an end. Neither branch of the government can or ought to be expected to move in effecting a compromise, *without being preceded by the voice of the people.* On the contrary, it becomes each branch to stand stern and steadfast by the rights of Maine, as heretofore asserted, until *the people* shall declare their willingness for some relaxation of those rights in exchange for rights claimed and relaxed by the adversary.

The question recurs, *What may those terms be?*

I answer, 1st. That Great Britain should acknowledge the title of the disputed territory to be in Maine, precisely to the extent Maine has claimed it.

2nd. That, when Great Britain shall do this, the federal government may regard itself as having the assent of Maine to cede to Great Britain the angle of territory lying north and west of the following described boundary, viz:

Commencing at a point formed by the junction of *Eel river* with the *river St. John;* thence extending up the latter river by the central thread or channel thereof to the debouchere or mouth of the *Madawaska river,* thence up the latter river by its thread or channel to *lake Temiscouata;* and from the most northerly shore of that lake, by the shortest route, to the highlands claimed by Maine for the true boundary.

3d. That Great Britain, on the other hand, shall cede to the United States, for Maine, all that portion of territory which lies south and east of the above-described line, and between the *St. John,* north of *Eel river,* and the boundary now recognised by the two countries; and pay to the United States, for the joint benefit of Maine and Massachusetts, such further indemnity for such exchange of territory as the government of the United States, through its treaty-making power, shall deem just and expedient.

4th. That Great Britain shall secure to the citizens of the United States the free navigation of the St. John to its mouth for the period of fifty years; and,

5th. That the United States government shall refund to the government of Maine its bill of expenditures heretofore incurred in defending the territory in dispute from British aggression.

Is there a citizen of Maine who will not, upon careful meditation, pronounce such a compromise honorable to both parties, advantageous to both parties, and founded in a just regard for the wants and rights of the respective parties?

Is there a citizen of any other State who will, on proper reflection, assert that the terms specified ask too much for Maine?

By the concession of title, and by that only, will her right and her honor be vindicated.

By an indemnity for the difference in the extent of territory exchanged, the exchange will be made equal; while, without it, it would be unequal.

By the free navigation of the St. John for a limited period, the territory acquired by Maine may be rendered useful to her other territory, and the convenience of Maine be consulted, as will be the convenience of the British government through the territory newly acquired by her.

By refunding to Maine her expenses incurred in defending the territory in dispute, the United States will be doing only what she should have done without the interposition of the State.

I appeal to the deliberate sense of the people of Maine to weigh these considerations as becomes men and Christians, lovers of justice and national peace. If approved, let the people, through public meetings and by memorials, direct their Representatives to reduce to better form and a proper consistency their sense of right and policy in this matter, and let a firm and energetic demand be made of the federal administration to give Great Britain the opportunity of honorable compromise, and therein to test her estimation of the benefits of peace with our people.

If she refuse the olive branch, upon her be the judgment of Heaven and the world, in terms of condemnation that will avert from her the sympathy of both Heaven and the world in the consequences that may ensue.

Already has a sister State, the chivalrous *Maryland,* asked Maine thus to show her willingness to yield to an honorable peace in this matter, and make the proper advance towards it,—still pledging the "lives and fortunes and sacred honor" of the citizens of that State, to stand by our people, let weal or woe betide us. The manifestations have been numerous that the same sense of the propriety of a movement on the part of the people of Maine, to adjust by compromise, while the way for it is open, as well as to defend by force, when no alternative is left, her territorial rights, is entertained by the other States of the Union. And can Maine seek more sincere friendship, or better advice, than emanates from such quarters—her sister States?

Regardless of party and party spirit, looking only to the country and its good, studying the comfort of all concerned in the administration of both State and national affairs, let this grave subject be approached by our people, and, with Heaven's blessing, another six months may terminate it amicably, and to the highest honor of all.

AGRICOLA.

We the more cheerfully give insertion to a pacific proposition for the settlement of the Boundary question, in consequence of the truly unfortunate relations which the political parties and papers bear to each other. We have wished the question might be kept free of all connexion with local politics; and though it be true that, in some measures, growing out of the dispute, party politics have been, for the moment, waived, and an entire unanimity witnessed, yet there have always been after-claps; and what the candidates for office have done or not done, and what they will do or not do, in relation to the Boundary dispute, is always among the topics urged on the notice of the people to influence them in giving their suffrages.

The moment, now, that the organs of either political party should propose a compromise, which should allow us to take any thing short of, or different from, the identical "pound of flesh," those of the other would load them with odium, as being ready to "sell our country to the British." And yet we believe the intelligent and considerate of both parties wish the dispute settled by other means than war. Within two years past we have put the question to distinguished men, as we have fallen in with them in stage-coach and elsewhere—men high in office and in the confidence of their respective parties, and belonging to different sections of the State—Supposing them to acknowledge the line established by the treaty of '83; what sacrifice of national honor could there be in a compromise which should give to the British the angle of our State so important to them, for an equivalent on this side the St. John, or wherever we can agree to take it? The answer was always prompt, and always the same—"No sacrifice at all."

We ask any fellow citizen, no matter who, to consider and answer the same question in the retirement of his closet. It hardly admits a doubt that all would come to the same result.

Why not act openly and manly on this conviction? The civil, economical, and moral results of a settlement, on some such basis as "Agricola" proposes, would be most auspicious, and very speedily realized. It would be a triumph of humanity, of principle, of Christianity, a thousand times more glorious than a victorious war.

It is too generally overlooked that the question must be settled, at last, by negotiation, though a ten years' war should intervene, unless we should resolve to be content with nothing short of the extermination of Englishmen, or at least their utter exclusion from the soil of North America. But who can compute the cost of such a work, or the time it would require to execute it? If national honor were at stake, we would not put such a question. This secure, it becomes solemnly obligatory to consult for the lives, the morals, the property, which would be put in jeopardy, utterly lost, by a long and bloody war.

At all events, it becomes us to keep the British in the wrong in this matter by doing right ourselves; and, by thus holding out the olive branch, if she rejects the overture, we shall show her to be wrong in the judgment of all the world. Then, if war should come, what could so nerve the American arm for the conflict? "Thrice is he armed who has his quarrel just."

As we are already thought to have no "surplus" love for old England, we trust our opinion on this matter will not be scouted without weighing it. We hope our friends in the different political parties will not think it for their interest to throw any obstacle in the way of a peaceable mode of adjusting this troublesome difficulty.—*Mirror.*

[From the Portland *Christian Mirror,* February 3, 1842.]

NORTHEASTERN BOUNDARY—WHY NOT SETTLE IT?

MR. EDITOR: In the two communications which I submitted to public consideration through your columns some weeks since, I endeavored to elucidate the expediency, favorable opportunity, and a mode of amicably adjusting, in a very short time, the perplexed question of boundary, in which our State is so largely interested. The very general circulation which the views then advanced readily obtained through the columns of the public prints in this State, without regard to party distinction, indicated the candid tone in which the public mind is prepared to entertain whatever may be feasible upon the subject, and not asking a positive sacrifice of the honor of the State. The confirmation also, which the view advanced has received in the report of the Land Agent of the State, is a gratifying evidence that the authorities of Maine will not hesitate to do in a spirit of conciliation all that can be requisite to terminate the dispute, while they can yield nothing to threats or military force. The Land Agent, among other views, well remarks as follows.[26]

"This subject having been a matter of negotiation between the two governments for many years, without appearing to approximate to any satisfactory result, it is quite probable that many years more will elapse before a conclusion can be reasonably apprehended under the protracted shifts of diplomacy.

"At the present day, few nations feel disposed to draw the sword and demand by force what is due by right, unless as the last resort, and until it shall be apparent that no honorable expedient for redress has been left untried.

"The question, therefore, seems to be one of expediency; whether it would be better to await the slow decision of this question under the action of the general government, or *to examine and see if some*

26. The Report of the Maine Land Commissioner [Elijah L. Hamlin], from which this excerpt was taken, is in the *Portland Advertiser* (w), Jan. 11, 1842. The *Advertiser* was a Whig journal.

new boundary line cannot be agreed upon without delay, that will be satisfactory to Maine and Massachusetts, and without compromitting the honor of the nation.

"From the personal knowledge I have of this territory, *I believe that a new line may be agreed upon, that will be advantageous to both governments, and by which Maine, in the end, would not be a loser.*

"Suppose the boundary line should be established today, as contended for by us, it may be worth the while to examine and see what our condition would be.

"The valley of the St. John extends across the northern section of our State, and, with the valley of the Aroostook, includes about one-third part of our whole territory. The natural outlet of this country, for trade and intercourse, will be through the province of New Brunswick. Unless, therefore, we possess some right in the navigation of the St. John, it is evident that we shall not be able to realize the full value of our timber on this river, and that the settlement of the territory will progress slowly.

"From the monument at the head of the St. Croix northward to the St. John, the boundary line crosses several rivers which have their sources within the limits of this State. It is important for the permanent prosperity of the settlements upon these rivers that Maine should own the narrow strip of land on the west side of the St. John, which embraces the mouths of those rivers.[27]

"The territory north of the St. John, above the Grand Falls, or that portion of it lying north and east of the British mail line of communication between the provinces, with the exception of some tracts of moderate width lying on the main river and some of its tributaries, is not particularly valuable for settlement or for timber, and might well be ceded to Great Britain, provided we received an equivalent in the cession of contiguous territory, the navigation of the river St. John, and such other recompense as shall be considered equitable and just.

"I think it must be apparent that this long protracted and embarrassing question can speedily be brought to a close, *when Maine and Massachusetts shall signify to the government their willingness to ac-*

---

27. This is another reference to the strip above Eel River. The Eel River proposal was early ruled out as a possibility in the actual negotiation by Lord Ashburton. *House Exec. Docs.* 27 Cong., 3 sess. (Ser. 418), No. 2, 51.

cept a boundary line varying from that defined by the treaty of 1783, upon the ground of receiving an equivalent.

"I would, therefore, suggest the propriety of the legislature, with the co-operation of Massachusetts, *presenting to the general government some basis for the settlement of a new boundary line upon reciprocal terms.*

"In proposing this plan for a final settlement of this question, it will evince a sincere desire on our part to settle the dispute upon the ground of reciprocity, and, if not met in the same spirit by the British government, it will give us an additional advantage in maintaining our present position, and must place our adversary more clearly in the wrong."

Since the above report appeared, or simultaneously with it, the boards of topographical survey, employed by the United States government for the past two years in a perambulation of the line claimed by us, have made a preliminary report, or announcement of the incompleteness of their labors, and that another season will be requisite to finish the survey. This confirms the opinion expressed by me formerly, and repeated above by the land agent, that, without a compromise of the dispute, "many years more will elapse before a conclusion can be reasonably apprehended under the protracted shifts of diplomacy."

Let us look at the grounds of this probability. Mr. Van Buren's administration proposed to the British government to make a new Commission of three American and three British members, I think, to settle the dispute, with authority, if need be, to make a joint survey of all the territory and disputed lines; and in case these commissioners could not agree on an adjustment, they should elect a single individual as umpire, whose decision should be conclusive. This, I understand from good authority, was the substance of the proposition.

It had not been acceded to by the British up to the time when the new administration came into power. It has not yet been accepted, but probably it may be with some qualification.

Now, in case of such a commission, it is wholly improbable that they will be influenced, if they consent at all to the use of the *ex parte* survey of the British government, or the *ex parte* survey of the American government. The consequence will be a new joint survey, embracing both sets of lines, and perhaps intermediate lines. There

170

is no probability that the commissioners of the two countries will make any greater progress, if agreed on, through the coming summer, than to organize, decide on preliminary proceedings, and agree on the necessity of a joint survey. This will not of a certainty be consummated in season for such survey to commence operations during the year 1842. Now, supposing it shall take the new surveyors to cover both lines, and all intermediate lines, only as long as the American survey will have been, when their next summer's work will have ended in surveying only a single line, three years more, or after 1842, will be requisite to get the return of the joint survey. This throws the dispute forward to the year 1846. Then the commissioners will not consume less than a year more in digesting these results, and ascertaining if they can or cannot agree upon the basis of an adjustment. It may be they will find it necessary to traverse the lines themselves afterwards. If they disagree after all, (which will be in 1847 probably before that shall be ascertained,) *an indefinite period* must be consumed thereafter in the selection of an umpire, in getting the evidence and arguments of each side before him, and in his making up judgment in the case. *Ten* or *twelve* years more at least will be spent by this process of amicable settlement; and, should any suspension of the good understanding that now exists between our Government and Great Britain take place in the meantime, or should the sovereign (who may be selected) be involved in war, or die, or be dethroned, as was the late umpire, the delay of the boundary adjustment will be proportionably extended.

In view of all these considerations, and many others which are appropriate to be mentioned, who can fail to appreciate the policy and wisdom of a more direct course to a compromise of the dispute? Let the Legislature of Maine, backed as she will be beyond doubt by that of Massachusetts, fearlessly advance to this point, and the people of both States will say AMEN to the movement.

I am pleased to recognise in the enlightened character and experience of the gentleman in our State Legislature who has been placed at the head of the joint Committee on the Boundary, additional signs of a politic and pacific course at this time in our Legislative Councils on this subject. In fact, the whole Committee is happily selected, it is believed, to guide with fearless prudence this troublesome topic to a right issue; and, while the honor of the State is preserved, an encouraging advance towards an early and satisfactory settlement may be hoped for at their hands.

AGRICOLA.

Reuel Williams to Daniel Webster.
(Copy in Smith's handwriting)

Private and Confidential   Augusta, February 12, 1842.

DEAR SIR, Since writing to you some days ago, I have endeavored to ascertain what may be expected from the Legislature of Me. in reference to the boundary question.

The point of honor and consistency on the part of the Legislature are in the way of arriving at what might be satisfactory to both countries.

Maine is confident of the justice and validity of her claim as advanced and insisted upon by her, and has no wish to change the *Treaty* line. Still I believe she wd release to Great Britain such portion of her territory in controversy as the convenience of the latter may require, in an offer of other territory in exchange, or other suitable equivalent.

In her view, Gt. Britain has interposed an unwarrantable claim to a portion of her territory, and has taken, and now holds part of it by military force.

To open the way to a friendly adjustment of the question, it would seem that Gt. Britain shd first withdraw all military occupation of the territory in controversy and then a proposition from her for an exchange of territory, and equivalents wd be met and carried out by Maine in a friendly spirit.

Aware of the difficulties urged by the gov't of Gt. Britain as standing in the way of her proposing a conventional line and equivalents to a party not authorized to agree to and establish such a line, the members of the Legislature, as well as the Govr of Me. as far as I can ascertain, wd agree to any course which can be honorably adopted to afford the parties an opportunity of understanding the objects and views of each other, and of arriving at a settlement of the long pending question of boundary, if possible, without resort to arbitration, indicated by the last, as well as the present Admn, as the only remaining course to be adopted.

If the information possessed by the Genl Govt wd enable you to propose to the Governor of Me. or the Legislature, a specific line of boundary, yielding to Me. territory, privileges of navigation, or other benefits equivalent to the territory which might be yielded to Gt Brn., in lieu of the line described by the Treaty of 1783, it wd be well recd. and acted upon by the Legislature as the general Govt. might justly expect from one of its members.

If that cannot be done, then I think that an appeal to Maine, as indicated in your letter, wd. receive some consideration and be acted upon with a strong desire to adopt the measure, if it shall be deemed consistent with the honor and just pretensions of the State.

Suggestions are made by some that altho' Gt. Britain has heretofore proposed to treat for a conventional line, *it is not known* that Lord Ashburton will be so instructed, and that if Maine shd authorize Comers to consider and agree upon a conventional line and its terms, and then learn that no such line or terms were to be *proposed by England,* Maine would then be placed where no American could wish to see her placed.

While I have thus given you the views of the dominant party in Maine, as fairly and fully as I can, it shd not be forgotten, that much will depend upon the course of the Whigs. Neither party, as such, will be inclined to encounter the united efforts of the other upon this great question. If the Whigs shall, as I think they will, sustain a reasonable proposition from the Genl Govt for authority to settle the question upon just grounds and with proper limitations it seems to me that the object may be attained, but I speak from appearances and not from authority. The Legislature propose to adjourn about the first of March.

> I am very respectfully
> Your obedient servant

F. O. J. Smith to Honorable Jonathan Smith.[28]

Washington, February 14, 1842.

DEAR SIR: Within the few days I have been spending in this city, I have become satisfied, from mingling with gentlemen who have the

28. Jonathan Smith was a member of the Maine Senate from Augusta.

best opportunities for judging, and *independently of all party politics and bias,* that the present time is regarded as a most favorable one for Maine to hasten an adjustment of our long-protracted boundary dispute, and that it is believed altogether advisable for the executive or legislative authorities of Maine, or both in concurrence, to appoint commissioners, say one from each political party, to visit Washington at this time, with ample powers to decide on terms that would be acceptable to Maine, for the settlement of the dispute.

That *now* is the propitious season for doing this, and enabling Maine, at the same time, to vindicate her own honor in respect to the title, and also, for a suitable compensation, to accede to a conventional line without the least detriment to herself, and that shall satisfy the adverse party, I have not the least doubt, from the information I have obtained on the subject. And seeing this so clearly, from being here upon the spot, I have deemed it a duty which I feel under, to the best interests of our State, so to advise and inform our citizens at home, that the opportunity now offered, in the favorable disposition and hopes on the subject, of the federal administration, may not be neglected by the proper authorities of Maine. I think if such prudent men as John Anderson, or Joseph Sewall, from the democratic party, and Gov. Kent, or Samuel Fessenden, from the whig party, were sent on as commissioners, to decide or negotiate the final and decisive terms upon which Maine would agree to a conventional line, the result would be most advantageous to Maine, and acceptable to her people, and satisfactory to the whole Union.

I pray you to reflect on the matter, and if you think favorably of it, cause the opportunity to be improved.

Most respectfully, your obedient servant,

Daniel Webster to F. O. J. Smith.

Private   Washington, April 10, 1842.

MY DEAR SIR: I yesterday addressed an important official letter to the Governor of Maine.[29] He will undoubtedly make the general con-

---

29. Webster refers to a letter dated April 11, 1842, to Governor Fairfield requesting the calling of the Maine legislature in special session to appoint commissioners with power, for the coming negotiation with Lord Ashburton. He sent a like

tents known, and I am informed will be very likely to consult Mr. ————, and other Portland friends. It is a moment likely to produce important results, and I must therefore pray your attention to the subject about which I have written the governor—that is, the boundary question. I verily believe the time has come for ending this controversy.

I am, dear sir, yours,

F. O. J. Smith to Daniel Webster.

Portland, April 13, 1842.

DEAR SIR: I have today had an interview with one of the State Senators of Maine (who is an influential friend of the State administration here), on the subject of an adjustment of the boundary. He is one to whom I wrote, while I was at Washington, on the same subject. He informs me, that he, and the leading men of the dominant party in this State, are decidedly in favor of compromising for a conventional line. But, upon careful search into the temperament of the House of Representatives, he and they became satisfied that a seemingly *voluntary* movement on the subject at that time in the legislature, though in terms as vague as the Massachusetts resolutions, would be almost certain of defeat in that branch; and that the only sure way of succeeding would be to have the legislature specially assembled, in case Ld. Ashburton should be found authorized and disposed to make a definite proposition such as would justify the Governor in convening the legislature for their consideration of it—

I have no doubt that there was much well-founded apprehension that led to this view; while I have no doubt that the idea of having an occasion for a special session influenced others to give seriousness to such apprehension.

---

letter to Governor John Davis of Massachusetts, but was confident Davis already had power to appoint commissioners with the advice of the Governor's Council. The letter to Fairfield appears in *Works of Daniel Webster* (6 vols., Boston, 1853), VI, 272–275. Webster's letter to Smith is in *House Reports*, 29 Cong., 1 sess. (Ser. 490), No. 684, 24. Though dated April 10, it was written after the one to Fairfield.

Every day assures me, however, that *now* is a more favorable time than has ever heretofore existed for effecting a compromise of the matter with the assent of Maine. And if the power of Ld. Ashburton over the matter does not fall short of your expectations, I think the result of your efforts will be most successful—My earnest prayers are for it, and for both your own sake and that of the Union—

I have the honor to be,
Your obedient servant,

Daniel Webster to F. O. J. Smith.

Private   Washington, May 7, 1842.[30]

My Dear Sir: I thank you for your letter, received yesterday. I am quite sorry Governor Fairfield has not published my letter. It will appear, from that letter, that not only can no agreement be subsequently submitted to Maine, but that no negotiation can be entered upon until we can assure the British minister that we are authorized to treat. I will send you a copy of the letter to-morrow. Meantime, I pray you let it be understood that we can do nothing unless commissioners come here free and untrammelled. If terms and restrictions be laid down beforehand, the British minister will say, "We treat on unequal terms. Before any propositions are made, you lay down positive conditions. This is not negotiating, but deciding without negotiation."

I have no hope of a successful result if the two States do not send commissioners in whom they can confide, and give them full powers

Yours, always truly,

F. O. J. Smith to Daniel Webster.

Private   Portland, August 12, 1842.

Dear Sir, I suppose we may consider our long disputed boundary as now settled, and the people of Maine feel that great credit is due to your efforts in bringing a forty years' dispute to a close. I feel

---

30. This letter appears in *House Reports*, 29 Cong., 1 sess. (Ser. 490), No. 684, 24–25.

gratified in the result from a conviction, of many years standing, that a new mode of approaching the subject, and such a one as you have adopted, would accomplish it, while another forty years of circuitous diplomacy would have availed nothing.

Considering the matter settled, I presume you can feel justified in enabling me to fulfil certain assurances which I made to a few individuals at different points in this State, whose services and influence I had occasion to resort to in order to adjust the tone and direction of the party presses,[31] and through them, of public sentiment, to the purpose so desirable of accomplishment under your administration.

For my own services, you can also make such allowance from the contingent fund as you may deem proper—merely remarking that all that was contemplated in my original letter to you of May [June], 1841, on the subject, has been happily realized, so far as Maine and the voice of her people, are concerned.

To the individuals alluded to above, three in number, I gave an assurance that in the event of a settlement of the boundary under your negotiation, they should be allowed *a reasonable* remuneration for their time and incidental expenses. And I should like to be able to remit them $100 or $125 each, if in my power. Nevertheless, I assumed no authority to bind your Department in any official manner on the subject; but the whole rests in my confidential intercourse with them—and I leave it, after stating the fact, wholly at your discretion. I presume the contingent fund will be ample, and your own control over it ample, to do whatever you may think just.

I send herewith a bill with entire consent for you to fill the blanks, as you may deem proper. And I do it thus seasonably, lest there be grounds for the rumor, (as I trust there is not) that you will shortly claim a right to retire from the administration of the State Department.

I beg you to believe that whether you remain in your present, or any other position of the public service, my best wishes will attend your efforts; and I shall be most happy in any opportunity of my being serviceable to you in this region of our country.

I am most truly,
Your friend and obedient servant

31. For a different rendering of the term "party presses" adopted by Smith after this letter had become public, see Documents, under date June 17, 1846.

[Enclosed in the above letter was this bill,
with blanks for Webster to fill in.]

State Department of the United

1842	States	
August	To Francis O. J. Smith, Dr.	
To Services as Special agent upon the N. E. Boundary from May 1841		$
To Services of assistants and their incidental expenses		

Supra Cr.	————
By cash Paid me, as per my receipt to Hon. D. Webster, of May 1841	$500
Bal. Rec'd of D. Webster	$ ————
Secretary of State	
Francis O. J. Smith	

[Copy of a Memorandum by disbursing agent of
State Department, August 24, 1842.][32]

(In Agent's writing)

Mr. Webster to a/c for	$9200
Less payment to Mr. Crittenden	1000
	$8200
Pay'ts certified by him	3610
	$4590

32. This "Copy of a Memorandum" and the accompanying copy of a note by Tyler are found in manuscript form in the National Archives, "Select Committee on Charges against Mr. Daniel Webster made by C. J. Ingersoll," labeled H.R., 29. No. 684, A–D, 24.1. The date of the memorandum is derived from the note of Tyler, dated August 25, 1842. The item in line two was accounted for by Webster five years later in a recollection that is unclear. He thought the money paid had probably been "without voucher for some time," but had afterward been receipted for by Crittenden. C. H. Van Tyne (ed.), *Letters of Daniel Webster,* (New York, McClure, Phillips and Co., 1902), 320.

(In Mr. Webster's writing) except the footing figures.

Smith	1500		
——— (not legible it may be assistants)	500		500
Albert Smith	200		
Sparks	250	×	
Sprague	250	×	500
Smith of (Va.)	200		
C. S. Daveis for map	200 ⎫		
for journey to Boston twice	100 ⎭	×	300
Various small items	100	×	100
	3300		1400

This is all, unless the President should think something more ought to be allowed to Mr. Sparks.

Reply of President Tyler.

Sir, In reply to your note of yesterday I can only say that I should regard $250 to Mr. Sparks for the map fully enough. I do not doubt but that it will satisfy him. If otherwise we can see more about it.

Yrs,
Signed J. Tyler
Aug. 25, 1842

Daniel Webster to F. O. J. Smith.[33]

Marshfield, June 28, 1843.

My Dear Sir: I left your last letter, by accident, at Boston, or I should have answered it before this time.

On the 15th of July I shall be in Boston, and wish you could come up. I desire to see you, first, to arrange an affair of business; and

33. This letter is in Folder No. 16, main file, F. O. J. Smith Papers, Maine Historical Society.

second to talk of public affairs a little. Please let me know, by letter addressed to me here, whether you can come.

Yours,

[House of Representatives. April 27, 1846.][34]

Mr. C. J. INGERSOLL spoke as follows:

Mr. Speaker: When Mr. Webster, in virulent terms, in Senate, assailed my truth, concerning transactions of which proofs ought to be in the Department of State, I went there in search of them for my vindication. As member of the Committee on Foreign Affairs, for some years, I have some freedom of access there, though probably none which any other member of Congress is not entitled to.

Searching for proofs, not to expose him, but vindicate myself, I fell most unexpectedly on others which led me, next day, to denounce him as a delinquent.

When the President's answer to the resolution of the House of Representatives refused certain documents, I repeated, in general assertion, the fact of his delinquency, and added that it is easily susceptible of proof. My friends advised me to go no further, supposing that Mr. Webster would challenge investigation.

Not having done so, but having again, with opprobrious language, in Senate, charged me with slander, and called on me to substantiate my accusation of him, I now submit a short statement, which may be tested as to truth.

There are three charges of delinquency:

First. Unlawful use of the fund appropriated for the contingent service of foreign intercourse, commonly called the secret service fund.

Secondly. Misapplying part of that fund to corrupt party presses.

Thirdly. Leaving the Department of State in default to that fund.

34. Ingersoll was chairman of the House Committee on Foreign Affairs. His charges against Webster appear in *Cong. Globe*, 29 Cong., 1 sess. (1845–1846), 729 (Apr. 27, 1846). For the background of the charges, see *ibid.*, pp. 636 ff. The cash figures he quotes are not always in accord with those given to the committee by Edward Stubbs, the disbursing clerk, in his "Memorandum." See Documents, under date Aug. 24, 1842. The entrance by Ingersoll into the State Department's secret archives was undercover. A Senate committee sought to determine who connived at it. It found that subordinates of the State Department had done so, not naming them. *House Reports*, 29 Cong., 1 sess. (Ser. 490), No. 686, 1–37. Webster believed Stubbs had been the culprit. Van Tyne (ed.), *Letters*, 326–327, 329.

First. Congress appropriates annually a small sum, commonly $30,000 for the contingent expenses of foreign intercourse; the disbursement of part of which is sometimes usefully clandestine, but never, as has been erroneously supposed, corrupt. Whenever, in the President's opinion, it would be wrong to make public how any part of it is disposed of, he so certifies, and, by act of Congress, his mere certificate is sufficient voucher at the treasury for the required settlement.

These funds have, for the last sixteen years, if not always, been in the hands of a clerk, called, by acts of Congress, the *disbursing agent* of the Department of State, who kept them in banks, *as agent.* The official routine is for the President, on the requisition of the Secretary of State, to authorize payment of the money from the treasury to the disbursing agent of the State Department. The disbursing agent is debited at the treasury with the sum drawn into the Department of State, keeps it to his credit as agent, in bank, and gives checks as required by the Secretary, for payment to any person he may designate.

In this way the first check I saw, when I went to the department, was drawn by the agent for the service at New York in McLeod's case, $1,000.

But, shortly after President Harrison's death, and before Vice President Tyler was at home in chief magistracy—in April, 1841—Mr. Secretary Webster began an entirely novel method of dealing with the secret service fund. Instead of directing the disbursing agent to pay *any third person*, Mr. Webster required the money to be paid *to himself.*

In this way he drew to himself from the disbursing agent twelve thousand dollars during the first nine months of Mr. Webster's incumbency as Secretary, about $1,300 a month, in 1841, and three thousand dollars more early in 1842.

Thus he took into his own hands fifteen thousand dollars in his first twelve months. The President, there is written evidence in the department to show, never authorized this, knew nothing of it, and when first apprized of it, more than fourteen months after it had been going on, to the large amount of fifteen thousand dollars, refused it his sanction.

It was not till July, 1842, as the evidence in the department shows, in Mr. Webster's handwriting, that he got a President's certificate for four thousand four hundred and sixty dollars, ($4,460).

That President's certificate, of which I took a minute, dated 19th July, 1842, is—

To J. J. Crittenden, for expenses of journey to New York	$100
To F. O. J. Smith, for services connected with the northeastern boundary	2,000
To Alexander Powell, for journey to and stay on the frontier in 1841, on the subject of the disturbances	1,000
With several other items.	

The first item in this short account concerning McLeod will show how I was led from that to other objects; and some of the other items will show the agents whom, as Secretary of State, Mr. Webster employed. Both houses of Congress, if not the public at large, have not been left in ignorance of the characters of some of those on whom the Secretary of State bestowed large sums of public money, if their receipts correctly vouch what they got.

In a memorandum of payments to Mr. Webster, by authority of the President, there is a minute dated June 23, 1842, "By cash *returned,* $5,000."

After drawing $15,000 to himself during fifteen months, during which period there is no trace of what he did with those large sums, he appears to have *returned* one-third of the amount withdrawn. Why return it, if taken for any *public* purpose? Where had it been kept? If in any place of deposite, was it separate from Mr. Webster's private funds? Did he *use* it?

These $5,000 were returned ten days after (according to the published correspondence) his negotiation with the British envoy extraordinary, began by conversational and confidential intercourse, without protocols or other usual records of such transactions.

In 1843 Mr. Webster took to himself $2,000 more, making altogether $17,000.

On closing his account, crediting the $5,000 *returned,* and various other sums, there remained a balance against him of $2,290 of the secret service fund. One of his credits against it was for $1,400, published in House documents (report No. 29) first session 28th Congress—report of Mr. Rogers for maps, charts, surveys, and expenses of bringing them to the seat of government, and for copies of transcripts, and for various agencies to procure information connected with the boundary treaty.

This inarticulate and comprehensive mixture of many incongruous items, without specification of prices, dates, or any apparent test of rectitude, Mr. Secretary Webster certified himself as a proper credit for himself, and deducted from his debit to the secret service fund. Without that credit his default to that fund would have been $3,690, instead of $2,290, which it was when he was removed from office.

The $17,000 were in his hands contrary to uniform usage; if used by him, contrary to the sub-treasury act. Whether so, is for him to make appear. The burden of proof is on him.

Secondly. Application of the secret service fund to corrupt party presses. The Ashburton treaty bears date the 9th August, 1842. Congress were then in session; and, as Mr. Adams has charged me lately, I confess I did what little I could as one of a small minority in the House of Representatives (we had forty votes, I think, under the previous question) to resist a treaty which Mr. Webster has lately stated in the Senate granted near half a million of dollars from the treasury of the United States to the people of Maine and Massachusetts. I then desired to contend, when put down by the previous question, that the House of Representatives had a constitutional right to pass on such a treaty.

What I am now enabled to add, of revelation from the Department of State, will prove that my instincts of aversion to the treaty were even truer than reason.

In the Department of State there is now a letter signed F. O. J. Smith, marked *private,* dated Portland, the 12th of August, 1842, addressed to Mr. Webster, Secretary of State, substantially as follows:

It begins by congratulating Mr. Webster on his settlement of the Maine boundary question by *a new mode of approaching the subject,* after forty years of diplomacy, without which *new mode* another forty years of diplomacy would have come to nothing.

(Mr. F. O. J. Smith seems to have suggested the boast with which his correspondent, Mr. Webster, hugged himself in his elaborate vindication in Senate.)[35]

35. The parenthetical remarks by Ingersoll relate to Webster's speech of April 6, 7, 1846, in the Senate in defense of the treaty. *Cong. Globe,* 29 Cong., 1 sess., 609–612, 616–621. For a full version see Webster, *Writings,* IX, 78–150.

Mr. Smith informs Mr. Webster by this letter that he had occasion to resort to services and *influences, in order to adjust the tone and direction of* THE PARTY PRESSES, and through them of public sentiment, to a purpose so desirable of accomplishment under Mr. Webster's administration.

Mr. Smith, therefore, submits a claim, or account, if I recollect right, in blank for Mr. Webster to fill up, of which he calls for payment out of the contingent fund. Mr. Smith presumes that the contingent fund will be ample, and Mr. Webster's control of it complete, to do whatever he may think just.

The sums Mr. Smith vouches as got by him from Mr. Webster are $2,000 for services connected with the northeastern boundary; and, two years after, he vouches $500 more, as will be shown.

Thirdly. Leaving the Department of State in debt to the secret service fund, $2,290.

The records of the department show this default beyond all denial or question.

They show, furthermore, that it was neither paid nor accounted for during nearly two years after Mr. Webster's removal from office.

They show several letters sent to him by President Tyler's direction, urging payment, and evasive letters of excuse from Mr. Webster for non-payment.

At length, a peremptory letter that exposure would or might be the consequence of more delay, produced reimbursement. But *settlement* did not take place till the 1st February, 1845, ten days before President Polk arrived in Washington to be inaugurated, when Mr. Webster produced another voucher from Mr. F. O. J. Smith, for an additional $500, and other vouchers, one from George Smith for $500.

George Smith, since dead, denied that he had ever been paid or vouched more than $150, to which sum Mr. Webster reduced the $500 at first demanded, as his agent, now in Washington, will prove.

Granting all the vouchers Mr. Webster produced, there was nevertheless a balance of about $1,200 due from him, at all events, when he left the department. That sum he was in default to the secret service fund, after crediting every thing in the way of repayment, offset, or voucher, that he claimed.

In all I have said in this affair, no allusion has been made to any private aggravation. Regretting the exposure forced from me, having afforded Mr. Webster several opportunities to meet the charges in his own way, that which he chose left me no alternative but this forbearing justification of myself.

A resolution, or committee, which I cannot institute, will soon test the truth of my statements.

F. O. J. Smith to Fletcher Webster.

Boston, May 8, 1846.

MY DEAR SIR: On Monday last I met our mutual friend Deblois[36] at Portland. I had previously written your father of my readiness and ability to explain Ingersoll's slanders. Give yourself no apprehension so far as I am concerned. My early letter to your father will cover more vouchers than he has filed, if need be, and bring the Govt in his debt. But this is *entre nous*, until I see you.

I think it best to force the Govt to summon me.[37] I have not yet been summoned, and don't wish to put myself in the position of a volunteer. But the Govt will readily appreciate the propriety of calling on me for explanation. They don't yet see Ingersoll's false scent.

I have not yet seen your father, and would if needful. But I know so well what is needed. You may trust all to the facts of the case, and my discretion until I have occasion to see you. The world, the present as well as future, will see in this whole matter naught but the envy of greatness, as in other days it was the envy of justice, that furnishes a moving history of persecution.

In haste, yours truly

Official Misconduct of the Late Secretary of State.
[Title of House of Representatives printed Report 684, June 9, 1846.]

Mr. Vinton, from the select committee, made the following Report:

The select committee of the House of Representatives appointed to investigate certain charges made by the honorable Charles J. Ingersoll

36. Refers probably to Thomas A. Deblois of the Portland law firm where Smith read law as a youth.
37. Refers to the investigation by a select committee of the House of Representatives for which see the next Document, under date June 9, 1846.

against the honorable Daniel Webster, for official misconduct while he held the office of Secretary of State of the United States, beg leave to report:

That they have given to the subject referred to them a patient and laborious investigation, and have collected a large mass of testimony, the result of which only, without going into its details, they deem it necessary to present to the House.

The committee in the first place directed their attention to the first charge against Mr. Webster, that without the knowledge of the President of the United States, and contrary to usage, he had taken out of the hands of the ordinary disbursing agent, and into his own, a portion of that part of the foreign intercourse fund commonly known as "the secret service fund," and appropriated it to his own use. The committee find that, by law, this fund is committed to the exclusive control of the President of the United States, who may, if he think proper, keep the money himself and disburse it from his own hands, or he may commit the keeping and disbursement of it to such agent or agents, under his direction, as he may deem it expedient to appoint. In consequence, as the committee presume, of the many and important duties which necessarily constantly occupy the whole time and attention of the President of the United States, so as to render it very troublesome and difficult for him in person to keep and disburse this fund, and make up its accounts, he has always, from the first establishment of the government, intrusted the discharge of these duties to other hands.

As the Secretary of State of the United States is peculiarly the confidential adviser of the President, in whatever concerns the foreign relations of the country, he would seem to be the natural and appropriate agent for the discharge of these duties, if he could perform them without detriment to other public business of higher importance. Accordingly, the committee find, that, in the administrations of General Washington, the elder Adams, and part of that of Mr. Jefferson, while the office of Secretary of State was held in succession by Mr. Jay, Jefferson, Randolph, Pickering, Marshall, and part of the time that Mr. Madison held that office under Mr. Jefferson, the whole of this fund was under the direction and supervision of the President of the United States, received, kept, and disbursed by the Secretary of State.

In the early part of Mr. Jefferson's administration, the Secretary of State, without any law requiring it, seems to have been relieved from the discharge of this duty; and the keeping and disbursing of this fund, under the President's direction, appears to have been passed over into the hands of agents, whose accounts, after receiving the sanction of the President, are settled at the treasury. But no change has been made in the law, or in the powers or duties of the President, in respect to this fund, from the time of General Washington to the present day. This change must have been made for the convenience of the Secretary of State, and not from any want of confidence which Mr. Jefferson had in Mr. Madison.

The Committee have examined Mr. Tyler, the late President of the United States; he testified that when he came into the presidency he found the foreign relations of the country in a very delicate condition in certain particulars, which the committee do not deem it expedient to specify, requiring, in his opinion, the employment of confidential agents; and for reasons assigned by him to the committee, he regarded his Secretary of State as the fittest person to select and employ them. Under an impression entertained both by him and Mr. Webster that this was the usual and proper mode, he suggested that the money should be disbursed by Mr. Webster, and for that purpose placed in his hands a portion of the foreign intercourse fund, which was then lying in deposite with Mr. Stubbs, the ordinary disbursing agent. This had not been done before for a long time.

A knowledge of the modern usage in respect to the keeping and disbursing this fund, it is not improbable, led Mr. Ingersoll into the erroneous belief that this money had come improperly, and without the President's sanction, at Mr. Webster's instance, into his hands. But there can be no doubt that the President had ample authority to commit to his Secretary the keeping and disbursing of this money, and that he alone had a right to judge of its expediency.

The committee find from the testimony, that all the money put into his hands was placed there with the knowledge and sanction, and by the order of the President; and so much of it as was necessary, was disbursed in accordance with his views. A balance, not needed for the purposes contemplated, was afterwards returned by Mr. Webster to Mr. Stubbs, the disbursing agent; with whom the testimony shows there is usually on deposit a larger amount of money than is required to meet present demands. With these remarks the committee dismiss this, and proceed to notice the second charge.

In that charge, Mr. Ingersoll accuses Mr. Webster with using the public money to corrupt the party presses. Among the agents employed by Mr. Webster, under the authority of the President, as above explained, was Mr. Francis O. J. Smith, of the State of Maine. There is, in the Department of State, among the papers relating to the secret service fund, a letter from that gentleman to Mr. Webster, which contains an expression that, unexplained, might justly lead to the impression that he (Mr. Smith) had used the money of the government in that way. The committee have fully investigated this charge. They do not deem it necessary or expedient to go into a specification of the acts of this agent, who was employed in a secret service, or to inquire into the propriety of employing agents for secret service within the limits of the United States, and paying them out of the contingent fund for foreign intercourse; but will content themselves with simply remarking, that the testimony they have taken fully explains whatever is of obscure or doubtful meaning in this letter, and removes every foundation for a belief, or even a suspicion, that the public money was used, or attempted to be used, to corrupt the party presses. This brings the committee to the third and last charge, that when Mr. Webster went out of office he was a public defaulter.

From an examination of his accounts, it appears that when he retired from office there was, of the moneys that had been intrusted to him, an apparent balance of $2,290 in his hands, as stated by Mr. Ingersoll. The expenditure of this sum remains to be accounted for by him. There seems to have been delay in procuring vouchers from the agents whom Mr. Webster had employed, for the moneys advanced by him to them. For a payment of a thousand dollars, which he claimed to have made out of the fund in his hands, he alleged the voucher had been lost, mislaid, or not procured; and it has not yet been found or obtained, though efforts were made by him to find or procure it. These causes occasioned a delay in the settlement of his accounts for some eighteen or twenty months.

In the autumn of 1844, the period having arrived when it was necessary for Mr. Stubbs to close his accounts at the treasury, and Mr. Webster not having then procured the necessary vouchers, he proposed to pay the apparent balance against him, with the understanding that the government should refund to him if he subsequently procured the evidence of his payments. This proposition, which proceeded from Mr. Webster, was acceded to by the President of the United States. In the month of November of that year Mr. Webster procured a voucher for a payment of $200, and paid in cash $2,090, the residue of the apparent balance in his hands. This money was remitted by him in part from Boston, and in part from Philadelphia. In the following winter he visited Washington, and, on the 1st of February, 1845, presented vouchers for payments made by him while in office, and not before credited to him, to the amount of $1,050, which the President of the United States directed to be refunded; and that amount was then repaid to him. Mr. Webster was urged by Mr. Stubbs to collect and transmit his accounts and vouchers, that he (Mr. Stubbs) might close his accounts with the treasury; but the committee find no evidence of any threat of exposure having been made by the President, which induced the payment of the apparent balance against him.

If it be assumed that Mr. Webster was correct in his impression that he had paid the above-mentioned thousand dollars out of the fund in his hands, and if to this amount be added the vouchers for $1,250, procured by him after his retirement from office—making, together $2,250—and this last amount be deducted from $2,290, the apparent balance against him, it will show that the real balance in his hands when he went out of office was $40 only. On reviewing his accounts, the keeping of which was for the most part intrusted by him to Mr. Stubbs, the disbursing agent, the committee have been led to doubt whether, on the final settlement, an item of $500 was not, by mistake, carried to his credit, which had been before allowed him. This error was pointed out to the committee by the disbursing agent, by whom the account was drawn up and the settlement made. He proves that it was at his own suggestion, and not at that of Mr. Webster, that this item was carried to his credit in the final settlement. It is not necessary to go into the particulars of the history of this item, and of the cause of the mistake, if one was made. The committee deem it sufficient to remark that no blame is imputable to Mr. Webster, who, they are satisfied, was not aware, and probably is not now, that this item had been before credited to him; nor is the disbursing agent who drew up the items of the final settlement, liable to the charge of negligence. If it be assumed that this item was twice allowed to him, and that the final settlement was in all other respects correct, then, in refunding to Mr. Webster, he should have been repaid $550 only, instead of $1,050. But if Mr. Webster was not mistaken in the belief that he had paid the thousand dollars above mentioned, then the government still owes him $500.

The committee deem any comment on the above facts, connected with this charge, unnecessary. In their opinion there is no proof in relation to any of the charges, to impeach Mr. Webster's integrity or the purity of his motives in the discharge of the duties of his office. The value of this opinion is perhaps, to some extent, enhanced by the fact that, in their investigation, the committee, in observance of the usage in similar cases, have taken the testimony without notice to him, in his absence, without communication with him, or explanation from him. In conclusion, they beg permission to remark that their investigation has brought out facts (which are embodied in the testimony) connected with the foreign relations of the country, the disclosure of which public policy would seem to forbid. On this subject they entirely concur with the President of the United States [Polk], in the views so fully and strongly enforced by him in his message at the present session, in answer to a resolution of the House requesting a communication to it of the same facts that are embodied in the testimony taken by the committee, and which, for reasons then assigned, he declined to communicate or make public, except with a view to an impeachment, and to furnish the proof necessary to attain the great ends of public justice. He expressed the opinion that, even in that case, the House should adopt all wise precautions to prevent the unnecessary exposure of matters the publication of which might injuriously affect the public interest. No dissent from the views of that message was expressed by the House. The committee therefore think that these facts were laid open to their view with an implied understanding, both on the part of the President and of the House, that they would be made public only in the event of an impeachment, and of their being necessary for bringing to justice great public delinquents. Inasmuch, therefore, as no evidence has been exhibited to the committee which can lay any foundation for an impeachment, all the reasons which induced the President to decline to make these facts public on the call of the House, return in their full force against their disclosure now.

They therefore recommend that they be discharged from the further consideration of this subject, and that the testimony taken by them (which accompanies this report) be sealed up, endorsed "confidential," and deposited in the archives of the House—not to be opened unless by its order. And they report resolutions accordingly.

Resolved, That the testimony taken in this investigation be sealed up by the clerk, under the supervision of the committee, endorsed "confidential," and deposited in the archives of the House; and that the same be not opened unless by its order.

Resolved, That this report be laid on the table and printed, and that the select committee be discharged from the further consideration of the subject.[38]

Signed and submitted by

> SAML. F. VINTON,
> JEFFER. DAVIS,
> DANIEL P. KING,
> SEABORN JONES.

Extracts from the deposition of John Tyler,[39] late President of the United States, taken before the select committee appointed to investigate certain charges of C. J. Ingersoll against Daniel Webster, for official misconduct while he held the office of Secretary of State.

Question by Mr. Jones. Please state what disbursements were made of the foreign intercourse fund during the time Mr. Webster was Secre-

38. These proposals by the majority of the select committee to print only the formal report and to seal up in the House archives all the testimony taken were challenged by Jacob Brinkerhoff, the minority member, whose report follows. He wished the testimony to be printed in its entirety. He forced the issue by including the letter of F. O. J. Smith to Webster of August 12, 1842, in the body of his report. A debate ensued in the House, the outcome of which was that all of Smith's testimony, including the August 12 letter, and Tyler's testimony, in highly expurgated form, were included as appendixes. For the majority report and its appendixes, see *House Reports,* 29 Cong., 1 sess. (Ser. 490), No. 684. For the debate in the House see *Cong. Globe,* 29 Cong., 1 sess. (1845–1846), 948, 988, 999–1000.

39. The testimony of Tyler was a defense of himself and of his Secretary of State against charges of having misused the foreign intercourse fund. Only a part, and not the more valuable part, was reproduced in the printed House document. The deleted portions, found at the National Archives in Select Committee Report, H.R. 29, No. 684, A–D 24.1, have been restored here to the printed version. The reconstructed document is basic to an understanding of the preliminaries of the Webster-Ashburton negotiation.

tary of State, and particularly those disbursements made relative to the settlement of the northeastern boundary, and to whom they were made, and for what services to be rendered.

Answer. The deponent expressed embarrassment in answering so much of the question as related to the names of individuals. To do so would be in violation of an implied understanding, in the absence of which no executive officer could hope to obtain the services of individuals in dangerous or delicate emergencies. He should reserve an answer to that part of the question for further consideration, and the future action of the committee. In answer to the general scope and design of the question, he would be permitted to say that, when deponent came to Washington to assume the duties of the Chief Executive office, the peace of the country was most seriously threatened. The spirit which had led to prior disturbances on the northern frontier had not subsided, but was, as was believed, greatly excited and increased by the arrest of McLeod, a British subject, who was at that moment in jail charged with the murder of Durfee, an American citizen; a *demand* for whose release had been emphatically made by the British government; a demand which it was impossible, if so inclined, for the government to have met.

The difficult question of the northeastern boundary, which had already produced a military array on the part of Maine, and as to which political parties in that State had not marshalled themselves against each other, but rather vied with each other in the effort to go farthest in the assertion of the territorial rights of that State, was calculated to arrest and unceasingly to claim the attention of the administration. (To add to its embarrassments, the agitating, and for the time, not a little dangerous condition of affairs in Rhode Island, occurring at a subsequent period, required great vigilance and the most delicate management.)[40]

The administration wanted information which would enable it to act with proper understanding upon all these subjects, and I placed at the disposal of Mr. Webster, the Secretary of State, from time to time, what was regarded as a suitable amount of funds to obtain such information. In what deponent should say, he did not mean to avoid

40. The sentence in parentheses is taken from the manuscript of Tyler's testimony. The same mode of completing the testimony is followed in the remainder of the "Extracts."

any responsibility which could properly attach to him, but stood ready to abide by any decision which might be pronounced of him or his acts, in connexion with this subject. The Secretary of State seemed to him every way the most suitable person, from his extensive acquaintance with the citizens of the northern States, and the fact of his being at the head of the department more directly intrusted with what related to the preservation of the public peace, to be selected as deponent's agent upon matters so interesting and yet so delicate and confidential. Accordingly, I placed at his disposal, from time to time, ample funds to enable him to employ agents who would be most likely to acquire for the government full and satisfactory information, and aid it in its efforts to secure and advance the general good. It was deemed also necessary to appoint agents to foreign parts, for purposes believed to be essential to the well being of the country. For those and other purposes, I placed at Mr. Webster's disposal, at different periods during his secretaryship, sums of money amounting in the whole to $15,000 (fifteen thousand dollars.)

While deponent felt reluctant to name individuals who were employed by the government, he had no hesitation in explaining to the committee the objects held in view by the government. He had already said enough to satisfy the committee of the objects contemplated in the appointment of secret agents upon the northern frontiers, and he would proceed to an explanation, which would be more directly responsive to the question which had been asked him, as to the expenditures touching the northeastern boundary.

This deponent had before said, that parties in Maine seemed to vie with each other as to which should be most extreme on the subject of the boundary. The public press there was but the exponent of this state of feeling. The administration had no press in Maine to enforce its views and wishes. It wanted merely to be heard and understood, and the only way which seemed to be opened to it was, by the employment of persons to make known its views by all proper means. Those views were, simply, to induce Maine to unite with the government in an effort to settle the questions in dispute, and that through commissioners to be appointed by the legislature, and who should come on to Washington and unite their counsels with those of the American negotiator, in the then shortly anticipated negotiation, and without whose concurrence nothing should be done. This was the great point to be gained, with the approbation of men of both the great parties of that day. It was gained; and the committee well knows the negotiation was crowned with success. In all this business a sum of between three and four thousand dollars, it is believed, was expended.

(The sums thus advanced to Mr. Webster were accounted for in part, from time to time, by Mr. Webster with Mr. Stubbs, the confidential clerk employed in the bureau, who reported to Deponent from time to time the progress of the settlement. When the vouchers were paid by Mr. Stubbs, all the items of expenditures with the exception of such as it was deemed proper to keep secret, more for the sake of the agents employed than for any other reason known to Deponent, took their places in the public accounts, and Deponent's orders in favour of Mr. Webster were cancelled, and Deponent's certificate was made to cover $4460 of this class of expenditures. Deponent was informed by Mr. Stubbs that Mr. Webster had returned a portion of the money thus advanced, which upon the settlement had been duly credited. Under what circumstances money was returned except as he shall state hereafter, or how or when drawn in virtue of the orders, he does not remember to have been informed. He knows nothing which was calculated to induce a belief that it had been used for private purposes or otherwise improperly employed.

Deponent further states that at the time Mr. Webster left the State Department Mr. Stubbs informed him that Mr. Webster had not settled his account, and that there was a balance of something, he thinks, exceeding $2000, which Mr. Webster stated to Mr. Stubbs he had also expended, but that he had either lost or mislaid his vouchers, and that so soon as he could lay his hands upon them he would settle it.

Some time afterwards Deponent directed Mr. Stubbs to write to Mr. Webster, and to inform him of Deponent's solicitude to have the account closed. He afterwards informed me that he had done so, and as well as Deponent remembers, stated that he had received a letter from Mr. Webster to the purport that he labored under the same disability which had attended him on leaving Washington and expressed the fear that he should have to have the vouchers renewed, which would of course give him great trouble. Some months afterwards Mr. Stubbs informed Deponent that Mr. Webster, not having procured his vouchers, had deposited with him a sum of money to cover his responsibilities, and which Mr. Webster said to him he must lose and class under the head of his misfortunes, if he did not procure suitable vouchers. Shortly afterwards Mr. Stubbs informed me that Mr. Webster had called on him with satisfactory vouchers, and recommended that the money deposited by Mr. Webster should be returned to him, which was accordingly directed to be done, and thereby the whole matter was settled and finally closed.)

Question by Mr. Brinkerhoff. Were the instructions given to, or the reports received from, the agent employed by Mr. Webster in relation to the northeastern boundary question, ever submitted to your inspection; and did you ever communicate personally with that agent?

Answer. I had conversed freely with Mr. Webster as to the objects to be attained by the appointment of agents, but did not see the instructions, nor were anything but results communicated to me. I have no knowledge of having conversed with the agents.

(Question by same. After Mr. Webster retired from the Department of State and after he had been written to by Mr. Stubbs under your direction in relation to his delinquency, did not Mr. Webster request or suggest that you should, without the requirement of further vouchers or payments from him, grant a certificate to cover the amount of that delinquency in order to enable him to close his accounts and did not you refuse such certificate?)

(Answer. I have no recollection that Mr. Webster made any communication to me except through Mr. Stubbs after his retirement from office. I was impressed very strongly with the belief that Mr. Stubbs informed me that Mr. Webster considered it was but reasonable that I should grant a certificate for the balance necessary to close his account upon his formal statement that expenditures to that amount for which his vouchers were lost had been made. I declined granting the certificate, from no want of confidence in Mr. Webster but because of my objection to cover up by my certificate, expenditures which might admit of publicity. He was my agent *pro tanto* and I did not think it proper to exempt him from rules which applied to all others.)

(Question by same. Were the letters which passed between Mr. Stubbs and Mr. Webster on the subject of his account after Mr. Webster's retirement from office submitted to your inspection as the correspondence progressed or were your communications with Mr. Stubbs on that subject verbal only?)

195

(Answer. I gave directions to Mr. Stubbs and received his verbal report, both of the contents of his letters and Mr. Webster's replies.)

Question by Mr. Jones. Were you advised by Mr. Webster of any particular need for the $15,000 which was ordered to be paid to him, and any particular use for it at the time of the orders; and did he give any reasons satisfactory to you why the usual mode should be departed from in having the money paid to him instead of being left with the confidential agent of the President, to be paid out as wanted?

Answer. I have already stated, in the body of my deposition, the reasons which led me to make Mr. Webster the agent for disbursing funds, and to that I refer. I deemed it proper to make the Secretary of State my confidant in matters which it was not desirable should be publicly known at the time. The advances were necessarily made in advance of the individual demands, since their object was, in part, to employ agents who had afterwards to be looked out for by the government. In other instances the demands were present and existing. When I first made an advance to Mr. Webster, I regarded it as a matter consistent with previous usage, and he was of the same impression; and I now regard it quite as regular as the constituting Mr. Stubbs the agent. The President is, according to the opinions of many, the only disbursing officer recognised by the law; but his appointment of agents is a work of necessity, and the field of selection is his own. When Mr. Webster applied for advances, he certainly assigned reasons which were regarded as sufficient.

(Question by the same. Did Mr. Webster give any reason which should authorize him to draw out the sum of $5000 in November, 1841, keep it in possession until June, 1842, and then return it, and did you know or were you informed by Mr. Webster of any circumstances requiring the money to be drawn and which ceased to exist when it was refunded?)

(Answer. He did, as will appear by the paper a copy of which is hereto appended, assign reasons for the advance. I know nothing of the time or manner in which the money was drawn nor the time of its return. That was between Mr. Webster and Mr. Stubbs—the latter of whom only communicated to me at some time or other that the sum of money had been returned. Mr. Webster never said anything to me about it.)

(Question by the same. What reason induced you to refuse your sanction to the certificate of $9200 asked for by Mr. Webster, and give one only for the sum of $4460, and to the certificate for $1290, also asked for by Mr. Webster?)

(Answer. I preferred that all items of expenditure that could be made public consistently with propriety, should take their place on the face of the regular quarterly accounts, and that my certificate should only be used in cases where concealment was necessary for the public good. Many of the items composing the expenditure of nine thousand two hundred dollars were of a character not injurious to be made public and I directed a separation to be made between them and those which it was improper to make public. The last class were covered by my certificate for $4460. I give the same answer to the latter part of the question.)

(Question by Mr. King. Had you any knowledge or suspicion that unsuitable agents were employed by the Secretary of State or that large sums of public money were bestowed by him as charged by Mr. Ingersoll, or do you know of any conduct of the Secretary in relation to the Boundary question which was dishonorable or liable to suspicion?)

(Answer. I have no such knowledge or suspicion).

(Question by same. Mr. Ingersoll charges upon Mr. Webster "an entirely novel method of dealing with the secret service fund. Instead of directing the disbursing agent to pay to any third person Mr. Webster required the money to be paid to himself." Was not Mr. Webster selected by yourself for reasons which appeared sufficient as your disbursing agent?)

(No answer.)

(Question by same. Were your orders to make advances to Mr. Webster before or after the purposes for which they provided were carried into execution, and if before, would it be known with certainty how much money would be necessary for those purposes?)

(Answer. The orders for advances were made both before and after the purposes for which they provided were carried into execution. When made before, it was next to impossible in some instances to know with certainty how much money would be required. The same thing holds true with the ordinary current expenses chargeable on the contingent fund for diplomatic intercourse. Mr. Stubbs most generally, if not always, had a fund on hand beyond existing demands.)

(Question by same. Mr. Ingersoll in his charges against Mr. Webster speaks of his having begun the negotiation with the British Minister by conversational and confidential intercourse without protocols or other usual records of such transactions. Please state if such was the fact, and if so, was the negotiation thus begun with or without your knowledge?)

(Answer. I had full knowledge upon the subject, and labor under a strong impression that it assumed that form upon my own suggestion. It seemed to me that enough had been said and written in the diplomacy on the subject in controversy, and that if it was to be settled it could be done only by avoiding commitments in writing so difficult to be recovered from on the part of the negotiators.)

(Question by same. Was Mr. Webster's time much engrossed with the duties of his office while he held the office of Secretary of State, and especially till the conclusion of the Boundary treaty?)

(Answer. It was a period of great labour. Mr. Webster was closely and most laboriously engaged.)

(Question by Mr. Vinton. Was or was it not wholly in your discretion, in giving a President's certificate for expenditures out of the foreign intercourse fund, whether you would require the production of vouchers for the same?)

(Answer. That is certainly my understanding of the powers of the President, but I did not think proper to exert it. I refer to what I have previously said upon this subject in answer to the above. Mr. Webster considered it proper and I concurred in the opinion. I am not prepared to admit that this was universal. The Secretary of State had been required to discharge similar, if not broader duties under previous administrations in regard to disbursements from the fund.)

Question by Mr. Vinton. Have you any knowledge or suspicions that the secret service fund, or any part of it, was applied by Mr. Webster to corrupt the party presses?

Answer. I have no such knowledge or suspicion.

JOHN TYLER.

I hereby certify that the foregoing deposition was taken and subscribed in the presence of the committee, between the 28th of May, 1846, and the 1st of June.

SAML. F. VINTON, *Chairman.*

JUNE 1, 1846.

The deposition of Francis O. J. Smith, taken before the select committee of the House of Representatives appointed to investigate certain charges made by C. J. Ingersoll against Daniel Webster.

The said Francis O. J. Smith being, on this twenty second day of May, 1846, first duly sworn by the chairman in the presence of said committee to testify the truth, the whole truth, and nothing but the truth, touching the matter now under investigation, deposeth and saith as follows, viz:

Question. Please inform the committee whether you were employed as an agent concerning the northeastern boundary question; and if so, by whom, when, and for what purpose were you employed; state fully what you did as such agent, and disclose, in particular, whether by yourself, or by any one else within your knowledge, the secret service fund, or any part of it, was employed or used to corrupt party presses; and if so employed, state fully all you know about it, and how the said secret service fund, or any and every part that came into your hands, or was disbursed through your agency and within your knowledge, was disbursed and employed, to whom paid, and for what purposes.

In answer to the general interrogatory propounded by the committee, the undersigned respectfully, and upon his oath, says: That he was employed by the honorable Daniel Webster, while Secretary of State, as agent of the government of the United States in Maine, from the early part of June, A. D. 1841, until August, 1842, in special relation to the adjustment of the northeastern boundary dispute.

The circumstances giving rise to that agency were as follows: Being at Mr. Webster's residence in Washington with a personal friend of mine, but who was his political opponent, and for the purpose, mainly, of a friendly call, in the latter part of May, 1841, the northeastern boundary dispute was spoken of as one of anxious concern to himself, Mr. Webster. In the course of the conversation that ensued, I expressed to him the outline of certain views I had urged upon Mr. Van Buren for the settlement of that dispute in 1837, early in the progress of his administration.[41] Mr. Webster appeared at once arrested by the suggestions made, and led on to a more extended discussion of the

41. For the letter to President Van Buren, see Documents, under date Dec. 7, 1837.

subject. The interview resulted in his requesting that I would submit to him in writing what I had expressed as feasible, and the method of accomplishing it in detail, and consent to engage in accomplishing the object. I promised to submit to him the suggestions desired, and did so by letter bearing date June 7, 1841, an exact copy of which I herewith submit, marked A.[42] This letter explains the whole length, breadth, height, and depth of all the influences I ever proposed to resort to, or ever did resort to, on the subject, at any time or with any person. It must speak for itself; and the history and provisions of the treaty subsequently made, and incontrovertibly approved by the mass of the citizens of Maine, as well as by the treaty-making power of the federal government, will demonstrate whether I reasoned correctly or not, honestly or not, and for the best interest of Maine and of the Union, or otherwise.

As that letter contemplated, so now do I solemnly protest that nothing was designed in it, and nothing done under it, to subserve any sinister motive, nor to effectuate any party purpose, nor to make political capital, and much less corruptly, for any person, beyond the credit which a worthy act accomplished in the settlement of a long protracted and greatly embarrassed national dispute would confer on the parties engaged in it.

In 1837, following up the suggestions and tendency of President Jackson's proceedings towards the adoption of a conventional boundary to end the dispute, I urged, in more detail even than in this letter to Mr. Webster, upon Mr. Van Buren, the expediency and feasibility of settling it by a conventional line, by abandoning reliance upon the circuitous artifices of ministerial diplomacy, and instituting a system of direct consultations with, and appeals to, the judgments, and interests, and co-operating common sense of the people themselves of the two local governments that were alone immediately interested in the matter. By local governments I mean the government of Maine and that of the adjacent province.

I do not find myself possessed of a copy of that letter to Mr. Van Buren, but I do not doubt that little pains will disclose the existence of it in the State Department at this date, if its exhibition be desirable. I had one or more private interviews with Mr. Forsyth, Mr. Van Buren's then Secretary of State, on the subject of that letter, *at his request.*

42. For this letter, see Documents, under date June 7, 1841.

Of them I have not had occasion to speak, and have not spoken, until now, because I designed at no time to make any efforts of mine to bring the boundary dispute to an end a matter of personal merit or of political capital. But as I have by me one of Mr. Forsyth's written requests for a confidential interview on the subject, I exhibit it to the committee, that they may not imagine I am speaking from recollection alone. The divergence which soon after took place between many of Mr. Van Buren's political friends, of whom I had been one, and himself, in respect to the sub-treasury and kindred matters, shut off inducements on both sides to pursue to a fair trial the proceedings I had suggested as the proper and only ones that could ever prove successful in the matter, and there they fell to the ground.

After my communication to Mr. Webster of the 7th of June, 1841, he renewed the request, in an interview I had with him at the State Department, that I would consider myself engaged in furthering the settlement as far forth as might be found practicable in the way suggested; taking new directions from such events and developments as might arise, and apprizing him from time to time of the condition and prospects of success; adding that I might consider my compensation as satisfactorily arranged in respect to time, services, and expenses.

I thenceforward made it a leading and primary engagement, by consultations and correspondence with men of well known influence in Maine of both political parties; for I then, politically, stood between the two parties, and identified myself with neither, yet betraying no official views, as such, that no jealousies might be excited, and endeavoring only to interest as many persons as possible to think and act for themselves, favorably to a conventional line.

The next letter, succeeding that of June 7th, that I wrote Mr. Webster on the subject, and of which I find any copy, I submit, marked B.[43] The printed enclosure therein is a form of petition, such as I enclosed and alluded to in my original to Mr. Webster. In this connexion let me say that this one printed sheet was the only line of print touching the boundary for which I paid any person whomsoever, at any time, either directly or indirectly, in person or by proxy; and that payment was made to a printer, who was in nowise connected with any party press or party newspaper. And in further response to this feature of the committee's interrogatory, I will add, that at no time did I per-

43. For this letter and its enclosure, see Documents, under date July 2, 1841.

sonally, nor through any sub-agency, pay or promise to pay, or suggest the idea of either pecuniary compensation or patronage of any kind, to any person whomsoever, for any publication or for the omission of any publication on the subject of the boundary, in any newspaper of any party or of any religion; nor do I recollect that I ever suggested to any person, or conceived in my own mind the necessity of so doing, or that it might become desirable so to do under any circumstances, and certainly never in any other sense than as for any business advertisement or communication. But the whole success of the effort for a conventional line from the beginning was at all times expressed by me, and at all times concurred in by Mr. Webster, as dependent on our successfully restraining the newspapers and politicians of all parties from imparting to the proposition any party color or hope of party advantage. And so well was this idea maintained at all times throughout the State, (however or by whomsoever conducted,) that the governor, in his message convening the special session of the legislature to act upon the question of compromise, declared it one void of party considerations, and "emphatically a State question."

The only press I selected through which to act upon the popular sense of Maine, or to which I was known as a contributor on the subject, was the Christian Mirror, of which I submit three numbers, dated November 18, 1841, December 2, 1841, and February 3, 1842, marked I,J,K, which contain the only articles I wrote for publication.[44] This press, then, ever had been, and still is, neutral in politics, and devoted mainly to the interests of a religious sect. But it was and is known as one of very wide circulation in the State, and of deservedly great influence. The editor, without fee and without reward, and alone from a sense of duty to the interests of the State, commended these publications in his columns, and they were very generally, in whole or in parts, recopied by the political presses of both parties in the State. On the appearance of the first number, I enclosed it to Mr. Webster in a letter, of which copy herewith submitted, marked C, dated November 20, 1841, is a true representation.[45]

I ask the special attention of the committee to the temper and sentiments of these published articles, and of this last-named letter, for a true exponent of the spirit, character, and design of all my efforts

44. For these articles, see Documents, under dates given.
45. For this letter, see Documents, under date given.

to act upon the popular judgment of Maine in furthering Mr. Webster's earnest desires to adjust the boundary dispute. In nothing different from these publications did Mr. Webster at any time ask, desire, or expect me to conduct my agency; and at no time did I depart from their general tone and policy.

It was this tone of abjuration of party politics in respect to the matter among all the party presses of Maine, this discouragement and displacement through the party presses, and starting with the influence of a press wholly neutral, that was alone sought, was alone aimed at, and was alone accomplished, so far as I accomplished anything in the matter, and to which, and to nothing beside, was the allusion made in my letter to Mr. Webster of August 12, 1842, hereinafter copied. It was to secure this end that I invoked the aid, and secured the aid, of persons of influence in party matters, who approved of both the motive and object themselves.

If need be, to illustrate yet further the spirit in which I pursued my efforts in the matter, I present the committee with a copy (marked D) of a letter I addressed from this city to a then senator of the Maine legislature, in session at Augusta,[46] under date of February 14, 1842, and with the knowledge and approval of Mr. Webster. The gentleman addressed was then, and still is, an adherent of the dominant party in Maine—not an original thinker, but an influential person in the ranks of his party. He was one with whom I had in other years been on terms of political friendship, though we were not so at the time; yet our relations were such as justified my expectations of his concurrence in a procedure involving no party designs. Of the result of that letter's suggestions, and at the same time as an index of the delicate and jealous temper of Maine politicians on the boundary question, I wrote Mr. Webster, in a letter dated April 13, 1842, of which an exact copy is hereto annexed, marked E.[47]

A request by Mr. Webster for a special session of the legislature was the alternative, and letters from him to myself, of which copies are herewith submitted (marked F and G) are all I find in my possession in relation to this stage of the proceedings, and will speak for themselves.[48]

46. For this letter to Senator Jonathan Smith, see Documents, under date given.
47. For this letter, see Documents, under date given.
48. For these letters, see Documents, under dates Apr. 10, May 7, 1842.

Subsequently, when the treaty had been consummated between Mr. Webster and Lord Ashburton, and rumor represented Mr. Webster as about to retire from the State Department, considering my agency at an end, I wrote the letter of August 12, 1842, of which a copy is herewith submitted (marked H) and being *the* letter that has been so widely misapprehended by Mr. Ingersoll.[49] Even had its allusions meant the *purchase* of party presses into an advocacy of a compromise of the boundary question, the scale of corruption must be thought quite *a small one* to be very effective upon a question that had been only a short time before of sufficient magnitude to put a large portion of all the troops of Maine in motion, led on by a valiant chief magistrate; for $375 (*three hundred and seventy-five dollars*) is all the letter calls for under this imagined branch of expenditure. But the whole history of my proceedings in the matter, as delineated in the letters of which I have given copies, will bear me out in declaring Mr. Ingersoll's construction of that letter wholly erroneous, and one which, on reflection, he will, I trust, withdraw and disavow as an error of temporary passion, and not of the heart.

As to the disbursement of the secret service fund inquired of by the committee, I answer that I know nothing beyond the fact, that when I engaged in the effort of effectuating a compromise of the boundary, I did it without reference to any particular fund, or with a view to any studied or necessary secrecy in respect to the matter, beyond the period while the subject was in progress. I always supposed the ordinary contingent fund of the State Department would be available. But my original letter to Mr. Webster, of June 7, 1841, expressly stated my terms of compensation to be $3,500 per annum and expenses. I forwarded to him my bill in blank,[50] as stated in letter marked H, and on which he made payment of $2,000, additional to $500 previously paid, without ever explaining to me, or my asking explanation of him, why the full amount stipulated for my services was not remitted, or whether a further allowance would not be made for expenses incurred by myself and by others. Until I saw Mr. Ingersoll's accusations published, I did not know, for I had never felt an occasion for looking into the public documents for the purpose of seeing, whether these payments to me had or had not been detailed in the published expendi-

49. For this letter, see Documents, under date Aug. 12, 1842.
50. For the bill, see Documents, under dates June 7, 1841, Aug. 12, 1842.

tures incident to the boundary adjustment, as well they might have been. I did not suppose that Mr. Webster, if he had kept in mind my original letter, considered these payments thus made to be in full; yet, during his continuance in the State Department, I did not have a convenient opportunity to recall to his mind the terms of my engagement, although I doubt not, if I had done so, they would have been fully complied with by him, and cheerfully. Had I been actuated by any venal motives, I should hardly have conducted thus negligently in a matter where the original stipulation was so explicit, and so clearly fixed my compensation. But I had never made my relation to the boundary a subject of remark myself, simply because I had not from the beginning any personal ends to accomplish in it beyond the consciousness of having endeavored well to bring the dispute to a close; and knowing that, if I ever had occasion to recur to it, the means of "setting history right" would not be lost; and that these, with the provisions of the treaty itself, would establish whatever claim to the credit of a useful adviser in the matter I might desire to prefer. I know of no act of my life that could have been performed with a more single eye to the public service, and with less of sinister motives, than this of which inquiry is now made; and if any person living has any letter of mine touching the matter, or has knowledge of any act of mine respecting it, militating in the slightest degree with my present representation, I absolve him from all injunction or seal of secrecy with which it may have been hitherto marked, and invoke its publication. The subject, while it lasted, occupied very much my whole time and attention. I made other engagements give way to it. It was one which had been long familiar to me in all its bearings; and from my acquaintance with the leading men of all parties in Maine being equal to, if not even more minute than that of any other individual in the State, my correspondence and communications with them were constant and continued, and directed to this one end, viz: to persuade the government and people of Maine to adopt a mode of settling this controversy of half a century old, which would only be effectual by keeping the subject entirely aloof from party jealousies and party influences.

And it is due to Mr. Webster from me to add, as I now do, that in all correspondence I had with him on the subject, whether verbal or written, he appeared governed by one great and leading desire, and for which he manifested intense anxiety; and it was, the settlement of the boundary dispute in a way honorable to the United States government, and satisfactory to the people of the States concerned.

Question by Mr. Brinkerhoff. I understand, from what you have said above, that the sum of $2,500 is the whole amount that ever came to your hands from Mr. Webster, or from the Department of State while he was at its head; do you intend to be so understood?

Answer. I do so intend to be understood.

Question by the same. Did you retain the whole of that sum for your own personal services and expenses; or was some part of it paid by you for the services of assistants?

Answer. I made no disbursements except for my travelling expenses and like incidental expenses, as I had never been informed of the fact that my account had been settled in full by the payments made, nor that any appropriation of those payments for other than my own services was in the contemplation of the Secretary. In other words, I had not been informed that my application for recompense to others had [not] been decisively acted upon by Mr. Webster, in the account I had furnished as before stated.

Question by same. I understand you, then, as saying that no part of this sum of $2,500 was ever paid to either of the three individuals alluded to in your letter to Mr. Webster, of the 12th of August, 1842?

Answer. It was not, for the reasons already stated.

Question by same. What were the particular "services" of those individuals?

Answer. Their services consisted in obtaining interviews with leading and influential men of their party, to induce favorable action on the subject of a compromise of the boundary on the part of the legislature, and procuring a favorable expression thereto on the part of the press, by republishing the articles first published in the Christian Mirror, as stated above, or otherwise. It would be impossible for me to say how much time was spent, or how much expense might be incurred in this way; but, either through the influences thus exerted, or without it, public attention was aroused on the subject; the party presses of Maine were brought to favor a compromise; and I should have felt like compensating several persons for the aid I supposed to have been rendered to my undertaking in the matter, had I been furnished with means and been authorized so to have done.

Question by same. Were either of these persons, and, if so, how many of them, in any way connected with the public press?

Answer. Neither of them. I have, in the body of my deposition, stated that to that class of persons I never promised, directly nor indirectly, the slightest recompense; nor were any such ever approached by me, nor by any one under me, for aid or influence, except from considerations of public duty, and the reasonableness of this proposition sought to be attained.

Question by Mr. King. Have you any knowledge of Mr. Webster employing unfit persons as agents in this business, or of his "bestowing large sums of public money," as charged by Mr. Ingersoll?

Answer. I had no knowledge of any of Mr. Webster's disbursements in respect to the boundary, beyond the statements I have already made, neither large nor small, and have not to this day.

Question by Mr. Vinton. Did Mr. Webster ever, either directly or indirectly, instruct, or express, or hint to you that he wished you to bribe or use any improper influence with the party presses or any of them?

Answer. He never did at any time, and in no mode of expression whatever.

Question by Mr. Vinton. Please look at the bill and receipt therefor, which are appended to the deposition of Edward Stubbs, and is part of paper marked A No. 6, purporting to have been presented by you to Mr. Webster, and receipted for by you, and state if it is a true copy of your bill and receipt; and, if any part of it was in blank when forwarded to Mr. Webster, how and by what authority the blanks were filled.

Answer. I have no doubt the paper inquired of is a true copy of the bill I forwarded to Mr. Webster in my letter of August 12, 1842, annexed to my deposition here, marked H, except that the sums of $2,000 and $500, first contained in that paper, were not filled up by me. In that letter of August 12, 1842, I expressly say to Mr. Webster—"I send herewith a bill, with entire consent for you to fill the blanks as you may deem proper." It was by such authority that the blanks were filled, but I never received any particular information how they

State Department of the United States —

1842
August —

To Francis O. J. Smith. Dr.

To services as special agent upon
the N. E. Boundary: from May
1841 — $2000

To services of assistants and their
incidental expenses ———— 500

$2500

[supra] be

By cash paid me, as he may
[receipt] to Hon. D. Webster, of May 1841 $500. —

Bal. Paid of D. Webster $
Secy of State.
Francis O. J. Smith.

F. O. J. Smith's bill for services in Maine. This is the original bill sent in
August 1842, with spaces later filled in by Webster. In "Letters to Presidents
Requesting Authorization of Disbursements," Bureau of Accounts, Records of
the State Department, Record Group 59, National Archives. A copy of this
was submitted to the House committee that investigated Webster in 1846.

were filled, or that the $2,000 additional was considered any thing more than a general payment on my account.[51]

Question by Mr. Brinkerhoff. Was or was not Mr. Webster acquainted with the names of the three individuals mentioned by you in your letter to him of the 12th of August, 1842?

Answer. He was not, nor with any name of any person with whom I corresponded on the subject, so far as I now recollect.

Question by Mr. Jones. As you appropriated the $2,500 paid you by Mr. Webster to your own use, under the belief expressed that it was for you, how have you been able to satisfy the three individuals referred to in your letter of the 12th of August, 1842, to whom you "gave an assurance that, in the event of a settlement of the boundary under Mr. Webster's negotiation, they should be allowed a *reasonable* remuneration for their time and incidental expenses," when you have never paid them any thing, and have never, since August, 1842, made any application for money to pay them the sums of $100 or $125 each, which you expressed a desire to pay them, as proper and reasonable for their services in bringing about the desirable result; and what have you informed them has prevented you from complying with their reasonable expectations?

Answer. I have never made any satisfaction to the persons spoken of as contemplated for them, and for the reasons heretofore stated in answer 2, as elsewhere in the body of my deposition. I supposed my account would have been settled upon the basis of my original stipulation of $3,500 per annum, and that fifteen months compensation was due; and that an allowance of the kind asked would have been made for the other persons. Having received but $2,500 in all, and knowing no reason for supposing the remainder would not be allowed, the whole matter has so remained unsettled to the present day; perhaps through my own, rather than any other person's neglect. I cannot recollect that I have either been asked by or have given any explanation to the persons in question, of the condition of my account with the government on the subject, or why allowance had not been obtained for them. I have seldom seen either, in person, since the treaty was consummated, and presume they have taken it for granted, as the

51. The bill, with figures supplied by Webster, showing that Smith received $2,000 in addition to the $500 advance of May 1841 is among the manuscripts at the National Archives as illustrated here.

fact has been, that had I received any knowledge of an allowance for them, they would have received it.

As the committee and the government now have all the facts before them, and are enjoying the benefits of a treaty that silenced disputes that had caused, and were still causing, the expenditure of hundreds of thousands of dollars, the propriety of fulfilling the stipulations of my agency in bringing it about will hardly admit of denial.

Further deponent saith not.

Francis O. J. Smith.

I certify that Francis O. J. Smith, esq., was sworn by me before the committee, as in the caption thereof is stated.

Saml. F. Vinton, *Chairman.*

May 25, 1846.

Report of the Minority [Jacob Brinkerhoff].

The undersigned, one of the members of the select committee of the House of Representatives, appointed to investigate the truth of the charges against Daniel Webster, late Secretary of State, made by Charles J. Ingersoll, a member of this House, finding himself unable to concur in all respects in the report of the majority of the committee, and believing that truth and justice require that some of the facts made to appear in the course of the investigation should be stated more fully than has been done in the report of the majority, begs leave briefly to present his views in the way of a minority report.

While it is true, as stated in the majority report, that it would appear from the testimony of ex-President Tyler that it was on his own suggestion that the moneys belonging to the secret service fund were placed in the hands of Mr. Webster, yet, from the testimony of Mr. Stubbs, the disbursing agent of that fund, and by the correspondence on the subject, copies of which were obtained by the committee, it is evident that the *modus operandi* was this: Mr. Webster verbally suggested to Mr. Stubbs that he should write a note to the President, suggesting the propriety and convenience of placing a part of this fund at the disposal of the Secretary of State. This Mr. Stubbs did; and Mr. Webster transmitted the note of Mr. Stubbs to the President, accompanied with one from himself approving the suggestion, and mentioning the amount which he supposed would be necessary for the then present purposes of the department.

At the conclusion of that part of the report of the majority of this committee which relates to the first charge of Mr. Ingersoll, it is said: "A balance not needed for the purposes contemplated was afterwards returned by Mr. Webster to Mr. Stubbs, the disbursing agent." In reference to this part of the subject it is but proper to say, that the whole amount of the secret service fund which came into the hands of Mr. Webster was seventeen thousand dollars. Five thousand dollars of this sum was received by him in November and December, 1841, and remained in his hands until the 23d day of June, 1842, when it was returned to the disbursing agent of the department. Whether, during the time which intervened, Mr. Webster made use of the whole or any part of this sum, or whether it lay untouched by him in the hands of his banker or elsewhere, there is, to the knowledge of the undersigned, no evidence whatsoever.

Proceeding to notice the second charge, the majority, in their report, say: "There is in the Department of State, among the papers relating to the secret service fund, a letter from that gentleman, (F. O. J. Smith, esq.,) which contains an expression that, unexplained, might justly lead to the inference that he (Mr. Smith) had used the money of the government in that way." The undersigned deems it but right that this letter should be given at large.[52]

It is hardly possible that any one reading this letter should come to any other conclusion than that arrived at by Mr. Ingersoll, and embraced in his second charge. Mr. Smith, however, in his examination before the committee, positively denies that any part of the sum of two thousand five hundred dollars, received by him out of the secret service fund, was ever paid or promised to any person in any way connected with the public press; and, from his testimony, it would appear that the object of his agency in Maine was to institute and prosecute a course of sysematic electioneering; and, by correspondence and confidential communication with the leading and influential political characters of both political parties, so to influence the public mind, and "adjust the tone and direction of the party presses," as to secure a majority in the legislature of that State favorable to the appointment

52. The letter of August 12, 1842, offered here by Brinkerhoff, is omitted, since it already appears in Documents, under date of Aug. 12, 1842.

of commissioners with full powers to bind the State in the anticipated negotiations. In this object it has been seen the agent claims to have been successful, and asks "$100 or $125 each" for his assistants. Accordingly, five hundred dollars were remitted to him; and, in the accounts relating to the secret service fund, Mr. Webster is credited with $500 paid to Mr. Smith for his "assistants." It is due to them, however, whoever they may be, to add, that Mr. Smith, at the time he received this remittance of $500, was not informed that it was specially intended for the payment of the "assistants," and having, as he thought, received no more, in all, than he was justly entitled to for his own services, retained the money in his own hands, and they yet remain unpaid. Whether this direct effort of the general government, through the agency of one of its high functionaries and the employment of pecuniary means for the purpose of influencing the legislative action of a State government, constitutes an impeachable offence in that functionary, the undersigned will not assume to decide.

In regard to the third charge, viz: that when Mr. Webster left the office of Secretary of State he was a public defaulter, the undersigned concurs with the majority of the committee, that "from an examination of his accounts, it appears" that, at that time, "there was of the moneys that had been intrusted to him an apparent balance of $2,290 in his hands, as stated by Mr. Ingersoll. The expenditure of this sum remained to be accounted for by him." But the undersigned knows of no evidence which came before the committee in any form whatever, other than the declarations of Mr. Webster himself, going to show that there was any "difficulty in procuring vouchers from the secret agents, whom Mr. Webster had employed, for the moneys advanced by him to them;" nor does he know of any other evidence of the loss or mislaying of any voucher "for a payment of a thousand dollars," nor of any "efforts" by Mr. Webster to obtain such voucher; though it is very true that such voucher "has not yet been found or obtained." The simple truth on this branch of the inquiry, so far as the undersigned is capable of seeing it, is substantially this: Mr. Webster went out of the State Department an apparent defaulter to the amount of $2,290. Afterwards, by direction of the President, he was written to by the disbursing agent, Mr. Stubbs, and urged to a settlement. For different reasons, and on various pleas, the matter was delayed, from time to time, until Mr.

Tyler approached the termination of his presidential term; when Mr. Webster having, in this correspondence, been reminded of the necessity that would exist for the publication of the public accounts, and the exposure which would result from that publication, if the account remained unadjusted, having been thus hinted at, suggested, in the first place, that the President should take the ex-Secretary's word for the expenditure of one thousand dollars, and grant him a certificate covering that amount; but, the President declining to act upon this suggestion, Mr. Webster then proposed to pay up the apparent balance against him; which proposal was, of course, accepted and Mr. Webster paid it up accordingly. Subsequently, however, Mr. Webster produced vouchers to the amount of $1,250, and was repaid to that amount, leaving $1,040 as the *real* amount of his defalcation at the time of his retirement from office; and of the expenditure of which sum in the *public* service there is (beyond the mere word of Mr. Webster) no evidence whatsoever.

It is true, Mr. Webster at first claimed to have paid this sum to a Mr. Healy; but, the disbursing agent having shown that he had himself paid that sum, and that Mr. Webster had already been credited with the amount paid to Mr. Healy, he still claimed to have paid it to some person employed in the public service; but there is no evidence before the committee that, subsequent to this time, Mr. Webster ever pretended to state specifically to whom, when, where, or for what purpose, the whole, or any part of this sum, was ever paid by him.

Whether he could have expended this sum for public purposes, and for purposes so important and delicate as to require a draft on the secret service fund, without being able, within two years thereafter, to designate, even to the President, whose agent he was, any of these particulars connected with its expenditure, the undersigned will leave it to the House to determine.

Having thus supplied what he deemed defective or erroneous in the report of the majority, and believing that no injury can result to the public service from the publication proposed, the undersigned begs leave to offer the following resolution:

Resolved, That the testimony and exhibits taken before the select committee of this House, instituted to investigate the charges against Daniel Webster, late Secretary of State, together with the reports of the majority and minority of said committee, be laid upon the table and printed; and that said committee be discharged from the futher consideration of the subject.

JACOB BRINKERHOFF.

[House of Representatives. June 19, 1846.]

Motion of Mr. Brinkerhoff.

Resolved, That all the testimony accompanying the report of the select committee appointed to investigate the charges made by Charles J. Ingersoll against Daniel Webster be printed.[53]

"The Webster Investigation" [an editorial in the Portland *Eastern Argus* (tw), June 17, 1846].

The Investigating Committee have made a Report, exculpating Mr. Webster from the charge of misappropriating the secret service fund. This is no cause for regret in any quarter. It is always a satisfaction to see friends or foes relieved from imputations against [*sic*] charges affecting their character for integrity. In regard to corrupting the party press of Maine, nothing appears but what is disclosed by the subjoined letter of Mr. Smith. The reader will perceive that the paragraph in relation to adjusting the tone of the "party *wishes*," reads differently from that which Mr. Ingersoll gave as a quotation from Smith's letter. In the latter it reads "party *presses*," not "party *wishes*." The letter reads as follows.[54]

The Committee say they do not deem it necessary or expedient to go into the acts of this agent, who was employed in a secret service, or to enquire into the propriety of employing agents for secret service

---

53. This motion, reported in *Cong. Globe,* 29 Cong., 1 sess. (June 17, 1846), 999–1000, was defeated by a margin of 77–57. Its sting was that it would have exposed the full Tyler testimnoy and that of the disbursing agent.

54. The editor of the *Eastern Argus* here reproduces the Smith letter of August 12, 1842, but makes one significant alteration. For the term "party presses" he substitutes the milder term "party wishes." The substitution is in contradiction of the evidence. The words in Smith's 1842 letter are unmistakably "party presses." The exculpatory change may have been suggested by Smith himself who had helped to bring the editor, Eliphalet Case, into control of the paper. See correspondence beween the two men for the period from November 29 to December 25, 1841, in the Smith Papers, numbered 312, 325, 326, 327, 336.

within the confines of the United States, and paying them out of the contingent fund for foreign intercourse, but will content themselves with simply remarking that the testimony they have taken fully explains whatever is of obscure or doubtful meaning in this letter, removes every foundation for a belief, or even a suspicion, that the public money was used, or attempted to be used to corrupt the party presses . . . Who the three individuals were who received $100 to $125 each, does not appear. Neither does the Report show what services Mr. Smith rendered for which he received at least $2125.

F. O. J. Smith to George Ticknor Curtis.[55]

Williamsburgh, New York, March, 1869.

DEAR SIR, On my visit to Maine last week, I found my file of papers relating to the settlement of the Northeastern Boundary Line by Mr. Webster, while Secretary of State of the United States, and I send you the originals, as they will confirm beyond question the pure and patriotic motives of all concerned in it.

In my testimony before the Ingersoll Congressional Committee upon charges preferred against Mr. Webster, I alluded to my previous proposition of the same mode of settlement, and of bringing it about, to President Van Buren in 1837, as follows:

"In 1837, following up the suggestions and tendency of President Jackson's proceedings towards the adoption of a conventional boundary to end the dispute, I urged, in more detail even than in this letter (June 7, 1841) to Mr. Webster, upon Mr. Van Buren, the expediency

55. George Ticknor Curtis was the literary executor and biographer of Webster. His two-volume *Life of Daniel Webster* (New York, 1870) is still standard. He was a notable legal scholar and historian. In politics he was a Whig and, as such, served in the Massachusetts House from 1840 to 1843. While at work on the biography of Webster he had applied to Smith for information regarding the preliminaries to the Ashburton negotiation, and he made some use of Smith's detailed reply. He described at length the debate in Congress following the Ingersoll charges and summarized the printed report of the special committee investigating those charges, but made no reference to the manuscript record of the committee's investigation containing Tyler's full testimony and that of the disbursing clerk of the State Department. His interest lay in clearing Webster of the charges of irregular and personal use of government funds. Smith's letter was a tacit plea to be acknowledged by Curtis as a contributor to Webster's achievement in the boundary settlement but Curtis made no such acknowledgment. Vol. II, 278, 282–284.

and feasibility of settling it by a conventional line, by abandoning reliance upon the circuitous artifices of ministerial diplomacy, and instituting a system of direct consultations with, and appeals to, the judgments, and interests, and co-operating common sense of the people themselves of the two local governments that were alone immediately interested in the matter. By local governments I mean the government of Maine and that of the adjacent province.

"I do not find myself possessed of a copy of that letter to Mr. Van Buren, but I do not doubt that little pains will disclose the existence of it in the State Department at this date, if its exhibition be desirable. I had one or more private interviews with Mr. Forsyth, Mr. Van Buren's then Secretary of State, on the subject of that letter, *at his request.*"

I then exhibited to the [Ingersoll] Committee one of Mr. Forsyth's letters I had at hand, confirmatory of my statement.

Now in this file, I find the original draft of my letter to President Van Buren, and all its details, and the instructions proposed therein to be given to the proposed agency. I enclose it to you, with such evident marks of its authenticity upon its face, as will not leave any doubt in your mind, of its identity, if its counterpart has not been seen by you in the State Department at Washington. I mark it A.1. including my proposed letter of instructions to the Government agent who might be appointed.

One of Mr. Forsyth's letters alluded to I also enclose, marked A.2.[56]

In my before named testimony, I explain why *my project* for a settlemet of this protracted boundary question was not followed up under Mr. Van Buren's administration, thus:—

"The divergence which soon after took place between many of Mr. Van Buren's political friends, of whom I had been one, and himself, in respect to the sub-treasury and kindred matters, shut off inducements on both sides to pursue to a fair trial the proceedings I had suggested as *the proper and only ones that could ever prove successful in the matter,* and they fell to the ground." See Rept. Ho. Rep. No. 684, 29th Cong., 1st Sess., Ho. Rep.

Let me retrospect a little, the better to present to your understanding the chronology of this matter.

In the latter part of President Jackson's administration, he proposed

56. The Forsyth letter was not published with the committee report; nor was a copy found in the Smith Papers.

to the British Government the constitution of a joint commission to settle the boundary line.

In the first message of President Van Buren in 1836–37, he states that this offer had been made, but not responded to.[57] During the subsequent years of his administration, negotiation between the two governments had so far progressed as to have arranged for a joint commission, and an ultimate reference to arbitrators, if needful.

In the meantime, however, constant excitement in Maine and the adjacent Provinces was kept up on the subject; and in the winter of 1838–39 it culminated in the assemblage of hostile troops by them upon the disputed border. By the dexterous interference of the Federal administration, through General Scott, actual collision was avoided, and the people of Maine, though acquiescing in the earnest desires of the Federal administration to preserve peace between the two countries, were restless and threatening, even towards Mr. Van Buren's administration under the goadings of the opposing party. It was at this crisis, that Hon. Albert Smith (now deceased) then a prominent democratic politician, received from Mr. Woodbury (also now deceased) of Mr. Van Buren's Cabinet, the despondent letter which, being the original, I enclose herewith, marked A.3, as an exponent of the embarrassing nature of the Boundary dispute at that time. I have forgotten under what circumstances this letter came into my possession.

When the new administration of President Harrison succeeded to the Government, with Mr. Webster as Secretary of State, this question of boundary had lost none of its perplexing characteristics, although a new party had come into charge of it.

Being, however, myself no less desirous than under Mr. Van Buren's administration to see it settled, and removed from the arena of party politics—being no less convinced than in 1837, that the true and only effective way of doing this had not yet been essayed, the subject was revived at my first personal interview with Mr. Webster after his succession to the chair of Mr. Harrison's premier, and as detailed in my before named testimony. And it was out of this interview that came my letter to him of June 7, 1841, marked A in the Congressional Committee's Report.[58]

57. James D. Richardson (comp.), *Messages and Papers of the Presidents* (10 vols., Washington, G.P.O., 1896–1898), III, 373.
58. For this letter, see Documents, under date given.

Having several conversations with Mr. Webster on this subject immediately after the writing of the programme of proceeding contained in the last named letter, and receiving not only his earnest approval of my views, but a no less earnest request that I would at once enter upon their execution according to my best judgment, I wrote from Washington several letters to leading politicians in Maine of each party, as stated in my before named testimony. I declined to furnish the Congressional Committee with the names of my correspondents, although I furnished the Committee with a copy of *one* such of my letters, (marked D in the Committee's Report) "to illustrate yet further the spirit in which I pursued my efforts in the matter," suppressing the name of the Senator to whom it was addressed. There is no longer occasion to suppress his name. It was to Hon. Jonathan Smith, then a democratic Senator in the State Legislature of Maine from Cumberland County, previously represented by myself in Congress. He is still living and will authenticate the letter, if desired.[59] It was not one of the original series written in 1841, while I was in Washington, but in the winter of 1842, while there to consult Mr. Webster, as to the mode of taking advantage of the progress which had been made during the preceding year, in reconciling the popular mind in Maine, and in the British Provinces, to a conventional settlement of the dispute and by a conventional line.

But to verify still further the perfect exemption from anything like recourse to any improper, or unpatriotic influences in this novel mode of *negotiating* an important National Treaty, on the part of either Mr. Webster, or myself, I will now send you herewith marked A 4, the original, by way of sample, of one other of my letters written at the very opening of the campaign for which I had obtained the sanction of Mr. Webster.

This was written, it will be observed, on the 12th of June, 1841, following my programme letter to Mr. Webster of the 7th of that month. It was addressed to Hon. John Hodgdon, of Bangor, who had been long an eminently influential politician in the State, State Land Agent, Senator, etc.[60] I know he can no longer have objections to my disclosing this correspondence, if at all essential to illustrate the history of the Northeastern Boundary Settlement, and in it the purity and patri-

59. For this letter, see Documents, under date Feb. 14, 1842.
60. For this letter, see Documents, under date June 12, 1841.

otism of Mr. Webster's motives in it. Mr. Hodgdon is no longer a resident of Maine, but of ——— in the State of ———. I also communicate his prompt answer, the original thereto, marked A 5.[61] Also my next letter to him, marked A 6. Also a copy, marked A 7, of the printed petition alluded to in my last named letter, for circulation among the people.[62]

I think I may assume without vanity that the correspondence thus conducted between myself and others who had the lead of the popular mind in their respective parties, and which this correspondence excited between still other parties throughout the State, and the timely articles published in the Christian Mirror of Nov. 18, 1841, Dec. 2, 1841, and Feb. 3, 1842, written by me over the signature of Agricola, with the strong endorsement, which I secured, of the universally respected in the State and adjacent Provinces, editor of that paper—"Father Cummings"—, and the extensively copied and approved circulation in all the political papers of the State of both parties—had fully prepared the people of the State for the next step, which I recommended to be taken in my letter to Mr. Webster of Feb. 14, 1842, marked E in the Congressional Committee's report.[63]

The resolutions of Maryland, referred to in my letter of June 12, 1841, to Mr. Hodgdon, were accompanied by an able report, drawn by Hon. B. C. Howard, a distinguished democrat formerly in Congress, and subsequently the well known Reporter of the Decisions of the Supreme Court of the United States. In that report, after ably and elaborately vindicating the title of Maine to the disputed territory, and pledging Maryland to stand by the United States and by Maine if need be in its defense, adds:

"*Resolved,* that if the British Government would acknowledge the title of the State of Maine to the territory in dispute, and offer a fair equivalent for the passage through it of a Military Road, it would be a reasonable mode of adjusting the dispute, and *ought to be satisfactory to the State of Maine.*" Session of 1841.[64]

61. For this letter, see Documents, under date June 17, 1841.
62. For the petition, see enclosure in Documents, under date July 2, 1841.
63. The letter is incorrectly dated by Smith. It appears under correct date (April 13, 1842) in the Documents. The letter was written subsequently to Webster's of April 10, 1842.
64. The full set of these resolutions is reproduced above, p. 140. For their source, see fn. 3.

The letter of Mr. Webster to the Governor of Maine of April, 1842,[65] urging an extra session of the State Legislature, for the appointment of Commissioners to agree upon a conventional boundary, and upon the terms of such agreement—urging, too, the unavoidable delays which must otherwise attend the negotiations for settlement—the consequent special session, held in May following, and the appointment of Commissioners, and the consequent conventional line agreed on, and the consequent early settlement of the dispute, by the Webster-Ashburton Treaty, all brought about exactly in the manner, and by the agencies, and within the short time, which, in my letter to Mr. Van Buren in 1837, again revived by Mr. Webster in 1841, were suggested and predicted, and at a trifling expenditure only, are all well known facts to you, and to the nation. The completeness with which the additional light and confirmations, which the documents now submitted to you, and never yet published, furnish of the patriotism, integrity, and purity of Mr. Webster's proceedings in the whole matter, must set history *permanently* right on the subject, never to be again disturbed by either malice, envy, or partisan prejudice. That so far as compensation was either sought or had by me, I was but poorly paid, much less corruptly paid, and for a service that did both state and nation great good, all who shall read the true history of the transaction cannot but fully admit.

You are at liberty to make such use of these documents, or this letter, as you may desire, only I wish, when no longer needed by you, the original papers I send herewith may be returned to me.

With great respect, I remain,
Your obedient servant

65. For this letter, see, *Works of Daniel Webster*, VI, 272–275.

LETTER

OF

MR. WALKER, OF MISSISSIPPI,

RELATIVE TO THE

ANNEXATION OF TEXAS:

IN REPLY TO

THE CALL OF THE PEOPLE OF CARROLL COUNTY, KENTUCKY, TO
COMMUNICATE HIS VIEWS ON THAT SUBJECT.

———————

WASHINGTON:

PRINTED AT THE GLOBE OFFICE.

1844.

LETTER.

WASHINGTON CITY, Jan. 8, 1844.

GENTLEMEN: Your letter, dated Ghent, Carrol county, Kentucky, November 25th, 1843, has been received. It contains the resolutions of a meeting of the people of that county, in favor of the annexation of Texas, and requesting the candidates for the presidency and vice presidency of the Union to make "known to (you) or to the public" their views on this subject. As a committee, you have transmitted me these proceedings, together with a special letter, addressed to me as a candidate for the "vice presidency," requesting my opinions on this question. I am not a candidate for the vice presidency. The only State in which my name has been designated, to any considerable extent, for this station, was my own; and knowing how many, with much older and better claims than mine, were named for this office, for this and other reasons, by letter dated November 20, 1843, addressed by me to the democratic convention which assembles this day in Mississippi, my name is withdrawn unconditionally.

The treaty by which Texas was surrendered to Spain, was always opposed by me; and in 1826, 1834, and 1835, various addresses were made by me, and then published, in favor of the reannexation of Texas; and the same opinions have been often expressed by me since my election, in 1836, to the Senate of the Union.

It was a revolution in Mexico that produced the conflict for independence in Texas. The citizens of Texas had been invited there by Mexico, under the solemn guaranty of the federal constitution of 1824. This constitution, to which Texas so long and faithfully adhered, was prostrated by the usurper Santa Anna. After a severe struggle, the people of Mexico were subdued by a mercenary army; the States were annihilated, and a military dictator was placed at the head of a central despotism. In the capital of Mexico, and of the state of Coahuila and Texas, the civil authorities were suppressed by the bayonet; the disarming of every citizen was decreed, and the soldiery of the usurper proceeded to enforce this edict. The people of Texas resolved to resist, and perish upon the field of battle, rather than submit to the despotic sway of a treacherous and sanguinary military dictator. Short was the conflict, and glorious the issue. The American race was successful; the armies of the tyrant were overthrown and dispersed, and the dictator himself was captured. He was released by Texas, and restored to his country, having first acknowledged, by a solemn treaty, the independence of Texas. After the fall of Santa Anna, and the total rout and dispersion of the Mexican army, and when a resubjugation had become hopeless, I introduced into the Senate the resolution acknowledging the independence of Texas. It was adopted in March, 1837, and the name of Texas inscribed on the roll of independent nations. Subsequently, France, England, and Holland, have recognised her independence; and Texas now has all the rights of sovereignty over her territory and people, as full and perfect as any other nation of the world. It was to Spain, and not to Mexico, that we transferred Texas by treaty; and it was by a revolution in Mexico, and the recognition of her independence, not by Spain, but by this republic and other nations, that Mexico acquired any title to Texas. It was by a successful revolution, and the expulsion of Spanish power, that Mexico, unrecognised by Spain, acquired all her right to this territory; and it is by a similar successful revolution that Texas has obtained the same territory. These principles have been recognised for many years by Mexico, and by this republic; and it is absurd in Mexico now to attempt to recall her unequivocal assent to these doctrines, and ask to be permitted to change the well-settled law of nations, and oppose the reannexation of Texas. It is an admitted principle of the law of nations, that every sovereignty may cede the whole or any part of their territory, unless restrained by some constitutional interdict; and which, if it exist, may be removed by the same sovereign power which imposed the limitation. There is, however, no such limitation in the constitution of Texas, which is a single central government, with the same authority to make the cession, as appertained to France or Spain, in the transfer of Louisiana or Florida. Nor does it change the question of power, that these were distant colonies; for the sovereignty extends alike over every portion of the nation: and this principle was fully recognised, when Mr. Adams, as President, and Mr. Clay, as Secretary of State, in 1825 and 1827, by instructions to our minister at Mexico; and General Jackson, as President, and Mr. Van Buren as Secretary of State, by subsequent similar instructions in 1829, endeavored to procure from Mexico the cession of Texas, then a contiguous and integral portion of the Mexican confederacy. And if a nation may cede a portion of her territory, being completely sovereign over the whole, she may certainly cede the whole; and, in any event this would be a question, not of our right to receive, but of the authority of the ceding nation to make the transfer, or simply an inquiry, whether we obtained a good or a bad title. In this case, the title would be unquestionable; for Texas being independent in fact, and so recognised by ourselves, and the great powers of Europe, as completely sovereign throughout her territory, Mexico could make no just objection to the transfer.

In 1836, this question, together with that of ratifying their constitution, was submitted by the constituted authorities to the people of Texas, who, with unparalleled unanimity, (there being but ninety-three dissenting votes,) decided in favor of reannexation.

Texas, then, has already assented to the reannexation, not merely by the act of all her authorities, but of her people, and made it a part and parcel of the organization of the government itself; and he who, with the knowledge of these facts, would now deny the power of Texas to assent to the reannexation, must reject and discard the great fundamental principle of popular sovereignty. Surely, then, no one will contend that monarchies may transfer, and we receive, their colonies and subjects, without and against their consent; but that the entire people of a single republic, in whom resides the only rightful sovereignty, cannot cede, nor we receive, their own territory, and that monarchs have more power than the people, and are more truly sovereign. Texas, then, having the undoubted right to transfer the whole, or any part of the territory, there can be no difference, as a *question of constitutional power,* between our right to receive a part or the whole of the territory.

The reannexation, then, can be accomplished by any one of three modes. 1st, by treaty; 2d, by an act of Congress, without a treaty; and 3d, by the authority reserved to each State, to extend their boundaries, and annex additional territory with the sanction of Congress.

1st. By treaty.—This right was established in the cession of Louisiana and Florida, and cannot now be questioned, without menacing the organization of the government and integrity of the Union; for, by virtue of this power, three States and several Territories now compose a part of the republic. In 1842, we acquired territory by treaty, and attached it to the States of New York and Vermont. There was there no disputed boundary, for the call was for a certain parallel of latitude—a mere question of measurement—which, when made, placed this territory within the undoubted limits of Canada; in consequence of which, we had abandoned the fortress erecting at Rouse's Point, and the ground it occupied, (which was a part of this territory,) which we acquired by the treaty of 1842. The question of the power of annexation by treaty is settled, and incorporated into the very existence of the government and of the Union.

2d. The object may be accomplished by act of Congress, without a treaty.—The language of the constitution is: "New States may be admitted by the Congress into this Union; but no new State shall be formed or erected within the jurisdiction of any other State; nor any State be formed by the junction of two or more States, or parts of States, without the consent of the legislatures of the States concerned, as well as of the Congress." The grant is unlimited, except that the boundary of an existing State cannot be disturbed by Congress without the assent of the State legislatures. "New States may be admitted by the *Congress* into this Union." This is the broad language of the constitution; and, to confine it to territory then acquired, is to interpolate most important words into that instrument. Nor could it have been the intention of the framers of the constitution to prevent the acquisition of new territory. Louisiana was not then a part of the Union, but it was a most important part of the valley of the Mississippi, containing New Orleans, and the whole of the western, and the most essential part of the eastern portion of that territory, with both banks of its great river for many hundred miles above its mouth, and the only outlet of the products of the mighty valley starting at the Youghiogany in Maryland, and the Alleghany in New York, uniting at Pittsburg, where they form the Ohio, to the outlet of all into the Gulf. If we look at the condition of many of the States when the constitution was framed, we will find it could never have been adopted had it forbidden the acquisition of the only outlet of all the products of the West. The waters of western Maryland, and of western New York, commingle with those of the Ohio and Mississippi. There stood Pittsburg at the head of the Ohio; and one-third of Pennsylvania is intersected by streams which water a part of the great valley. Virginia then included Kentucky; three-fourths of her territory was within the great valley, and the Ohio and Mississippi itself were its boundary for more than a thousand miles. North Carolina then included Tennessee, and was bounded for hundreds of miles by the river Mississippi; and Georgia then embraced Alabama and Mississippi, and was not only bounded for several hundred miles by the great river, but advanced to within a few miles of the city of New Orleans. Is it possible that all these States, in forming the constitution, could have intended to prohibit forever the acquisition of the mouth of the Mississippi, then in the hands of a hostile and despotic foreign power? The constitution contains no such suicidal provision; and all the historical facts, both before and after its adoption, are against any such anti-American restriction. As to a treaty, it is only necessary as indicating the assent of the ceding nation; and if that has been given already, as in the case of Texas, without a treaty, our acceptance may be made by Congress. Suppose the constitution of Texas forbid the cession, except by Congress: when their Congress passed the assenting law, could not we accept, by act of Congress? Or suppose Texas, or any other contiguous territory, was vacant and unclaimed by any power: could we not annex it by act of Congress? One of the grounds assumed in Congress, and by our government, in defence of our title to Oregon, is its alleged discovery and occupancy by us, (long before the treaty with France,) being one of the acknowledged modes by which nations acquire territory; but if we can only acquire territory by treaty, then this ground, upon which we claim title to Oregon, must be abandoned. It would be strange, indeed, if the treaty-making power (which, under our constitution, is purely an executive power) could annex territory, and yet that the Executive, and both Houses of Congress combined, could not. Then, if France or Spain had forever refused to cede to us Louisiana or New Orleans, could we never—no, not even by conquest in war—have occupied and annexed them by act of Congress? Congress, then, having the undoubted power to annex territory, and admit new States, and Texas having assented in advance, may be either admitted at once, as a Territory, or a State, or States, or Congress may provide for the prospective admission of one or more States from Texas, as has often heretofore been done as to other new States, the whole question of annexation not being one whether *this government* has the power, but only how it must be exercised; and whether only by one of the branches of this government, or by all combined. And if the power vested in Congress by the constitution to admit new States, does not of itself embrace territory then constituting a part of the Union, as well as all future acquisitions, there is no power to admit new States, except out of territory which was a part of the Union when the constitution was formed; but as this interpretation cannot prevail without expelling three States from the Union, and forbidding the admission of Iowa, it must be conceded that this power of *Congress* to admit new States does extend to future acquisitions. This being the case, what can be more clear than that Congress may admit a State or States out of Texas, if her assent is given, as we perceive it has been, in a form as obligatory as a treaty? In truth, the power to annex territory by treaty does not so much exist as a mere implication from the treaty-making power, as from the grant to Congress to admit new States out of any territory whatever, although not then a part of the Union; and the right to annex by treaty results mainly as a means of obtaining, when necessary, the assent of another government, especially when that assent can be obtained in no other manner.

Something like this was done by the annexation, by Congress, of the Florida parishes to the State of Louisiana. They had been claimed, and remained for many years after the cession of Louisiana, in the exclusive occupancy of Spain, when the American settlers revolted, assembled their convention, declared their independence, and, by a successful revolution, wrested this territory from the dominion of Spain, and Congress recognised the acts, and assumed and paid the debts of the insurgent convention; and the legislature of Louisiana, after the adoption of her constitution, and admission into the Union, without this territory, subsequently, by mere legislative enactment, with the consent of Congress, annexed it to the State of Louisiana.

3d. The annexation may be accomplished by one of the States of the Union, with the sanction of Congress.—That each of the States possessed the power to extend her boundaries before the adoption of the constitution, will not be denied; and that the power still exists, is certain, unless it is abandoned by the State in forming the government of the Union. Now, there is no such abandonment, unless it is found in the following clause of the constitution: "No State shall, without the consent of Congress, enter into any agreement or compact with another State, or with a foreign power." Each State, then, may, with the consent of Congress, "enter into any agreement or compact with another State, or with a *foreign power*." Texas, if not ours, is a foreign power; and if she, by law, assents to the reannexation, in whole or in part, to Louisiana, or to Arkansas, and those States, by law, agree to the annexation, it is "an agreement or compact" between a foreign power and a State of the Union, and is clearly lawful, with "the consent of Congress." It would not be a treaty, which is the exercise of an executive power, but a compact by law, and precisely similar to the numerous compacts, so called, by which, by acts of Congress and of a State legislature, so many agreements, especially with the new States, have been made by mere legislative enactments. Nor need the assent of Congress be given in advance; it was not so given on the admission of Tennessee, Arkansas, and Michigan; but if given subsequently, it would ratify the previous extension of their boundaries by Louisiana or Arkansas. There are, then, these three modes, by any one of which Texas may be reannexed to the American Union. 1st. By treaty; 2d. By act of Congress, without a treaty; and, 3d. By the act of a State, with the sanction of Congress. But, if it be otherwise, and the constitution only applies to territories then attached to the Union, and delegates no power for the acquisition of any other territory, nor prohibits the exercise of the pre-existing power of each State to extend her boundaries, then there would remain in each State the reserved right of extension, beyond the control of Congress. I have not asserted the existence of such a right in a State; but, if the clauses quoted do not confer the authority on Congress, and the reannexation is refused on that ground, then the annexing power, as a right to enlarge their boundaries, would result to any one of the States, and, with the consent of Texas, could be exercised. Perceiving, then, what power results to the States, from the denial of the power of annexation by Congress, let us agitate no such question in advance of a denial of its own authority by Congress, but discuss the question on its merits alone.

Is it expedient to reannex Texas to the American Union? This is the greatest question, since the adoption of the constitution, ever presented for the decision of the American people. Texas was once our own; and, although surrendered by treaty to Spain, the surrender was long resisted by the American government, and was conceded to be a great sacrifice. This being the case, is it not clear that, when the territory, which we have most reluctantly surrendered, can be reacquired, that object should be accomplished? Under such circumstances, to refuse the reannexation is to deny the wisdom of the original purchase, and to reflect upon the judgment of those who maintained, even at the period of surrender, that it was a great sacrifice of national interests.

Texas, as Mr. Jefferson declared, was as clearly embraced in the purchase by us of Louisiana as New Orleans itself; and that it was a part of that region, is demonstrated by the discovery, by the great Lasalle, of the source and mouth of the Mississippi, and his occupancy for France west of the Colorado. Our right to Texas, as a part of Louisiana, was asserted and demonstrated by Presidents Jefferson, Madison, Monroe, and John Quincy Adams. No one of our Presidents has ever doubted our title; and Mr. Clay has ever maintained it as clear and unquestionable. Louisiana was acquired by a treaty with France, in 1803, by Mr. Jefferson; and in the letter of Mr. Madison, the Secretary of State, dated March 31, 1804, he says, expresing his own views and those of Mr. Jefferson, that Louisiana "extended westwardly to the Rio Bravo, otherwise called Rio del Norte. *Orders* were accordingly obtained from the *Spanish* authorities for the delivery of *all* the posts on the west side of the Mississippi." And in his letter of the 31st January, 1804, Mr. Madison declares that Mr. Laussat, the French commissioner who *delivered the possession of Louisiana to us*, announced the "Del Norte as its true boundary." Here, then, in the delivery of the possession of Louisiana by Spain to France, and France to us, Texas is included. In the letter of Mr. Madison of the 8th July, 1804, he declares the opposition of Mr Jefferson to the "*relinquishment* of *any* territory whatever eastward of the Rio Bravo." In the letter of James Monroe of the 8th November, 1803, he incloses documents which he says "prove *incontestably*" that the boundary of Louisiana is "the Rio Bravo to the west;" and Mr. Pinckney unites with him in a similar declaration. In a subsequent letter—not to a foreign government, but to Mr. Madison—of the 20th April, 1805, they assert our title as unquestionable. In Mr. Monroe's letters, as Secretary of State, dated January 19, 1816, and June 10, 1816, he says none could question "our title to Texas;" and he expresses his concurrence in opinion with Jefferson and Madison, "that our title to the Del Norte was as clear as to the island of New Orleans." In his letter, as Secretary of State, to Don Onis, of the 12th March, 1818, John Quincy Adams says: "The claim of France always did extend westward to the Rio Bravo;" "she *always* claimed the territory which you call Texas as being within the limits, and forming a part, of Louisiana." After demonstrating our title to Texas in this letter, Mr. Adams says: "Well might Messrs. Pinckney and Monroe write to M. Cevallos, in 1805, that the claim of the United States to the boundary of the Rio Bravo was as clear as their right to the island of New Orleans." Again, in his letter of the 31st October,

1818, Mr. Adams says our title to Texas is "established beyond the power of further controversy."

Here, then, by the discovery and occupation of Texas, as a part of Louisiana, by Lasalle, for France, in 1685; by the delivery of possession to us, in 1803, by Spain and France; by the action of our government, from the date of the treaty of acquisition to the date of the treaty of surrender, (avowedly so on its face;) by the opinion of all our Presidents and ministers connected in any way with the acquisition, our title to Texas was undoubted. It was surrendered to Spain by the treaty of 1819; but Mr. Clay maintained, in his speech of the 3d April, 1820, that territory *could not be alienated* merely by a treaty; and consequently that, notwithstanding the treaty, Texas was *still our own.* In the cession of a portion of Maine, it was asserted, in legislative resolutions, by Massachusetts and Maine, and conceded by this government, that no portion of Maine could be ceded by treaty without the consent of Maine. Did Texas assent to this treaty, or can we cede part of a territory, but not of a State? These are grave questions; they raise the point whether Texas is not now a part of our territory, and whether her people may not now rightfully claim the protection of our government and laws. Recollect this was not a question of settlement, under the powers of this government, of a disputed boundary. The treaty declares, as respects Texas, that we "*cede to his Catholic majesty.*" Commenting on this in his speech before referred to, Mr. Clay says it was not a question of the power in case of dispute "of fixing a boundary previously existing." "It was, on the contrary, the case of an avowed cession of territory from the United States to Spain." Although, then, the government may be competent to fix a disputed boundary, by ascertaining as near as practicable where it is; although, also, a State, with the consent of this government, as in the case of Maine, may cede a portion of her territory,—yet it by no means follows that this government, by treaty, could cede a Territory of the Union. Could we by treaty cede Florida to Spain, especially without consulting the people of Florida? and, if not, the treaty by which Texas was surrendered was, as Mr. Clay contended, *inoperative.*

By the treaty of 1803, by which, we have seen, Texas was acquired by us from France, we pledged our faith to France, and to the *people of Texas,* never to surrender that territory. The 3d article of that treaty declares: "the inhabitants of the ceded territory *shall be* incorporated in the *Union of the United States,* and admitted as soon as possible, according to the principles of the federal constitution, to the enjoyment of all the rights, advantages, and immunities of *citizens of the United States; and* in the *mean time* they shall be protected in the free enjoyment of their liberty, property, and the religion which they profess." Such was our pledge to France and to the *people of Texas,* by the treaty of purchase; and if our subsequent treaty of cession to Spain was not unconstitutional and invalid, it was a gross infraction of a previous treaty, and of one of the fundamental conditions under which Texas was acquired.

Here, then, are many grave questions of constitutional power. Could the solemn guaranty to France, and to the people of Texas, be rescinded by a treaty with Spain? Can this government, by its own mere power, surrender any portion of its territory? Can it cut off a territory without the consent of its people, and surrender them and the territory to a foreign power? Can it expatriate and expel from the Union its own citizens, who occupy that territory, and change an American citizen into a citizen of Spain or Mexico? These are momentous questions, which it is not necessary now to determine, and in regard to which I advance at this time no opinion. Certain, however, it is, that, with the consent of the people of Texas, Congress can carry out the solemn pledges of the treaty of 1803, and admit one or more States from Texas into the Union.

The question as to Texas is, in any aspect, a question of the re-establishment of our ancient boundaries, and the repossession of a territory most reluctantly surrendered. The surrender of territory, even if constitutional, is almost universally inexpedient and unwise, and, in any event, when circumstances may seem to demand such a surrender, the territory thus abandoned should always be reacquired whenever it may be done with justice and propriety. Independent of these views, we have the recorded opinion of John Quincy Adams as President, and Henry Clay as Secretary of State, and also of Gen. Andrew Jackson as President, and Martin Van Buren as Secretary of State, that Texas ought to be reannexed to the Union. On the 26th of March, 1825, Mr. Clay, in conformity with his own views, and the *express directions of Mr. Adams* as President, directed a letter to Mr. Poinsett, our Minister at Mexico, instructing him to endeavor to procure from Mexico a transfer to us of Texas to the Del Norte. In this letter Mr. Clay says, "the President wishes you to effect that object." Mr. Clay adds: "The line of the Sabine approaches our great western mart nearer than could be wished. Perhaps the Mexican government may not be unwilling to establish that of the Rio Brassos de Dios, or the Rio Colorado, or the Snow Mountains, or the Rio del Norte, in lieu of it." Mr. Clay urges, also, the importance of having entirely within our limits "the Red river and Arkansas, and their respective tributary streams."

On the 15th of March, 1827, Mr. Clay again renewed the effort to procure the cession of Texas. In his letter of instruction, of that date, to our minister at Mexico, he says: "The *President* has thought the present might be an auspicious period for urging a negotiation at Mexico, to settle the boundary of the two republics." "If we could obtain such a boundary as we desire, the government of the United States might be disposed to pay a reasonable pecuniary compensation. The boundary we prefer is that which, beginning at the mouth of the Rio del Norte in the sea, shall ascend that river to the mouth of the Rio Puereo, thence ascending this river to its source, and from its source by a line due north to strike the Arkansas; thence following the southern bank of the Arkansas to its source, in latitude 42° north; and thence by that parallel of latitude to the South sea." And he adds, the treaty may provide "for the incorporation of the inhabitants into the Union."

Mr. Van Buren, in his letter, as Secretary of State, to our minister at Mexico, dated August 25, 1829, says: "It is the wish of the President that you should, without delay, open a negotiation with the Mexican government for the purchase of so much of the province of Texas as is hereinafter described." "He is induced, by a *deep* conviction of the *real necessity* of the proposed acquisition, not only as a *guard* for our western frontier, and the *protection of New Orleans,* but also to secure forever to the inhabitants of the valley of the Mississippi the undisputed and undisturbed possession of the navigation of that river." "The territory, of which a cession is desired by the United States, is all that part of the province of Texas which lies east of a line beginning at the Gulf of Mexico, in the centre of the desert, or grand prairie, which lies west of the Rio Nueces." And Mr. Van Buren adds, the treaty may provide "for the incorporation of the inhabitants into the Union." And he then enters into a long and powerful argument of his own, in favor of the reacquisition of Texas.

On the 20th of March, 1833, General Jackson, through Mr. Livingston as Secretary of State, renews to our minister at Mexico the former "instructions on the subject of the proposed cession." On the 2d of July, 1835, General Jackson, through Mr. Forsyth as Secretary of State, renews the instructions to obtain the cession of Texas, and expresses "an anxious desire to secure the very desirable alteration in our boundary with Mexico." On the 6th of August, 1835, General Jackson, through Mr. Forsyth as Secretary of State, directs our minister at Mexico to endeavor to procure for us, from that government, the following boundary, "beginning at the Gulf of Mexico, proceeding along the eastern bank of the river Rio Bravo del Norte, to the 37th parallel of latitude, and thence along that parallel to the Pacific." This noble and glorious proposition of General Jackson would have secured to us, not only the whole of Texas, but also the largest and most valuable portion of upper California, together with the bay and harbor of San Francisco, the best on the western coast of America, and equal to any in the world. If, then, it was deemed, as it is clearly proved, most desirable to obtain the reannexation of Texas, down to a period as late as August, 1835, is it less important at this period?

We find the administration of Messrs. Adams and Clay in 1825 and 1827, and that of Jackson and Van Buren, in 1829, and subsequently in 1833 and 1835, making strenuous efforts to procure the reannexation of Texas, by a purchase from Mexico, at the expense of millions of dollars. Let us observe also the dates of these efforts: That of the first, by Messrs. Adams and Clay, in March, 1825, was within three years only after the recognition of the independence of Mexico by this country, and prior to its full recognition by other powers; and it was within less than five years subsequent to the final ratification of the treaty by which we surrendered Texas, not to Mexico, but to Spain. Now, as Spain had not then recognised the independence of Mexico, and the war was still waging between those nations, the only title which Mexico had to Texas, was by a successful revolution, and is precisely the same title, and depending on the same principles, as that now possessed by Texas. The same remarks apply to the subsequent efforts of Messrs. Adams and Clay in 1827, and of Jackson and Van Buren in 1829, to acquire Texas by purchase from Mexico. And even at the latest period, no more time had elapsed between the date of the recognition of the independence of Mexico, and the proposed purchase from her, than the time (now about seven years) since our recognition of the independence of Texas. Throughout the period of all these proposed treaties, the war was waging between Mexico and Spain. The brave Porter, our own gallant commodore, commanded the Mexican navy, aided by many American officers and crews. In the earlier part, also, of the conflict on the land, the gallant Perry, and the brave Magee, an American officer, with a combined American and Mexican army, had defeated the royal forces of Spain in many a glorious conflict. Throughout this whole period, Mexico was *soliciting* and *obtaining* the aid of our countrymen, on the ocean and on the land; and it is more than doubtful whether, in the absence of that assistance, Mexico would yet have achieved her independence. On the 27th July 1829, Barradas, with a Spanish army of four thousand men, captured the Mexican city of Tampico, which he held until the 10th September of the same year. Yet, on the 25th August, 1829, whilst the fate of this expedition was yet undetermined, the administration of Jackson and Van Buren, as we have seen, proposed the purchase of Texas from Mexico. If, then, there be any force in the objections, that Texas was aided in her conflict by American citizens, that the war is still waging, (which it is not,) or that the independence of Texas is still unrecognised by Mexico, or that a treaty with Mexico (as we had with Spain) had been ratified,—all these reasons apply with far greater force against the proposed purchase of Texas from Mexico in 1825, 1827, and 1829, when Mexico was yet unrecognised by Spain; when our treaty, surrendering Texas to Spain, was unrescinded, except by the revolution in Mexico; and when our citizens were still aiding, as they always had done, the people of Mexico in their struggle for independence. It is true, that, in 1837, within a few weeks or months succeeding our recognition of the independence of Texas, and before her recogniton by any foreign powers, it might have subjected us to unjust imputations; and therefore might have been deemed inexpedient, at *such a time*, and *under such circumstances*, to reannex Texas by a treaty to this Union. But now, when seven years have elapsed since our recognition of the independence of Texas; and she has been recognized for many years as an independent power by the great nations of Europe; and her sovereignty fully established, and fully acknowledged, there can be no objection to such a treaty at this period.

The reasons assigned in 1825, 1827, 1829, 1833 and 1835, for the reannexation of Texas, apply now with full force. These reasons were, that the Sabine, as a boundary, was too near New Orleans; that the defence of that city was rendered insecure; and that the Arkansas and Red river, and all their tributaries, ought to be in our own exclusive possession. The present boundary is the worst which could be devised. It is a succession of steps and curves, carving out the great valley of the West into a shape that is absolutely hideous. It surrenders the Red river, and Arkansas, and their numerous tributaries, for thousands of miles, to a foreign power. It brings that power upon the Gulf, within a day's sail of the mouth of the Mississippi, and in the interior, by the curve of the Sabine, within about one hundred miles of the Mississippi. It places that power, for many hundred miles, on the banks of the Red river, in immediate contact with sixty thousand Indian warriors of our own, and with very many thousand of the fiercest savage tribes in Texas, there to be armed and equipped for the work of death and desolation. It enables a foreign power, with such aids, to descend the Red river, to the junction of the Mississippi, there to cut off all communication from above or below, to arrest at that point all boats which were descending with their troops and munitions of war for the defence of New Orleans, and fall down suddenly on that city, thus isolated from the rest of the Union, and subjected to certain ruin.

From the mouth of the Mississippi to the Sabine there is not a single harbor where an American vessel of war could find shelter; but westward of the mouth of the Sabine, in Texas, are several deep bays and harbors; and Galveston, one of these, has a depth of water equal to that at the mouth of the Mississippi. Looking into the interior, along this extraordinary boundary, we find a foreign power stretching for many hundred miles along the Sabine to the Red river; thence west several hundred miles along that river to the western boundary of our Indian territories; thence north to the Arkansas, and up that stream to the southern boundary of the territory of Oregon, and at a point which, according to the recent most able survey of Lieutenant Fremont, is within twenty miles of the pass of the Rocky mountains, which secures the entrance to Oregon. We thus place a foreign power there, to move eastward or westward, upon the valley of the Columbia or Mississippi. We place this power north of St. Louis, north of a portion of Iowa, and south of New Orleans, and along this line for several thousand miles in our rear.

Such is the boundary at present given to the valley of the West; such the imminent dangers to which it is subjected of Indian massacre; such the dismemberment of the great valley, and of many of the noblest streams and tributaries of the Mississippi; such the surrender of so many hundred miles of our coast, with so many bays and harbors; such the hazard to which New Orleans is subjected, and the outlet of all our commerce to the gulf. Such is our present boundary; and it can be exchanged for one that will give us perfect security, that will place our own people and our own settlements in rear of the Indian tribes, and that will cut them off from foreign influence; that will restore t) us the uninterrupted navigation of the Red river and Arkansas, and of all their tributaries; that will place us at the north, upon a point to command the pass of Oregon, and, on the south, to secure New Orleans, and render certain the command of the Gulf of Mexico. In pursuing our ancient and rightful boundary, before we surrendered Texas, along the Del Norte, we are brought, by a western curve of that great river, to a point within four hundred miles of the Pacific ocean, and where the waters of the Del Norte almost commingle with those that flow into the Western ocean. Up to this point on the Del Norte it is navigable for steamboats; and from that point to the Pacific is a good route for caravans, and where, it is believed, the Pacific may be united with the Del Norte and the Gulf by a railroad, not longer than that which now unites Buffalo and Boston; and where, even now, without such a road, we could command the trade of all the northern States of Mexico, and of a very large portion of the western coast of America.

The importance of Texas is thus described by Mr. Clay, in his speech of the 3d of April, 1820:

"All the accounts concurred in representing Texas to be extremely valuable. Its superficial extent was three or four times greater than that of Florida. The climate was delicious; the soil fertile; the margins of the rivers abounding in live-oak; and the country admitting of easy settlement. It possessed, moreover, if he were not misinformed, one of the finest ports in the Gulf of Mexico. The productions of which it was capable, were suited to our wants. The unfortunate captive of St. Helena wished for ships, commerce, and colonies. We have them all, if we do not wantonly throw them away. The colonies of other countries are separated from them by vast seas, requiring great expense to protect them, and are held subject to a constant risk of their being torn from their grasp. Our colonies, on the contrary, are united to, and form a part, of our continent; and the same Mississippi, from whose rich deposite the best of them (Louisiana) has been formed, will transport on her bosom the brave, the patriotic men from her tributary streams, to defend and preserve the next most valuable—the province of Texas." "He was not disposed to disparage Florida; but its intrinsic value was incomparably less than that of Texas."

In the letter of instructions from Mr. Madison, as Secretary of State, of the 29th July, 1803, he says, "the acquisition of the Floridas is still to be pursued." He adds, the exchange of any part of western Louisiana, which Spain may propose for "the cession of the Floridas," "is inadmissible." "In intrinsic value there is no equality." "We are the less disposed also to make sacrifices to obtain the Floridas; because their position and the manifest course of events *guaranty an early and reasonable acquisition of them.*" In Mr. Madison's letter, also, as Secretary of State, of the 8th July, 1804, he announces the opposition of Mr. Jefferson "to a perpetual relinquishment of *any territory* whatever eastward of the Rio Bravo." In the message of President Houston of the 5th May, 1837, he says that Texas contains "four-fifths of all the live oak now in the world." Cotton will be its great staple, and some sugar and molasses will be produced. The grape, the olive, and indigo, and cocoa, and nearly all the fruits of the tropics will be grown there also. In Texas are valuable mines of gold and silver; the siver mine on the San Saba having been examined and found to be among the richest in the world.

In the recent debate in the British Parliament, Lord Brougham said: "The importance of Texas could not be overrated. It was a country of the greatest capabilities, and was in extent full as large as France. It possessed a soil of the finest and most fertile character, and it was capable of producing all tropical produce; and its climate was of a most healthy character. It had access to the gulf, to the river Mississippi, with which it communicated by means of the Red river." The possession of Texas would ensure to us the trade of Santa Fe and all the northern States of Mexico. Above all, Texas is a large and indispensable portion of the valley of the West. That valley once was all our own; but it has been dismembered by a treaty formed when the West held neither of the high executive stations of the government, and was wholly unrepresented in the cabinet at Washington. The Red river and Arkansas, divided and mutilated, now flow, with their numerous tributaries, for many thousand miles, through the territory of a foreign power; and the West has been forced back along the gulf, from the Del Norte to the Sabine. If, then, it be true that the sacrifice of Texas was made with painful reluctance, all those who united in the surrender will rejoice at the reacquisition.

This is no question of the purchase of new territory, but of the re-annexation of that which once was all our own. It is not a question of the extension of our limits, but of the restoration of former boundaries. It proposes no new addition to the valley of the Mississippi; but of its reunion, and all its waters, once more, under our dominion. If the Creator had separated Texas from the Union by mountain barriers, the Alps or the Andes, these might be plausible objections; but he has planed down the whole valley, including Texas, and united every atom of the soil and every drop of the waters of the mighty whole. He has linked their rivers with the great Mississippi, and marked and united the whole for the dominion of one government and the residence of one people; and it is impious in man to attempt to dissolve this great and glorious Union. Texas is a part of Kentucky, a portion of the same great valley. It is a part of New York and Pennsylvania, a part of Maryland and Virginia, and Ohio, and of all the western States, whilst the Tennessee unites with it the waters of Georgia, Alabama, and Carolina. The Alleghany, commencing its course in New York, and with the Youghiogany, from Maryland, and Monongahela, from Virginia, merging with the beautiful Ohio at the metropolis of western Pennsylvania, embrace the streams of Texas at the mouths of the Arkansas and Red river, whence their waters flow in kindred union to the gulf. And here let me say, that New York ought to reclaim for the Alleghany its true original name, *the Ohio*, of which it is a part, and so marked and called by that name in the British maps, prior to 1776, one of which is in the possession of the distinguished representative from the Pittsburg district of Pennsylvania. The words "Ohio" and "Alleghany," in two different Indian dialects, mean *clear*, as designating truly, in both cases, the character of the water of both streams; and hence it is that New York is upon the Ohio, and truly stands at the head of the valley of the West. The treaty which struck Texas from the Union, inflicted a blow upon this mighty valley. And who will say that the West shall remain dismembered and mutilated, and that the ancient boundaries of the republic shall never be restored? Who will desire to check the young eagle of America, now refixing her gaze upon our former limits, and repluming her pinions for her returning flight? What American will say, that the flag of the Union shall never wave again throughout that mighty territory; and that what Jefferson acquired, and Madison refused to surrender, shall never be restored? Who will oppose the re-establishment our glorious constitution, over the whole of the mighty valley which once was shielded by its benignant sway? Who will wish again to curtail the limits of this great republican empire, and again to dismember the glorious valley of the West? Who will refuse to replant the banner of the republic, upon our former boundary, or resurrender the Arkansas and Red river, and retransfer the coast of the gulf? Who will refuse to heal the bleeding wounds of the mutilated West, and reunite the veins and arteries, dissevered by the dismembering cession of Texas to Spain? To refuse to accept the reannexation, is to *resurrender* the Territory of Texas, and redismember the valley of the West. Nay, more: under existing circumstances, it is to lower the flag of the Union before the red cross of St. George, and to surrender the Florida pass, the mouth of the Mississippi, the command of the Mexican gulf, and finally Texas itself, into the hands of England.

As a question of money, no State is much more deeply interested in the reannexation of Texas than your own great Commonwealth of Kentucky. There, if Texas becomes part of the Union, will be a great and growing market for her beef and pork, her lard and butter, her flour and corn; and there, within a very short period, would be found a ready sale for more than a million dollars in value, of her bale-rope and hemp and cotton-bagging. Nor can it be that Kentucky would desire, by the refusal of reannexation, to mutilate and dismember the valley of which she is a part; or that Kentucky would curtail the limits of the republic, or diminish its power and strength and glory. It cannot be that Kentucky will wish to see any flag except our own upon the banks of the Sabine and Arkansas and Red river, and within a day's sail of the mouth of the Mississippi, and the outlet of all her own commerce in the Gulf. Many of her own people are within the limits of Texas, and its battle-fields are watered with the blood of many of her sons. It was her own intrepid Milam, who headed the brave three hundred who, armed with rifles only, captured the fortress of the Alamo, defended by heavy artillery, and thirteen hundred of the picked troops of Mexico, under one of their best commanders. And will Kentucky refuse to re-embrace so many of her own people? nor permit them, without leaving Texas, to return to the American Union? And if war should ever again revisit our country, Kentucky knows that the steady aim of the western riflemen, and the brave hearts and stout hands, within the limits of Texas, are, in the hour of danger, among the surest defenders of the country, and especially of the valley of the West. The question of reannexation, and of the restoration of ancient boundaries, is a much stronger case than that of the purchase of new territory. It is a stronger case also than the acquisition of Louisiana or Florida; not only upon the ground that these were both an acquisition of new territory, but that they embraced a foreign people, dissimilar to our own, in language, laws, and institutions; and transferred without their knowledge or consent, by the act of a European king. More especially, in a case like this, where the people of Texas occupy a region which was once exclusively our own; and this people, in whom we acknowledge to reside the only sovereignty over the whole and every portion of Texas, desire the reannexation—that we cannot re-establish our former boundaries, and restore to us the whole or any part of the territory which was once our own, is a proposition, the bare statement of which is its best refutation.

Let us examine, now, some of the objections urged against the reannexation of Texas. And here, it is remarkable that the objections to the purchase of Louisiana are the same now made in the case of Texas; yet all now acknowledge the wisdom of that great measure; and to have ever opposed it, is now regarded as alike unpatriotic and unwise. And so will it be in the case of Texas. The measure will justify itself by its results; and its opponents will stand in the same position now occupied by those who objected to the purchase of Louisiana. The objections, we have said, were the same, and we will examine them separately. 1st. The extension of territory; and 2d, the question of slavery.

As to the extension of territory, it applied with much greater force to the purchase of Louisiana. That purchase annexed to the Union a territory double the size of that already embraced within its limits; whilst the reannexation of Texas, according to the largest estimates, will add but one-seventh to the extent of our territory. The highest estimate of the area of Texas is but 318,000 square miles, whilst that of the rest of the Union is 2,000,000 square miles. Now, the British territory, on our own continent of North America, exclusive of the West Indies, and north of our northern boundary, is 2,800,000 square miles, being 500,000 more than that of our whole Union, with Texas united. Indeed, we may add both the Californias to Texas, and unite them all to the Union, and still the area of the whole will be less than that of the British North American possessions. And is it an American doctrine, that monarchies or despotisms are alone fitted for the government of extensive territories, and that a confederacy of States must be compressed within narrower limits? Of all the forms of government, our confederacy is most specially adapted for an extended territory, and might, without the least danger, but with increased security, and vastly augmented benefits, embrace a continent. Each State, within its own limits, controls all its local concerns, and the general government chiefly those which appertain to commerce and our foreign relations. Indeed, as you augment the number of States, the bond of union is stronger; for the opposition of any one State is much less dangerous and formidable, in a confederacy of thirty States, than of three. On this subject experience is the best test of truth. Has the Union been endangered by the advance in the number of States from thirteen to twenty-six? Look also at all the new States that have been added to the Union since the adoption of the constitution, and tell me what one of all of them, either in war or peace, has ever failed most faithfully to perform its duties; and what one of them has ever proposed or threatened the existence of the government, or the dissolution of the Union? No rebellion or insurrection has ever raised its banner within their limits, nor have traitorous or union-dissolving conventions, in war or in peace, ever been assembled within the boundary of any of the new States of the West; but in peace, they have nobly and faithfully performed all their duties to the Union; and in war, the spirit of party has fled before an ardent patriotism, and all have rushed to the standard of their common country. From the shores of the Atlantic and the lakes of the North; from the banks of the Thames and the St. Lawrence, to those of the Alabama and the Mississippi; from the snows of Canada to the sunny plains of the South—the soil of the Union is watered with the blood of the brave and patriotic citizen soldiers of the West. And is it England would persuade us our territory and population will be too great to permit the reannexation of Texas? Let us see how stands the case with herself and other great powers of the world. The following facts are presented from the most recent geographies:

British empire—area, 8,100,000 square miles; population 200,000,000.

Russian empire—area, 7,500,000 square miles; population 75,000,000.

Chinese empire—area, 5,500,000 square miles; population 250,000,000.

Brazil—area, 3,000,000 square miles; population 6,000,000.

United States (including Texas)—area, 2,318,000 square miles; population 19,000,000.

Here is one monarchy, (the British empire,) nearly four times as large as the United States, including Texas; and one monarchy and three depotisms combined, largely more than ten times, our area, also including Texas; and to assert, under these circumstances, that our government is to be overthrown or endanged by an addition of one-seventh to its area, is to adopt the exploded argument of kings and despots against our system of confederated States.

President Monroe, a citizen of one of the old thirteen States, in his message of 1823, thus speaks of the effects of the purchase of Louisiana:

"This expansion of our population, and accession of new States to our Union, have had the happiest effect on all its highest interests. That it has eminently augmented our resources, and added to our strength and respectability as a power, is admitted by all. It is manifest, that by enlarging the basis of our system, and increasing the number of States, the system itself has been greatly strengthened in both its branches. Consolidation and disunion have thereby been rendered equally impracticable. Each government, confiding in its own strength, has less to apprehend from the other; and in consequence, each, enjoying a greater freedom of action, is rendered more efficient for all the purposes for which it was instituted." It is the system of confederate States, united, but not consolidated, and incorporating the great principle which led to the adoption of the constitution—of *reciprocal free trade* between all the States—that adapt such a government to the extent of a continent. The greater the extent of territory, the more enlarged is the power, and the more augmented the blessings of such a government. In war it will be more certain of success, and therefore wars will be less frequent; and in peace, it will be more respected abroad, and enjoy greater advantages at home, and the less unfavorable will be the influence on its prosperity, of the hostile policy of foreign nations. It may then have a home market, which, as the new and exchangeable products of various soils and climates are augmented, will place its industry less within the controlling influence of foreign powers. Especially is this important to the great manufacturing interest, that its home market, which is almost its only market, should be enlarged and extended by the accession of new territory, and an augmented population, embraced within the boundaries of the Union, and therefore constituting a part of the domestic market. By the census of 1840, the total product of the mining and the manufactures of the Union, was $282,194,985; and of this vast amount, by the treasury report, but $9,469,962 was exported, and found a market abroad. Almost its only market was the home market, thus demonstrating the vast importance to that great interest of an accession of territory and population at home.

Nor is it only the mining and manufacturing interests that would feel the influence of such a new and rapidly augmenting home market; but agriculture, commerce, and navigation, the products of the forest and fisheries, the freighting and ship-building interests, would all feel a new impulse; and the great internal communications, by railroads and canals, engaged in transporting our own exchangeable products, would find a great enlargement of their business and profits, and lead onward to the completion of the present and the construction of new improvements—thus identifying more closely all our great interests, bringing nearer and nearer to each other the remotest portions of the mighty whole, multiplying their trade and intercourse, breaking down the barriers of local and sectional prejudice, and scouting the thought of disunion from the American heart, and leaving the very term obsolete. Indeed, if we measure distance by the time in which it is traversed, this Union, with Texas reannexed, is much smaller in territory than the Union was at the adoption of the constitution. Then, the journey from the capital to the then remotest corner of the republic could not be traversed in less than a month; while now, much less than one-half that time will take us to the mouth of the Del Norte,

11

the extreme southwestern limit of Texas. Such are the conquests which steam has already effected, upon the water and upon the land; and, when we consider the wonderful advance which they are still making, we must begin to calculate a journey upon land, by steam, from the Atlantic to the Del Norte, by hours, and not by weeks or months. And he who, under such circumstances, would still say that Texas was too large or distant for reannexation to the Union, must have been sleeping since the application of steam to locomotion.

But if Texas is too large for incorporation into the Union, why is not Oregon also, which is nearly double the size of Texas? and if Texas is too remote, why is not. Oregon also, when ten days will take us to the mouth of the Del Norte, whereas three months by land, and five months by sea, must be required for the journey to the mouth of the Columbia. Texas, also, is a part of the valley of the Mississippi, watered by the same streams, and united with it by nature, as one and indivisible; whereas Oregon is separated from us by mountain barriers, and pours its waters into another and distant ocean. And if Oregon, although disputed, and occcupied by a foreign power, is, as I believe it to be, in truth and justice, all our own, Texas was once, and for many years, within our limits, and may now again become our own by the free and unanimous consent, already given, of all by whom it is owned and occupied. I have not thus contrasted Texas and Oregon with a view to oppose to oppose the occupation of Oregon; for I have always been the ardent friend of that measure. I advocated it in a speech published long before I became a member of the Senate, and now, since the death of the patriotic and lamented Linn, I am the oldest surviving member of the special committee of the Senate which has pressed upon that body, for so many years, the immediate occupation of the whole Territory of Oregon. There, upon the shores of the distant Pacific, if my vote can accomplish it, shall be planted the banner of the Union; and, with my consent, never shall be surrendered a single point of its coast, an atom of its soil, or a drop of all its waters. But while I am against the surrender of any portion of Oregon, I am also against the resurrender of the territory of Texas; for, disguise it as we may, it is a case of resurrender, when it once was all our own, and now again is ours, by the free consent of those to whom it belongs, already given, and waiting only the ceremony of a formal acceptance. Let not those, then, who advocate the occupation of Oregon, tell us that Texas is too distant, or too inaccessible, or too extensive for American occupancy. Let the friends of Oregon reflect, also, that Texas, at the head of the Arkansas, is contiguous to Oregon, and within twenty miles of the pass which commands the entrance through all that territory, and the occupation of which pass by a foreign power, would separate the people and Territory of Oregon from the rest of the Union, and leave them an easy prey to the army of an invader. In truth, Texas is nearly as indispensable for the safe and permanent occupation of Oregon, as it is for the security of New Orleans and the Gulf.

The only remaining objection is the question of slavery. And have we a question which is to curtail the limits of the republic—to threaten its existenct—to aim a deadly blow at all its great and vital interests—to court alliances with foreign and with hostile powers—to recall our commerce and expel our manufactures from bays and rivers that once were all our own—to strike down the flag of the Union, as it advances towards our ancient boundary—to resurrender a mighty territory, and invite to its occupancy the deadliest (in truth, the only) foes this government has ever encountered? Is anti-slavery to do all this? And is it so to endanger New Orleans, and the valley and commerce and outlet of the West, that we would hold them, not by our own strength, but by the slender tenure of the will and of the mercy of Great Britain? If anti-slavery can effect all this, may God, in his infinite mercy, save and perpetuate this Union; for the efforts of man would be feeble and impotent. The avowed object of this party is the immediate abolition of slavery. For this, they traverse sea and land; for this, they hold conventions in the capital of England; and there they brood over schemes of abolition, in association with British societies; there they join in denunciations of their countrymen, until their hearts are filled with treason; and they return home, Americans in name, but Englishmen in feelings and principles. Let us all, then, feel and know, whether we live North or South, that this party, if not vanquished, must overthrow the government, and dissolve the Union. This party propose the immediate abolition of slavery throughout the Union. If this were practicable, let us look at the consequences. By the returns of the last census, the products of the slaveholding States, in 1840, amounted in value to $404,429,638. These products, then, of the South, must have alone enabled it to furnish a home market for all the surplus mannfactures of the North, as also a market for the products of its forests and fisheries; and giving a mighty impulse to all its commercial and navigating interests. Now, nearly all these agricultural products of the South which accomplish all these great purposes, is the result of slave labor; and, strike down these products by the immediate abolition of slavery, and the markets of the South, for want of the means to purchase, will be lost to the people of the North; and North and South will be involved in one common ruin. Yes, in the harbors of the North (at Philadelphia, New York, and Boston) the vessels would rot at their wharves for want of exchangeable products to carry; the building of ships would cease, and the grass would grow in many a street now enlivened by an active and progressive industry. In the interior, the railroads and canals would languish for want of business; and the factories and manufacturing towns and cities, decaying and deserted, would stand as blasted monuments of the folly of man. One universal bankruptcy would overspread the country, together with all the demoralization and crime which ever accompany such a catastrophe; and the notices at every corner would point only to sales on execution, by the constable, the sheriff, the marshal, and the auctioneer; whilst the beggars would ask us in the streets, not for money, but for bread. Dark as the picture may be, it could not exceed the gloomy reality. Such would be the effects in the North; whilst in the South, no human heart can conceive, nor pen describe, the dreadful consequences. Let us look at another result to the North. The slaves being emancipated, not by the South, but by the North, would fly there for safety and protection; and three millions of free blacks would be thrown at once, as if by a convulsion of nature, upon the States of the North. They would come there to their friends of the North, who had given them freedom, to give them also habitation, food, and clothing; and, not having it to give, many of them would perish from want and exposure;

[231]

whilst the wretched remainder would be left to live as they could, by theft or charity. They would still be a degraded caste, free only in name, without the reality of freedom. A few might earn a wretched and precarious subsistence, by competing with the white laborers of the North, and reducing their wages to the lowest point in the sliding scale of starvation and misery; whilst the poor-house and the jail, the asylums of the deaf and dumb, the blind, the idiot and insane, would be filled to over-flowing; if, indeed, any asylum could be afforded to the millions of the negro race whom wretchedness and crime would drive to despair and madness.

That these are sad realities, is proved by the census of 1840. I annex in an appendix a table, marked No. 1, compiled by me entirely from the official returns of the census of 1840, except as to prisons and paupers which are obtained from city and State returns, and the results are as follows:

1st. The number of deaf and dumb, blind, idiots, and insane, of the negroes in the non-slaveholding States, is one out of every 96; in the slaveholding States, it is one out of every 672, or seven to one in favor of the slaves in this respect, as compared with the free blacks.

2d. The number of whites, deaf and dumb, blind, idiots, and insane, in the non-slaveholding States, is one in every, 561, being nearly six to one against the free blacks in the same States.

3d. The number of negroes who are deaf and dumb, blind, idiots, and insane, paupers, and in prison in the non-slaveholding States, is one out of every 6, and in the slaveholding States, one out of every 154; or twenty-two to one against the free blacks, as compared with the slaves.

4th. Taking the two extremes of north and south, in Maine, the number of negroes returned as deaf and dumb, blind, insane, and idiots, by the census of 1840, is one out of every twelve, and in slave-holding Florida, by the same returns, is one of every eleven hundred and five; or ninety-two to one, in favor of the slaves of Florida, as compared with the free blacks of Maine.

By the report of the secretary of state of Massachusetts (of the 1st November, 1843) to the legislature, there were then in the county jails, and houses of correction in that State, 4,020 whites, and 364 negroes; and adding the previous returns of the State prison, 255 whites and 32 blacks ; making in all 4,275 whites, and 396 free blacks; being one out of every one hundred and seventy of the white, and one out of every twenty-one of the free black population: and by the official returns of the census of 1840, and their own official returns to their own legislature, one out of every thirteen of the free blacks of Massachusetts was either deaf and dumb, blind, idiot, or insane, or in prison—thus proving a degree of debasement and misery, on the part of the colored race, in that truly great State, which is appalling. In the last official report to the legislature of the warden of the penetentiary in eastern Pennsylvania, he says: "The whole number of prisoners received from the opening of the institution, (October 25, 1829,) to January 1, 1843, is 1,622; of these, 1,004 were white males, 533 colored males; 27 white females, and 58 colored females!" or one out of every 847 of the white, and one out of every sixty-four of the negro population; and of the white female convicts, one out of every 16,288; and of the colored female convicts, one out of every 349 *in one prison*, showing a degree of guilt and debasement on the part of the colored

females, revolting and unparalleled. When such is the debasement of the colored females, far exceeding even that of the white females in the most corrupt cities of Europe, extending, too, throughout one-half the limits of a great State, we may begin to form some idea of the dreadful condition of the free blacks, and how much worse it is than that of the slaves, whom we are asked to liberate and consign to a similar condition of guilt and misery. Where, too, are these examples? The first is in the great State of Massachusetts, that, for 64 years, has never had a slave, and whose free black population, being 5,463 in 1790, and but 8,669 at present, is nearly the same free negro population, and their descendants, whom for more than half a century she has strived, but strived in vain, to elevate in rank and comfort and morals. The other example is the eastern half of the great State of Pennsylvania, including Philadelphia, and the Quakers of the State, who, with an industry and humanity that never tired, and a charity that spared not time or money, have exerted every effort to improve the morals and better the condition of their free black population. But where are the great results? Let the census and the reports of the prisons answer. Worse—incomparably worse, than the condition of the slaves, and demonstrating that the free black, in the midst of his friends in the North, is sinking lower every day in the scale of want and crime and misery. The regular physicians' report and review, published in 1840, says the "facts, then, show an *increasing* disproportionate number of colored prisoners in the eastern penitentiary." In contrasting the condition, for the same year, of the penitentiaries of all the non-slaveholding States, as compared with all the slaveholding States in which returns are made, I find the number of free blacks is fifty-four to one, as compared with the slaves, in proportion to population, who are incarcerated in these prisons. There are no paupers among the slaves, whilst in the non-slaveholding States great is the number of colored paupers.

From the Belgian statistics, compiled by Mr. Quetelet, the distinguished secretary of the Royal Academy of Brussels, it appears that in Belgium the number of deaf and dumb was one out of every 2,180 persons; in Great Britain, one out of every 1,539; in Italy, one out of every 1,539; and in Europe, one out of every 1,474. Of the blind, one out of every 1,009 in Belgium; one out of every 800 in Prussia; one out of every 1,600 in France; and one out of every 1,666 in Saxony; and no further returns, as to the blind, are given.—[*Belgian Annuaire*, 1836, *pages* 213, 215, 217.] But the table shows an average in Europe of one of every 1,474 of deaf and dumb, and of about one out of every 1,000 of blind; whereas our census shows, of the deaf and dumb whites of the Union, one out of every 2,193; and of the blacks in the non-slaveholding States, one out of every 656; also, of the blind, one out of every 2,821 of the whites of the Union, and one out of every 516 of the blacks in the non-slaveholding States. Thus we have not only shown the condition of the blacks of the non-slaveholding States to be far worse than that of the slaves of the South, but also far worse than the condition of the people of Europe, deplorable as that may be. It has been heretofore shown that the free blacks in the non-slaveholding States were becoming, in an *augmented* proportion, more debased in morals as they increased in numbers; and the same proposition is true in other respects. Thus, by the census of 1830, the number of deaf and dumb of the free blacks of the non-slaveholding States, was one out of every 996; and of blind, one out of every 893; whereas we have seen, by the census of 1840, the number of free blacks, deaf and dumb, in the non-slaveholding States, was one out of every 656; and of blind, one out of every 516. In the last ten years, then, the alarming fact is proved, that the *proportionate* number of free black deaf and dumb, and also of blind, *has increased about fifty per cent.* No statement as to the insane or idiots is given in the census of 1830.

Let us now examine the future increase of free blacks in the States adjoining the slaveholding States, if Texas is not reannexed to the Union. By the census of 1790, the number of free blacks in the States (adding New York) adjoining the slaveholding States, was 13,953. In the States (adding New York) adjacent to the slaveholding States, the number of free blacks, by the census of 1840, was 148,107; being an aggregate increase of nearly eleven to one in New York, New Jersey, Pennsylvania, Ohio, Indiana, and Illinois. Now, by the census and table above given, the aggregate number of free blacks who were deaf and dumb, blind, idiot or insane, paupers, or in prisons, in the non-slaveholding States, was 26,342, or one in every six of the whole number. Now if the free black population should increase in the same ratio, in the aggregate, in New York, New Jersey, Pennsylvania, Ohio, Indiana, and Illinois, from 1840 to 1890, as it did from 1790 to 1840, the aggregate free black population in these six States would be, in 1890, 1,600,000; in 1865, 800,000; in 1853, 400,000; and the aggregate number in these six States of free blacks, according to the present proportion, who would then be deaf and dumb, blind, idiot or insane, paupers or in prison, would be, in 1890, 266,666; in 1865, 133,333; and in 1853, 66,666; being, as we have seen, one-sixth of the whole number. Now, if the annual cost of supporting these free blacks in these asylums, and other houses, including the interest on the sums expended in their erection, and for annual repairs, and the money disbursed for the arrest, trial, conviction, and transportation of the criminals, amounted to fifty dollars for each, the annual tax on the people of these six States, on account of these free blacks, would be, in 1890, $13,333,200; in 1865, $6,666,600; and in 1853, $3,333,300.

Does, then, humanity require that we should render the blacks more debased and miserable, by this process of abolition, with greater temptations to crime, with more of real guilt, and less of actual comforts? As the free blacks are thrown more and more upon the cities of the North, and compete more there with the white laborer, the condition of the blacks becomes worse and more perilous every day, until we have already seen, the masses of Cincinnati and Philadelphia rise to expel the negro race beyond their limits. Immediate abolition, whilst it deprived the South of the means to purchase the products and manufactures of the North and West, would fill those States with an inundation of free black population, that would be absolutey intolerable. Immediate abolition, then, has but few advocates; but if emancipation were not immediate, but only gradual, whilst slavery existed to any great extent in the slaveholding States bordering upon the States of the North and West, this expulsion, by gradual abolition, of the free blacks into the States immediately north of them, would be very considerable, and rapidly augmenting every year. If this process of gradual abolition only doubled the number of free blacks, to be thrown upon the States of the North and West, then, a reference to the tables before presented, proves that the number of free blacks in New York, Pennsylvania, New Jersey, Ohio, Indiana, and Illinois would be, in 1890, 3,200,000; in 1865, 1,600,-000; and in 1853, 800,000; and that the annual expenses to the people of these six States, on account of the free blacks would be, in 1890, $26,666,400; in 1865, $13,333,200; and in 1853, $6,666,600.

It was in view, no doubt, of these facts, that Mr. Davis, of New York, declared, upon the floor of Congress, on the 29th December, 1843, that "the abolition of slvaery in the southern States must be followed by a *deluge of black population to the North*, filling our *jails* and *poor houses*, and bringing *destruction* upon the *laboring portion of our people.*" Dr. Duncan also, of Cincinnati, Ohio, in his speech in Congress on the 6th January, 1844, declared the result of abolition would be to inundate the North with free blacks, described by him as "paupers, beggars, thieves, assassins, and desperadoes; all, or nearly all, penniless and destitute, without skill, means, industry, or perseverance to obtain a livelihood; each possessing and cherishing revenge for supposed or real wrongs. No man's fireside, person, family, or property, would be safe by day or night. It *now requires* the whole energies of the law and the whole vigilance of the police of all our principal cities to restrain and keep in subordination the few straggling *free negroes* which now infest them." If such be the case now, what will be the result when, by abolition, gradual or immediate, the number of these free negroes shall be doubled and quadrupled, and decupled, in the more northern of the slaveholding States, before slavery had receded from their limits, and nearly the whole of which free black population would be thrown on the adjacent non-slaveholding States. Much, if not all of this great evil, will be prevented by the reannexation of Texas. Since the purchase of Louisiana and Florida, and the settlement of Alabama and Mississippi, there have been carried into this region, as the census demonstrates, from the States of Delaware, Maryland, Virginia, and Kentucky, half a million of slaves, including their descendants, that otherwise would now be within the limits of those four States. Such has been the result as to have diminished, in two of these States nearest to the North, the number of their slaves far below what they were at the census of 1790, and to have reduced them at the census of 1840, in Delaware, to the small number of 2,605. Now, if we double the rate of diminution, as we certainly will by the reannexation of Texas, slavery will disappear from Delaware in ten years, and from Maryland in twenty, and have greatly diminished in Virginia and Kentucky. As, then, by reannexation, slavery advances in Texas, it must recede to the *same extent* from the more northern of the slaveholding States; and consequently, the evil to the northern States, from the expulsion into them of free blacks, by abolition, gradual or immediate, would thereby be greatly mitigated, if not entirely prevented. In the District of Columbia, by the drain to the new States and Territories of the South and Southwest, the slaves have been reduced from 6,119 in 1830, to 4,694 in 1840; and if, by the reannexation, slavery receded in a double ratio, then it would disappear altogether from the District in twelve years; and that question, which now occupies so much of the time of Congress, and threatens so seriously the harmony, if not the existence of the union, would be put at rest by the reannexation of Texas. This reannexation, then, would only change the locality of the slaves, and of the slaveholding States, without augmenting their number. And is Texas to be lost to the Union, not by the question of the existence of slavery, but of its locality only? If slavery be considered by the States of the North as an evil, why should they prefer that its location should be continued in States on their border, rather than in the more distant portions of the Union. It is clear that, as slavery advanced in Texas, it would recede from the States bordering on the free States of the North and West; and thus they would be released from actual contact with what they consider an evil, and also from all influx from those States of a large and constantly augmenting free black population. As regards the slaves, the African being from a tropical climate, and from the region of the burning sands and sun, his comfort and condition would be greatly improved, by a transfer from northern latitudes to the genial and most salubrious climate of Texas. There he would never suffer from that exposure to cold and frost, which he feels so much more severely than any other race; and there, also, from the great fertility of the soil, and exuberance of its products, his supply of food would be abundant. If a desire to improve the condition and increase the comforts of the slave really animated the anti-slavery party, they would be the warmest advocates of the reannexation of Texas. Nor can it be disguised that, by the reannexation, as the number of free blacks augmented in the slaveholding States, they would be diffused gradually through Texas into Mexico, and Central and Southern America, where nine-tenths of their present population are already of the colored races, and where, from their vast preponderance in number, they are not a degraded caste, but upon a footing, not merely of legal, but what is far more important, of actual equality with the rest of the population. Here, then, if Texas is reannexed throughout the vast region and salubrious and delicious climate of Mexico, and of Central and Southern America, a large and rapidly increasing portion of the African race will disappear from the limits of the Union. The process will be gradual and progressive, without a shock, and without a convulsion; whereas, by the loss of Texas, and the imprisonment of the slave population of the Union within its present limits, slavery would *increase* in nearly all the slaveholding States, and a change in their condition would become impossible; or if it did take place by sudden or gradual abolition, the result would as certainly be the sudden or gradual introduction of hundreds of thousands of free blacks into the States of the North; and if their condition there is already deplorable, how would it be when their number there should be augmented tenfold, and the burden become intolerable? Then, indeed, by the loss of the markets of Texas—by the taxation imposed by an immense free black population, depressing the value of all property—then, also, from the competition for employment of the free black with the white laborer of the North,—his wages would be reduced until they would fall to ten or twenty cents a day, and starvation and misery would be introduced among the white laboring population. There is but one way in which the North can escape these evils; and that is the reannexation of Texas, which is the only safety-valve for the whole Union, and the only practicable outlet for the African population, through Texas, into Mexico and Central and Southern America. There is a congenial climate for the African race. There

cold and want and hunger will not drive the African, as we see it does in the North, into the poor-house and the jail, and the asylums of the idiot and insane. There the boundless and almost unpeopled territory of Mexico, and of Central and Southern America, with its delicious climate, and most prolific soil, renders most easy the means of subsistence; and there they would not be a degraded caste, but equals among equals, not only by law, but by feeling and association.

The medical writers all say, (and experience confirms the assertion,) that ill-treatment, overwork, neglect in infancy and sickness, drunkenness, want, and crime, are the chief causes of idiocy, blindness, and lunacy; whilst none will deny that want and guilt fill the poor-house and the jail. Why is it, then, that the free black is (as the census proves) much more wretched in condition, and debased in morals, than the slave? These free blacks are among the people of the North, and their condition is most deplorable in the two great States of Maine and Massachusetts, where, since 1780, slavery never existed. Now, the people of the North are eminently humane, religious, and intelligent. What, then, is the cause of the misery and debasement of their free black population? It is chiefly in the fact that the free blacks, among their real superiors—our own white population—are, and ever will be, a degraded caste, free only in name, without any of the blessings of freedom. Here they can have no pride, and no aspirations—no spirit of industry or emulation; and, in most cases, to live, to vegetate, is their only desire. Hence, the efforts to improve their condition, so long made, in Massachusetts, Pennsylvania, and many other States, have proved utterly unavailing; and it grows worse every year, as that population augments in numbers. In vain do many of the States give the negro the right of suffrage, and all the legal privileges of the whites: the color marks the dreadful difference which, here, at least, ages cannot obliterate. The negroes, however equal in law, are not equal in fact. They are nowhere found in the colleges or universities, upon the bench or at the bar, in the muster, or the jury-box, in legislative or executive stations; nor does marriage, the great bond of society, unite the white with the negro, except a rare occurrence of such unnatural alliance, to call forth the scorn or disgust of the whole community. Indeed, I could truly say, if passing into the immediate presence of the Most High, that, in morals and comforts, the free black is far below the slave; and that, while the condition of the slave has been greatly ameliorated, and is improving every year, that of the free blacks (as the official tables demonstrate) is sinking in misery and debasement at every census, as, from time to time, by emancipation and other causes, they are augmented in number. Can it, then, be sinful to refuse to change the condition of the slaves to a position of far greater wretchedness and debasement, by reducing them to the level of the free-negro race, to occupy the asylums of the deaf and dumb, the blind, the idiot and insane; to wander as mendicants; to live in pestilent alleys and hovels, by theft or charity; or to prolong a miserable existence in the poor-house or the jail? All history proves that no people on earth are more deeply imbued with the love of freedom, and of its diffusion everywhere, among all who can appreciate and enjoy its blessings, than the people of the South; and if the negro slave were improved in morals and comforts, and rendered capable of self-government, by emancipation, it would not be gradual, but immediate, if the profits of slavery were tenfold greater than they are. Is slavery, then, never to disappear from the Union? If confined within its present limits, I do not perceive when or how it is to terminate. It is true, Mr. George Tucker, the distinguished Virginian, and professor in their great university, has demonstrated that, in a period not exceeding eighty years, and probably less, from the density of population in all the slaveholding States, hired labor would be as abundant and cheap as slave labor, and that all *pecuniary* motive for the continuance of slavery would then have ceased. But would it, *therefore*, then disappear? No, it certainly would not; for, at the lowest ratio, the slaves would then number at least ten millions. Could such a mass be emancipated? And if so, what would be the result? We have seen, by the census and other proof, that one-sixth of the free blacks must be supported at the public expense; and that, at the low rate of $50 each, it would cost $80,000,000 per annum to be raised by taxation to support the free blacks then in the South requiring support, namely: 1,666,666, if manumission were permitted; but as such a tax could not be collected, emancipation would be as it now is, *prohibited by law*, and slavery could not disappear in this manner, even when it became unprofitable. No, ten millions of free blacks, permitted to roam at large in the limits of the South, could never be tolerated. Again, then, the question is asked, is slavery never to disappear from the Union? This is a startling and momentous question, but the answer is easy, and the proof is clear; *it will certainly disappear if Texas is reannexed to the Union;* not by abolition, but against and in spite of all its frenzy, slowly, and gradually, by diffusion, as it has already thus nearly receded from several of the more northern of the slaveholding States, and as it will continue thus more rapidly to recede by the reannexation of Texas, and finally, in the distant future, without a shock, without abolition, without a convulsion, disappear into and through Texas, into Mexico and Central and Southern America. Thus, that same overruling Providence that watched over the landing of the emigrants and pilgrims at Jamestown and Plymouth; that gave us the victory in our struggle for independence; that guided by His inspiration the framers of our wonderful constitution; that has thus far preserved this great Union from dangers so many and imminent, and is now shielding it from abolition, its most dangerous and internal foe—will open Texas as a safety-valve, into and through which slavery will slowly and gradually recede, and finally disappear into the boundless regions of Mexico, and Central and Southern America. Beyond the Del Norte, slavery will not pass; not only because it is forbidden by law, but because the colored races there preponderate in the ratio of ten to one over the whites; and holding, as they do, the government, and most of the offices in their own possession, they will never permit the enslavement of any portion of the colored race which makes and executes the laws of the country. In Bradford's Atlas, the facts are given as follows:

Mexico—area, 1,690,000 square miles; population 8,000,000—one-sixth white, and all the rest Indians, Africans, mulattoes, zambos, and other colored races.

Central America—area, 186,000 square miles; population nearly 2,000,000—one-sixth white, and the rest negroes, zambos, and other colored races.

South America—area, 6,500,000 square miles; population 14,000,000—1,000,000 white, 4,000,000 Indians; and the remainder, being 9,000,000, blacks and other colored races.

The outlet for our negro race, through this vast region, can never be opened but by the reannexation of Texas; but in that event, there, in that extensive country, bordering upon our negro population, and four times greater in area than the whole Union, with a sparse population of but three to the square mile, where nine-tenths of the population is of the colored races, there, upon that fertile soil, and in that delicious climate, so admirably adapted to the negro race, as all experience has now clearly proved, the free black would find a home. There, also, as slaves, in the lapse of time, from the density of population and other causes, are emancipated, they will disappear from time to time west of the Del Norte, and beyond the limits of the Union, among a race of their own color; will be diffused throughout this vast region, where they will not be a degraded caste, and where, as to climate, and social and moral condition, and all the hopes and comforts of life, they can occupy, among equals, a position they can never attain in any part of this Union.

The reannexation of Texas would strengthen and fortify the whole Union, and antedate the period when our own country would be the first and greatest of all the powers of the earth. To the South and Southwest it would give peace and security; to agriculture and manufactures, to the products of the mines, the forest, and fisheries, new and important markets, that otherwise must soon be lost forever. To the commercial and navigating interests, it would give a new impulse; and not a canal or a railroad throughout the Union, that would not derive increased business, and augmented profits; whilst the great city of New York, the centre of most of the business of the Union, would take a mighty step in advance towards that destiny which must place her above London in wealth, in business and population. Indeed, when, as Americans, we look at the city of New York, its deep, accessible and capacious harbor, united by canals and the Hudson, with the St. Lawrence and the lakes, the Ohio, and the Mississippi, with two-thirds of the imports, and one-third of the exports of the whole Union, with all its trade, internal, coastwise, and foreign, and reflect how great and rapidly augmenting an accession to its business would be made by the reannexation of Texas; and know that, by the failure of this measure, what is lost to us is gained by England, can we hesitate, or do we never wish to see the day when New York shall take from London the trident of the ocean, and the command of the commerce of the world? Or do we prefer London to New York, and England to America? And do the opponents of reannexation suppose that a British Parliament, and not an American Congress, sits in the capitol of the Union. Shall, then, Texas be our own, with all its markets, commerce, and products, or shall we drive it into the arms of England, now outstretched to receive it, and striving to direct its destiny? If we refuse the reannexation, then, by the force of circumstances, soon passing beyond the control as well of this country as of Texas, she will pass into the hands of England. The refusal of reannexation will, of course, produce no friendly feelings in Texas towards this country. United with this will be the direct appeal of England to the interests of Texas. She will offer to Texas a market in England, free of duty, for all her cotton, upon the assent of Texas to receive in exchange British manufactures free of duty; and such a treaty would no doubt soon be concluded. The ships and merchants and capital of England will be transported to the coast of Texas. Texas has neither ships, nor capital, nor manufactures, but England will supply all, and receive in return the cotton of Texas. Two nations with reciprocal free trade are nearly identical in feeling and interest, except that the larger power will preponderate, and Texas become a commercial dependency of England, and isolated from us in feelings, in interest, in trade, and intercourse. Texas would then be our great rival in the cotton markets of the world, and she would have two vast advantages over the cotton-growing interests of the Union: 1st, in sending to England her cotton, free of duty, which is an advantage of 7½ per cent., augmented five per cent. thereon by the act of 15th May, 1840, 3 Victoria, chap. 17, which made the duties paid in England on our cotton crop of 1840, $3,247,800, and all which, to the extent of their crop, would be saved to the planters of Texas, giving them this great advantage over our planters, carried out into all the goods manufactured in England out of the free cotton of Texas, and also depriving our cotton manufacturers of the advantage they now enjoy from this duty, over the cotton manufacturers of England. 2d. In enabling the planters of Texas to receive, in exchange for their cotton, the cheap manufactures of England free of duty. These two causes combined, would give the Texas cotton planters an advantage of at least 20 per cent. over the cotton planters of the Union. Such a rivalry we could not long maintain; and cotton planting would gradually decline in the Union, and with that decline, would be lost the markets of the South for the hemp, and beef, and pork, and flour of the West, and the manufactures of the North. Now, is it just, is it safe or expedient, to place the South and the Southwest in a position in which they will constantly behold an adjacent cotton-growing country supplanting them in the culture and sale of their great staple, for the reason that the one is, and the other is not, a part of the Union? Must we behold Texas every day selling her cotton to England free of all duty, whilst our cotton is subjected to a heavy impost? and must we also perceive Texas receiving in exchange the manufactures of England free of duty, whilst here they are excluded by a prohibitory tariff? Can the tariff itself stand such an issue; or, if it does, can the Union sustain the mighty shock? Daily and hourly, to the South and Southwest, would be presented the strong inducement to unite with Texas, and secure the same markets free of duty for their cotton, and receive the same cheap manufactures, free of duty, in exchange. Nor would these be the only dangers incurred, and temptations presented, by this fearful experiment. We would see the exports of Texas carried directly abroad from their own ports, and the imports brought into their own ports directly in exchange; thus building up their own cities, and their own commerce, whilst here, they would see that same business transacted for them, chiefly in New York, Boston, and Philadelphia. They would see New York receiving annually one hundred millions of imports, nearly fifty millions of which was for resale to them, and all which they would receive directly in their own ports if united with Texas, thus striking down nearly one half the commerce of the great city of New York, and transferring it to the South and Southwest.

The South and Southwest, whilst they would perceive the advancing prosperity of Texas, and their own decline, would also feel, that the region with which they were united had placed them in this position, and subjected them to these disasters by the refusal of reannexation. Whatever the result may be, no true friend of the Union can desire to subject it to such hazards; and this alone ought to be a conclusive argument in favor of the reannexation of Texas. One of three results is certain to follow from the refusal of reannexation: 1st. The separation of the South and Southwest from the North, and their reunion with Texas. Or, 2d. The total overthrow of the tariff. Or, 3d. A system of unbounded smuggling through Texas into the West, and Southwest. Accompanying the last result, would be a disregard of the laws, and an utter demoralization of the whole country, a practical repeal of the tariff, and loss of the revenues which it supplies, and a necessary resort to direct taxation to support the government.

As a commercial dependency, Texas would be almost as much under the control of England, as if she were a colony of England; and in the event of war between that nation and this, the interests of Texas would all be on the side of England. It would be the interest of Texas, in the event of such a war, to aid England to seize New Orleans, or at least in blockading the mouth of the Mississippi, so as to exclude the cotton of the West from a foreign market, and leave to Texas almost the entire monopoly. Even if Texas were neutral, certainly our power would not be as strong in the gulf for the defence of New Orleans, and the mouth of the Mississippi, as if we owned and commanded all the streams which emptied into it—as if their people were our countrymen, and all the rivers and harbors and coast of Texas were our own. We should be weaker, then, without Texas, even if she remained neutral; but I have shown it would be her interest to exclude our cotton from foreign markets, and to co-operate with England for that purpose. But if she did remain neutral, could she preserve, or would England respect, her neutrality? Without an army, ships, or forts, no one will pretend that her neutral position could be maintained; and England could enter any of her streams or harbors, and take possession of any of her soil at pleasure. Would she do so in the event of a war with America? Let the events of the last war answer the question. Then, within sight of Valparaiso, within the waters of neutral Spain, she captured the Essex, after a sanguinary and glorious defence. This was as complete a violation of the neutral rights of Spain, under the law of nations, as if she had entered upon her soil to molest us. At Fayal, Porto Praya, and Tunis, she captured other American vessels, within the harbors and under the guns of the forts of neutral powers; and, indeed, as to neutral ships and goods, and all the maritime rights of neutral nations, she acted the part of the outlaw and buccaneer, rather than of a civilized kingdom; and violated the neutral rights of all the world. Nor were her lawless acts confined to the coasts and harbors of neutral powers, but extended also to an actual use and occupation of their soil. During the last war, Spain was at peace with England and America; but England, in open violation of the neutral rights of Spain, seized upon a portion of Florida, (then a Spanish territory,) whence she fulminated her incendiary appeals to the slaves for a servile insurrection and massacre; and commenced, at Pensacola, her first preparations for the attack of New Orleans. And such, precisely, would be the conduct of Great Britain, in the event of another war with America. She would land suddenly at any point of the coast of Texas, and move along the Sabine, in the Territory of Texas, to the great bend, where it approaches within about one hundred miles of the Mississippi; and the intermediate territory being but thinly settled, she could advance rapidly across, seize the passage of the Mississippi, and cut off all communication from above, and descend upon New Orleans. Or she might proceed a little further, through the territory of Texas to Red river, the southern bank of which is within the limits of Texas, and equip her expedition; then by water descend the Red river, exciting a servile insurrection, and seize the Mississippi at the mouth of Red river. All these movements she might and would make through Texas. In this way she would seize and fortify her position on the Mississippi, and New Orleans must fall, if cut off from all communication from above. But, even if she only retained the single point on the Mississippi, it would as effectually command its outlet, and arrest its commerce ascending or descending, as if possessed of New Orleans. Whatever point she seized on the Mississippi, there she would entrench and fortify, and tens of thousands of lives, and hundreds of millions of dollars, would be required in driving her from this position. All this would be prevented by the reannexation of Texas. The Sabine and Red river would then be all our own, and no such movement could be made for the seizure of the Mississippi. Nor should it be forgotten, that, when she reached the Red river, and at a navigable point upon its southern bank in Texas, there she would meet sixty thousand Indian warriors of our own, and half as many of Texas, whom her gold, and her intrigues and promises would, as they always have done, incite to the work of death and desolation. If we desire to know what she would do under such circumstances, let us look back to Hampton and the Raisin, and they will answer the question. If for no other reason, the fact that for many hundred miles you have placed these Indians on the borders of Texas, separated only by the Red river, and on the frontiers of Louisiana and Arkansas, demands that, as an act of justice to these States, and as essential for their security and that of the Mississippi, you should have possession of Texas. Our boundary and limits will always be *incomplete*, without the possession of Texas; and without it the great valley and its mightiest streams will remain forever dismembered and mutilated. Now, if we can acquire it, we should accomplish the object; for, in all probability, the opportunity, now neglected, will be lost forever. There may have been good reasons, a few weeks or months succeeding the recognition of the independence of Texas, and before it was recognised by any other power, why it might then have been premature to have reannexed the territory; but now, when eight years have elapsed since the declaration and establishment of the independence of Texas, and seven years since it was recognised by us, and several years since the recognition by France, Holland, and England, there can be no possible objection to the measure.

I have shown that, in the event of a war with England, Texas, if we repelled her from our embrace, would become a complete dependency of England, alienated from us in feeling, in trade and intercourse, and identified in all with England. But would it rest here? No. Texas would first become a dependency, and then, in fact, a colony of Eng-

2

land; and her arms, and ships, and power, would be thus transported to the mouth of the Mississippi. The origin of the immense empire of England in India, was in two small trading establishments. Then followed a permanent occupancy of part of the coast; and India in time became a British colony. And so will it be with Texas, which can furnish England—what it is *now ascertained* India never can—a supply of cotton. The largest vote ever given in Texas was about 12,000. Of this the British emigrants and British party now number about 1,000; which, by the unfriendly feelings created by a final refusal of reannexation, and the necessity of seeking another alliance, would be immediately increased to four thousand, leaving a majority of 4,000 only against a union with England. Immediately a rapid emigration from England to Texas would be commenced under their colonization laws, which give the emigrant a home, and make him a voter in six months, and five thousand English emigrants would overcome the majority of 4,000, and give England, through the ballot-box, the command of Texas. The preperation for this colonization of Texas from England has already been made. One English contract has already been signed with the government of Texas, for the emigration there of one thousand families; and three thousand one hundred more would give the *majority to England*. It may be, to avoid the difficulty as to slavery at home, the nominal government for local purposes would be left with Texas, or rather with English voters and merchants in Texas; but in all that concerns the commerce and foreign relations of Texas, in all that concerns the occupancy and use of Texas in the event of war, the supremacy and authority of the British Parliament would be acknowledged. Much is concealed as regards the ultimate designs of England in regard to Texas; for to acknowledge them now would be to defeat them, by insuring reannexation to the Union; but enough has transpired to prove her object. Let us examine the facts. Three treaties were made between Great Britain and Texas, viz: on the 13th, 14th, and 16th of November, 1840. The preamble of one of these is as follows:

"Her Majesty, the Queen of the United Kingdom of Great Britain and Ireland, being desirous of putting an end to the hostilities which still continue to be carried on between Mexico and Texas, has *offered* her mediation to the contending parties, to bring about a pacification between them."

Article 1. "The republic of Texas agrees that if, by means of the mediation of her Britannic Majesty, an unlimited truce shall be established between Mexico and Texas, within 30 days after this present convention shall have been communicated to the Mexican government by her Britannic Majesty's mission at Mexico; and if, within six months from the day that communication shall have been so made, Mexico shall have concluded a treaty of peace with Texas, then, and in such case, the republic of Texas will take upon itself a portion amounting to £1,000,000 sterling of the capital of the foreign debt contracted by the republic of Mexico, before the 1st of January, 1835?"

The first article of the next treaty declares: "There shall be reciprocal liberty of commerce and navigation between and amongst the citizens of the republic of Texas and the subjects of her Britannic Majesty." The third article authorizes *British merchants* to carry on their business in Texas, and *British vessels of war* to enter freely all her ports. Next comes a treaty between Great Britain and Texas, which grants to England the *right of search* as fully and effectually, and in terms more obnoxious, than the celebrated quintuple treaty to which it refers, and adopts. It grants to the vessels of war of both parties, the right of searching merchant vessels by either party, and expressly provides for the exercise of this right, "IN THE GULF OF MEXICO." It provides also for the exercise of this right, whenever either of the parties shall have reason to *suspect* that the vessel *is* or *has been* engaged in the slave-trade, or has been *fitted out* for the said trade; and all this is to be done, whether the vessel carries the flag of Texas or not. For saving us from the consequence of the quintuple treaty, and the right of search which it granted, by inducing France to refuse to ratify that treaty, General Cass, our minister there, has received and deserved the thanks of the whole American people. He demonstrated that such a right of search would be fatal to the free navigation of the ocean, and subject the commerce of the world to the supervision of British cruisers. But here is a treaty, containing all the obnoxious provisions of the quintuple treaty, in regard to the right of search, and others that are still more dangerous. That treaty was made, too, with nations differing in language, and in many other respects, from our own; and therefore more easily distinguishable than the people and vessels of Texas. As the flag is not to designate the national character of the vessel, how can these vessels of Texas, that are thus to be *searched* on *suspicion*, be distinguishable; and what is to prevent American vessels and American crews from being carried for condemnation within the ports of England? Recollect, also, that under this treaty, the cruisers of England and, indeed, the whole British navy, or any part of it, may be brought into the *Gulf of Mexico*, and stationed in the narrow pass, commanding the whole outlet of the gulf, and all the commerce to and from the Mississippi. To the right of search, under whatever name or form, especially within our own seas, and upon our own coasts, we never have assented, and never can assent; but here, under pretext of searching the vessels of Texas, the navy of England, or any part of it, may occupy the only outlet of the gulf of Mexico, and all our vessels entering the gulf, or returning from the mouth of the Mississippi, must pass by and under the supervision of British cruisers, subject to seizure and detention, on suspicion of being Texas vessels, concerned in the slave-trade. The British navy may thus also be quartered on the southern coast of Florida, and along the coasts of Cuba and Mexico, to seize upon Cuba whenever an opportunity presents. Such is the influence which it is thus proved, by official documents, Great Britain has already obtained in Texas. It is here proved, that Great Britain "offered her mediation" to Texas to obtain peace with Mexico, and that she has already induced Texas to assume, conditionally, one million pounds sterling of the debt which Mexico owes in England, with all the accumulating interest from the 1st of January, 1835. A nation so feeble as Texas, which should owe so heavy a debt in England, with the payments secured by treaty, would be as completely within British influence as though already a British colony, especially when we consider the other most extraordinary privileges which she has already granted to England, including the right of search. In the official proclamation of June 15, 1843, President Houston says: "An official communication has been received at the department of State, from her *Britannic* Majesty's chargé d'affaires near this government, founded upon a des-

patch he had received from her Majesty's charge d'affaires in Mexico, announcing to this government the fact that the President of Mexico would forthwith order a cessation of hostilities on his part; therefore, I, Sam. Houston, President of the Republic of Texas, do hereby declare and proclaim that an armistice is established, to continue during the pendency of negotiations between the two countries, and until due notice of an intention to resume hostilities (should such an intention hereafter be entertained by either party) shall have been formally announced through *her Britannic Majesty's* chargé d'affaires at the respective governments." Is not Texas *already dependent upon England*, when England obtains for her an armistice, and the President of Texas announces that this will continue until its termination be announced *by England*?

In the message of the President of Texas of the 12th of December, 1843, he speaks of the "generous and friendly disposition, and active and friendly offices of England." He speaks, also, of "injuries and indignities inflicted" by this government upon Texas, and declares "that reparation has been demanded." Such *is* the wonderful advance in Texas of the influence of England, that she has succeeded in having it announced in an executive message to the people of Texas that *England is their friend, and that we are their enemies.* If all this had been predicted three years since, it would have been deemed incredible; and if Texas is not reannexed, she is certain, within a few years more, to become first a commercial dependency, and then a colony, in fact, if not in name, of England. When we regard the consequences which have already followed the mere apprehension of the refusal of reannexation, what will be the result in Texas when reannexation is positively and forever rejected? When this is done, and Texas is repulsed with contempt or indifference, when her people are told, The flag of the Union shall never wave over you, go!—go where you may, to England, if you please,—who can doubt the result? To doubt is wilful blindness; and whilst we will have lost a most important territory, and an indispensable portion of the valley of the West, England will have gained a dependency first, and then a colony; and we shall awake from our slumbers when, amid British rejoicings and the sound of British cannon, the flag of England shall wave upon the coast and throughout the limits of Texas; and a monarchy rises up on our own continent and on our own borders, upon the grave of a republic. Yes, this is not a question merely between us and Texas, but a question between the advance of British or American power; and that, too, within the very heart of the valley of the West. It is a question also between the advance of monarchy and republicanism throughout the fairest and most fertile portion of the American continent, and is one of the mighty movements in deciding the great question between monarchy and republicanism, which of the two forms of government shall preponderate throughout the world. In the North, the flag of England waves from the Atlantic to the Pacific over a region much more extensive than our own; and if it must float also for several thousand miles upon the banks of the tributaries of the great Mississippi, and along the gulf, from the Sabine to the Del Norte, we will be surrounded on all sides by England in America. In the gulf, her supremacy would be clear and absolute; and in the great interior, she would hang on the rear of Louisiana and Arkansas, and within two days march of the Mississippi, while her forts would stand, and her flag would wave, for more than a thousand miles, on the banks of the Arkansas, the Sabine, and Red river, and in immediate contact with sixty thousand Indian warriors of our own, and half as many more of what would then be British Indians, within the present limits of Texas. If any doubt her course as to the Indians, let them refer to her policy in this respect during the revolution and the last war, and they will find that the savage has always been her favorite ally, and that she has shed more American blood, by the aid of the tomahawk and scalping-knife, than she ever did in the field of fair and open conflict. And has she become more friendly to the American people? Look at her forts and her traders, occupying our own undoubted territory of Oregon; look at her press in England and Canada, teeming with abuse of our people, government, and laws; look at her authors and tourists, from the more powerful and insidious assaults of Alison, descending in the scale to the falsehoods and arrogance of Hall and Hamilton, and down yet lower to the kennel jests and vulgar abuse of Marryatt and Dickens, industriously circulated throughout all Europe; and never was her hostility so deep and bitter, and never have her efforts been so great to render us odious to all the world. The government of England is controlled by her aristocracy, the avowed enemies of republican government, wherever it may exist. And never was England endeavoring to advance more rapidly to almost universal empire, on the ocean and the land. Her steamers, commanded by naval officers, traverse nearly every coast and sea, whilst her empire extends upon the land. In the East, the great and populous empires of Scinde and Affghanistan have been virtually subjected to her sway, whilst yet another province now bleeds in the claws of the British lion. Though saturated with blood, and gorged with power, she yet marches on her course to universal dominion; and here, upon our own borders, Texas is next to be her prey. By opium and powder, she has subdued China, and seized many important positions on her coast. In Africa, Australasia, and the Isles of the Pacific, she has wonderfully increased her power; and in Europe, she still holds the key of the Mediterranean. In the Gulf of Mexico, she has already seized, in Honduras, large and extensive possessions, and most commanding positions, overlooking from the interior the outlet of the gulf; while British Guiana, in South America, stretching between the great Oronoco and the mighty Amazon, places her in a position (aided by her island of Trinidad, at the mouth of the Oronoco) to seize upon the outlet of those gigantic rivers. With her West India islands, from Jamaica, south of Cuba, in a continuous chain to the most northern of the Bahamas, she is prepared to seize the Florida pass, and the mouth of the Mississippi; and let her add Texas, and the coast of Texas, and her command of the gulf will be as effectual as of the British channel. It would be a *British sea;* and soon, upon the shores of the gulf, her capital would open the great canal which must unite (at the isthmus) the Atlantic and Pacific, and give to her the key of both the coasts of America. Her possessions in the world are now nearly quadruple the extent of our own; with more than tenfold the population, and more than our area on our own continent; and, while she aims openly at the possession of Oregon on the north, Texas on the west is to become hers by a policy less daring, but more certain in its results. We can yet rescue Texas from her grasp, and, by reannexation, insure at least the command of our own great sea, and the outlet of our own great river. And shall we neglect the reacquisition, and throw Texas, and the command of the gulf, into the arms of England? Whoever would do so, is a monarchist, and prefers the advance of monarchical institutions over our own great valley: he is also an Englishman in feelings and principle, and would recolonize the American States.

And when Texas, by the refusal of reannexation, shall have fallen into the arms of England, and the American people shall behold the result, let all who shall have aided in producing the dread catastrophe flee from the wrath of an indignant nation, which will burst forth like lava, and roll in fiery torrents over the political graves of all who shall thus have contributed to the ruin of their country. And who would place England at New Orleans or the mouth of the Mississippi? Who would place England on the banks of the Sabine, the Arkansas, and Red river? Who would place England along the coasts, and bays, and harbors, and in the great interior of Texas, and see her become a British colony, or—what is the same to us—a British commercial dependency? Could Texas be a power friendly to us, even if not a British colony? Would our refusal of reannexation secure her friendship? Would her rivalry in our great staple insure her good will? Would the monopoly of her trade by England increase her attachment to ourselves? No! Let reannexation be now finally refused; and she becomes a foreign and a hostile power, with all her interests antagonistical to our own. Indeed, all history tells us that there is no friendship between foreign and contiguous nations, presenting so many points of collision, so many jarring interests, and such a rivalry in the sale and production of the same great staple.

Much is now urged in many of the States in favor of securing a home market for our manufactures. Now here in Texas is a home market, that may be secured forever, of incalculable and rapidly increasing value—a market that is already lost to us for the present, as the table of exports demonstrates, and, all must admit, will be thrown, by the rejection of reannexation, into the possession of England; for, whether Texas does or does not become a British colony, it is certain that a treaty of reciprocal free trade would secure to England the monopoly of her markets and commerce. The cotton of Texas would find a market free of duty in England, and her manufactures a market free of duty in Texas, whilst discriminating imposts on our vessels and cargoes would effectually exclude them from her ports. Although England might not, so long as her treaty with us remained uncancelled, receive gratuitously the cotton of Texas free of duty; yet we concede the principle, and act upon it, that she may do it, not gratuitously, but for a consideration, viz: that Texas receives in return British manufactures free of duty;—and such we know is to be the first result of the final rejection of reannexation. Thus England would effectually monopolize the commerce and business of Texas, and in her harbors would float the flag of the English mercantile marine, soon to be the precursor of the next step in the drama of our disgrace and ruin; when the flag of England would float over a British province, carved out of the dismembered valley of the West. But if this last result were not certain; if it were only probable and contingent,—is it not wise and patriotic to arrest the danger, and remove all doubt by the sure preventive remedy of reannex-

action? But if Texas should only become a British commercial dependency, and not a colony, the danger to us, we have seen, would be nearly as great in the event of war, in the one case, as in the other. But even if not a dependency, we have seen she would be too feeble to guard her rights as a neutral power; and that England, as she always heretofore has done in the case of neutrals, would seize upon her soil, her coast, her harbors, her rivers, and our and her Indians, in her invasion of the valley of the West; and the only certain measure of defence and protection is the reannexation of Texas.

The defence of the country and of all its parts against the probable occurrence of war, is one of the first and highest duties of this government. For this we build forts and arsenals, dry docks and navy-yards, supply arms and ordnance, and maintain armies and navies at an annual expense of many millions of dollars; and for this we guard great cities and important bays and harbors. From the organization of the government under the constitution, up to the latest period in 1843, for which detailed statements are given, we have expended for the War Department, $374,-888,899, and for the Naval Department, $173,236,-569—being for both $548,125,468; for the civil list, $61,385, 373, for foreign intercourse, $35,051,772. miscellaneous, $61,578,168;—making for these three last items, $157,915,310; and for the public debt, $451,749,003;—making the total expenditures $1,157,-789,781. Now if, to the expenditures for the defence of the country, as above given—$548,125,468—we add that portion of the public debt which may be fairly estimated as having been incurred for the defence of the country, it would make $948,125,-468 expended for the defence of the country; and leave $209,664,313 expended for all other purposes. The defence of the country was the great object for which the government was founded, and for this purpose, nearly all the moneys collected from the people have been expended; and yet, of this vast amount, but $2,208,000 have been expended for fortifications in Louisiana; and New Orleans and the mouth of the Mississippi are still to a great extent undefended. When we consider that nearly the whole commerce of the West floats through this outlet, amounting now to $220,000,000 per annum, and rapidly augmenting every year, has not the West a right to demand a defence, complete and effectual, of this great river? Now, Mr. Adams and Mr. Clay, in 1825 and 1827, in attempting to secure the reannexation of Texas, say: "the line of the Sabine *approaches our great Western mart* nearer than could be wished;" and in 1829, General Jackson and Mr. Van Buren announce "the *real necessity* of the proposed acquisition," "as a *guard* for the western frontier, and the *protection of New Orleans.*" If, then, the defence of the country be one of the main objects and highest duties of this government, and to accomplish which it has expended nearly all the moneys collected from the people, can it be unconstitutional or improper to acquire Texas, as a mere question of defence and protection, when we are assured, that the acquisition is a matter of "*real necessity,*" "as a *guard* for the frontier and the *protection* of New Orleans?" And surely this protection is as necessary now as it was in 1825, 1827, 1829, 1833, and 1835; and New Orleans and Texas, and the frontier and the Sabine, stand precisely where they did at those periods. Indeed, I have now before me a letter of General Jackson, almost fresh from his pen, in which he announces his opinion that the reannexation of Texas "*is essential to the United States.*" Although some of my countrymen may differ from me as to the exalted opinion which I entertain of the high civil qualifications of General Jackson, none will dispute his extraordinary military talents, and that no man living can know so well what is necessary to the protection of New Orleans, as its great and successful defender. If, then, the reannexation of Texas be more essential to the safety and defence of New Orleans and the mouth of the Mississippi, than all the fortifications which could be, but have not been, and will not be, erected in that quarter, has not the West a right to demand, on this ground alone, the reacquisition of Texas? The money of the West, as the treasury reports above quoted demonstrate, is now freely disbursed, and has been expended by hundreds of millions, for the defence of the Atlantic States; and will not those States feel it a duty and a pleasure to defend the West, and their own products, which float upon its mighty rivers, by the repossession of a territory which is essential for our security and welfare? To refuse the reannexation, is to refuse the defence of the West in the only way in which that defence will be complete and effectual; for you may extend your fortifications along the whole coast of the gulf, and New Orleans, and the mouth of the Mississippi, and the Florida pass will remain undefended, so long as Texas is in the possession of a foreign power, and we are open to attacks from the rear through that region. Fortifications, also, may sometimes be captured by a great superiority of guns and force, by squadrons upon the sea; and with a sufficient time and adequate force, if not by storm, by mine and siege, they may be always taken by assaults upon the land—even Gibraltar and the Moro castle not having always proved impregnable. But Texas, our own, and in the possession of the brave and practised marksmen of the West, would be a position where, against all attacks from the rear, every inch of ground would be fiercely contested, and every advance would be marked by the blood of the invader; and if New Orleans should be invaded in other directions, our countrymen in Texas, over whom would then float the flag of the Union, would rush to the rescue of their own great city, and, uniting with their brethren in arms from other States of the same great Union, would re-enact, upon the banks of the Mississippi, the victories of San Jacinto and New Orleans. If, then, we are true to the West and Southwest, we will, if there were no other reasons, as a question of defence, reacquire the possession of Texas: or do patriotism, and love of the whole country, and of all its parts, exist only in name? Does the American heart yet beat with all their glorious impulses? or are they mere idle words, fitted only to round off a period, or fill up an address? And have we reached that point in the scale of descending degeneracy, when the inquiry is, not what will best strengthen and defend the whole, but what will most effectually impair the strength, retard the growth, and weaken the security of the valley of the West?

Let us now examine the effect of the reannexation of Texas on the whole country. The great interests of the Union, as exhibited in the census of 1840, are shown in the products of agriculture, of the mines and manufactures, of the forests and fisheries, of commerce and navigation. I hereto append tables marked Nos. 2 and 3, compiled from the census of 1840, the first exhibiting the products that year of agriculture, manufactures, commerce, mining, the forest and fisheries; and the second showing the number of persons then employed in agriculture, manufactures, commerce, mining, navigating the ocean, and internal navigation. I have also compiled from the official report of the Secretary of the Treasury in 1840, a table marked No. 4, representing for the year preceding, for each State, the imports and exports of each, distinguishing the domestic from the foreign exports; also the number of American vessels which entered or cleared from each State; the American crews employed; the foreign vessels which entered and cleared from each State; the vessels built in each State, and tonnage owned by each. Table No. 5, compiled from the same report, exhibits, for the same year, our exports to each of the countries of the world, distinguishing the foreign and domestic exports, with the number of American vessels and foreign vessels employed in our trade with each country, together with the imports from each, and the excess in our trade with any of them, of exports to over imports from them. Table No. 6, compiled from the same report, presents all the exports of our own products that year to Texas, ranged under the heads of the products of agriculture, manufactures, forest and fisheries, distinguishing the articles thus exported, and their value. With these facts before us, which are all official, let us proceed to the examination of this great question. Our chief agricultural exports to Texas, as the table shows, were pork, ham, bacon, lard, beef, butter, cheese, flour, bread, and bread stuff, amounting to $163,641. In looking at the census of 1840, the population of each State and section, and the amount of these products in each State, we will find that the chief surplus of these products raised for sale beyond their limits, were in the middle States, composed of New York, New Jersey, Pennsylvania, Delaware, and Maryland, including the District of Columbia; and in the northwestern States, composed of Missouri, Kentucky, Ohio, Indiana, Illinois, and Michigan, including also Wisconsin and Iowa. The middle and northwestern States derived, then, the principal profit in the sale of agricultural products to Texas. In the sale of domestic manufactures to Texas, the New England States came first; and next in their order, the middle, and the northwestern States; and in looking at the principal items of which these exported manufactures to Texas were composed, I find that of the surplus produced and sold to Texas, Massachusetts stood first, and Pennsylvania second. Next as to commerce, as connected with Texas, the middle States stood first, and then the New England and northwestern States; and here New York stood first, Massachusetts second, and next Pennsylvania, Maryland, and Ohio. But here we must remark the special interest which Louisiana, through her great port of New Orleans, has in commerce as connected with Texas. The total products from commerce in Louisiana in 1840 were 7,-868,898, being one-tenth of that of the whole Union, and consequently the interest of New Orleans, as connected with the reannexation of Texas, must soon be measured by millions every year. The great city of New York, into which was received, in round numbers, one hundred millions of the one hundred and forty-three millions of all our imports in the year referred to, and one-third of the exports, has a vast and transcendent interest in this question; for it is, in truth, a question to be settled in our favor by the reannexation of Texas, whether New York or Liverpool shall command her commerce. Next as to the products of mining, the middle States stand first; and next the Northwestern and New England States. And here Pennsylvania stands at the head of the list, having $17,666,146, or nearly one-half of the whole mining interest of the Union. Texas,

having no mines of coal or iron, must become a vast consumer of the products of the mines of Pennsylvania. In cables, bar-iron, and nails, and other manufactures of our iron, Texas imported from us, in the year referred to, the value of $120,184. Now, of cast-iron, Pennsylvania produced, in 1840, 98,395 tons, being largely more than one-third of the amount produced in the whole Union; and next came Ohio, Kentucky, New York, Virginia, Tennessee, New Jersey, Massachusetts, and Maryland. Of bar-iron, the amount produced in Pennsylvania was 87,244 tons, being very nearly one-half of the whole produced in the Union; and next came New York, with 53,693 tons, or more than one-fourth of the whole; and then Tennessee, Maryland, Ohio, New Jersey, Massachusetts, Virginia, Kentucky, and Connecticut. As connected with her vast interests in iron, must be considered also the coal in Pennsylvania, not only as an article of sale abroad, but as consumed at home, in producing her iron; the number of tons thus consumed in 1840, of her own mines, being 355,903 tons, or very nearly one-fourth of that of the whole Union. Coal and iron are scattered in juxtaposition, throughout nearly the whole of Pennsylvania; and, as the markets for her iron are augmented, in the same proportion will increase the consumption of the coal used in producing that iron. Now, in 1840, the amount of anthracite coal produced in the whole Union was 863,489 tons; of which Pennsylvania produced 859,686, or nearly the whole. Of bituminous coal, the total product of the Union was 27,603,191 bushels; of which Pennsylvania produced 11,620,654, or nearly one-half the whole. Let us observe here, also, the remarkable fact, that the three adjacent States of Delaware, New Jersey, and New York, produced no coal, either anthracite or bituminous; and the future interest of Pennsylvania, as connected with that great article, becomes of transcendent importance; and this, together with iron, and the manufactures connected with them, is to determine the value of her public works, and fix her future destiny. Up to a certain point of density, an agricultural State, with a rich soil, advances most rapidly; but when all the lands are cleared and cultivated, this augmentation ceases. It is otherwise, however, with a State possessing, throughout nearly every portion, inexhaustible mines of coal and iron, and wonderful adaptation to manufactures. There, when the soil has been fully cultivated, the development of the mines and manufactures, and the commerce and business connected with them, only fairly begins. Agriculture is limited by the number of acres; but for the products of mines and manufactures, such as Pennsylvania has within her boundaries, there is no other limit than the markets she can command; and this is not merely theory, but is demonstrated by the comparative progress of the various nations of the world. Look, then, at the great amount—certainly not less than three hundred thousand dollars—of the products of the industry of Pennsylvania, consumed by Texas in her infancy, with a population of less than two hundred thousand in 1839, and when those products were, to a considerable extent, excluded by the then existing tariff of Texas, and without which she certainly would then have consumed at least half a million of the products of the industry of Pennsylvania, had she been a state of the Union. But in ten years succeeding the reannexation, at the lowest rate of progress of population to the square mile of the other new States, she would contain a population of two millions; and consequently consume five millions of the products of the industry of Pennsylvania, or one-fifth of all the surplus products of the mines and manufactures of that great State, sold beyond her limits in 1840. The principal products of Texas will be cotton and sugar, and besides the iron used in all agricultural implements, as well as in the manufactures consumed by an agricultural people, the use of iron in the cotton and sugar mills is very great. There all the great iron apparatus and machinery connected with the cotton gin and press, and the iron boilers and kettles and grates and furnaces used in the making of sugar, is greater than in any other employment. Together with this, is the steam engine, now universally employed in making sugar, and being employed also in the ginning of cotton; and the iron that must be used by Texas, as she developes her resources, must be great indeed; and the question depending on the reannexation, is, whether Texas shall become a part of our home market, and whether England, or Pennsylvania and other States, shall supply her wants. There is another fact which must lead to a vast consumption of coal in Texas, and that is this: that from the banks of the Red river to the coast of the gulf, excepting only the cross timbers, and some other points, chiefly along her streams, Texas is almost exclusively a prairie country; and yet, (what is not very usual, except in northern Illinois, and some other portions of the West,) the soil of these prairies is inexhaustibly fertile. From these causes, wood and fuel must be scarce in Texas, and the coal of Pennsylvania and other States must find a market there of almost incalculable value.

We come next to the products of the forest: and here the middle States stand first, and then the New England and northwestern States. New York here stands first, and then, in their order, Maine, North Carolina, Pennsylvania, and Ohio. From Olean point on the Alleghany river, in New York, and down that stream through Pennsylvania, the lumber that now descends the Mississippi is very considerable, and of which, including the products from the forest from other quarters of the Union, Texas already took from us, as the table shows, in 1839, to the value of $157,474. The product of the fisheries of the whole Union, in 1840, was $11,996,-008, of which New England produced $9,424,555, and the middle States $1,970,030. Of the products of these fisheries, Texas already took, in 1839, to the value of $43,426, which, as Texas has no fisheries, must be vastly augmented hereafter. By the treasury report of 1840, as exhibited in table No. 4, the number of vessels built that year in the whole Union was 858; and here the New England States stood first, and then the middle and northwestern States; and Massachusetts was first, and then, in their order, Maine, Maryland, New York, New Jersey, Pennsylvania, Ohio, and Connecticut. Now, by table No. 5, it is shown that the clearances of American vessels to Texas, from the United States, and of entries into the United States of American vessels from Texas, was, in the whole, in 1839, 608, being two-thirds of the whole number of vessels built in that year in the United States; and our crews employed in navigating these American vessels thus employed that year in our trade with Texas, were 4,727. The number of American vessels which cleared for Texas in 1839, was greater than to any one of fifty-seven out of sixty-three of all the enumerated countries of the world. It was greater, also, than the whole aggregate number of our vessels which cleared that year for France, Spain, Russia, Prussia, Sweden, Norway, Denmark,

Belgium, and Scotland combined. The same disproportion also exists as regards the crews, and also in the American vessels which entered the United States from Texas, and the crews employed. The same tables demonstrate that, of the foreign vessels which entered the United States from Texas, in 1839, eighteen only, out of 4,105, entered our ports from Texas; and sixteen foreign vessels only cleared from the United States in that year for Texas, out of 4,036; showing that our trade with Texas, in 1839, stood nearly upon the footing of our great coastwise trade, and was conducted almost exclusively in American vessels. Having shown the large number of American crews concerned in the trade with Texas, and the great amount of wages they must have earned, let us now look at the States which made these profits. By the census of 1840, the whole number of persons employed in navigating the ocean was 56,021, of which number 42,154 were from New England, and 9,713 from the middle States. And here Massachusetts stood first, and then Maine, and next, in their order, New York, Connecticut, Pennsylvania, Rhode Island, Louisiana, and New Jersey. In looking, also, to the States which owned the tonnage employed in this navigation, we find, by table No. 4, from the treasury report, that the New England States stood first, and then the middle States; and that the largest amount was owned by Massachusetts, and next, in their order, by New York, Maine, Maryland, Pennsylvania, Louisiana, Connecticut, and New Jersey. When we consider the products of the fisheries consumed, and that will be consumed, by Texas, and the tonnage and crews employed in that trade, the reannexation must greatly augment our mercantile marine, and thus enable it to supply our navy, whenever necessary, with an adequate number of skilful, brave, and hardy seamen, to defend, in war, our flag upon the sea. The number of persons employed in internal navigation, (including our lakes, rivers, and canals,) by the census of 1840, was 33,076; more than one half being from the middle States, and next the States of the Northwest. The largest number was from New York, and, next, in their order, Pennsylvania, Ohio, Virginia, Maryland and Missouri. Here, the States which have constructed great canals, on which are transported the exchangeable products of the Union, have a vast interest in the reannexation of Texas. Of these canals, the great works in New York, Pennsylvania, and Ohio, are already completed; and those of Indiana, and Illinois approach a completion, whilst Maryland and Virginia are pausing in the construction of their great works, the value of all of which would be greatly augmented, and business increased, by the reannexation of Texas. And here let me say one word of the Old Dominion. She borders upon the Ohio and Atlantic, and when her great works shall unite their waters by one direct and continuous canal, her connection with the West, and with Texas, as a part of it, will be most intimate and important; and through the very heart of the State would float a vast amount of the commerce connected with the Ohio and the Mississippi. And she also has other great and peculiar interests connected with the reannexation of Texas. The amount of cast and bar iron furnished by her in 1840, was 24,696 tons; of bituminous coal, 10,622,345 bushels; and of domestic salt, 1,745,618 bushels; of wheat, $3,345,783 in value; of the product of animals, $8,952,278; and of cotton manufactures $1,692,040; of all of which articles Texas, as the table of exports shows, is a very large consumer.

From the official treasury report of 1840, I give the table No. 6, for the year commencing the 1st of October, 1838, and closing on the 30th of September, 1839, showing our commerce that year with Texas, and all the other nations of the world. This shows that the total of our exports of domestic produce to Texas that year, was $1,379,065, and the total of all our exports to Texas that year, $1,687,082; that the imports the same year from Texas were $318,-116, leaving an excess in our favor, of exports over imports, of $1,368,966. Thus the extraordinary fact is exhibited, that in the very infancy of her existence, the balance of trade in our favor with Texas, exceeded that of each of all the foreign countries of the world—*two only excepted*; and these two were colonies of an empire, our trade to the whole of which presented a balance of several millions against us. Texas then, that year, furnished a larger balance of exports over imports in our favor, than any other *one of the empires of the world.* The totality of our exports that year to Texas was greater than to either Russia, Prussia, Sweden and Norway, Denmark, Belgium, Scotland, Ireland, Spain, Portugal, Italy, Sicily, or China. It was greater also than to each of fifty-six of the sixty-six enumerated countries of the world. It was greater also than the aggregate of all our exports to Spain, Prussia, Denmark, Italy, Sweden and Norway, Portugal, New Grenada, Australasia, French Guiana, Sardinia, Morocco and Barbary States, and Peru combined.

By table No. 6, it appears that the exports of our domestic products in 1839 to Texas was—of the fisheries $43,426; of the products of the forest $157,474; of the products of agriculture $205,860; and of our manufactures $929,071. Now, by table No. 6 of the treasury report, the total exports, the same year, of the products of the fisheries to all the world, except Texas, was $1,864,543; and consequently the exports of the products of the fisheries to Texas, that year, amouted to about 2½ per cent. of those exports to all the rest of the world. The exports of the products of the forest, that year, to all other countries, except Texas, by the same table, was $5,607,085; consequently the export of those products, that year, to Texas, amounted to 3 per cent. of those exports to all the rest of the world. The exports of our agricultural products, (excluding cotton, rice, and tobacco,) that year, to all other countries, except Texas, (and including molasses, inaccurately placed in the table of manufactures,) was $11,156,057; and consequently the exports of these products that year to Texas, amounted to more than 2 per cent. of the agricultural exports that year to all the rest of the world. By the same table, the export of all our manufactures in 1839 (exclusive of gold and silver coin) to all other countries, except Texas, was $3,217,562. Now, the exports of our domestic manufactures, that year, to Texas being $929,071, consequently TEXAS CONSUMED OF OUR DOMESTIC MANUFACTURES, IN 1839, AN AMOUNT LARGELY EXCEEDING ONE-FOURTH, AND NEARLY EQUAL TO ONE-THIRD OF OUR DOMESTIC MANUFACTURES EXPORTED ABROAD, AND CONSUMED THAT YEAR, BY ALL THE REST OF THE WORLD. Such are the astounding results established by the official report of the Secretary of the Treasury, under date of June 25th, 1840, and to be found in vol. 8 Senate documents for that year, No. 577. Such was our trade with Texas the year ending 30th September, 1839, before her independence was recognised by any other power except by this republic, and before she had entered into commercial treaty with any other power; and therefore stood to us in the rela-tion, in many respects, as regards her trade, as a territory of the Union. Now, the treaty of amity and commerce between France and Texas was signed at Paris on the 25th of September, 1839; the treaty of amity and commerce between Holland and Texas was signed at the Hague on the 18th of September, 1840; the treaty of commerce between Great Britain and Texas was signed at London on the 13th of November, 1840: all which have been long since ratified. Now, let us observe the effect upon our trade with Texas, of her introduction into the family of nations, by the recognition of her independence by other nations, and treaties of commerce with them; thus placing her towards us in the attitude of a foreign state. The resolution offered by me in the Senate of the United States for the recognition of the independence of Texas, was adopted on the 2d of March, 1837; and with that year commence the tables of our exports to Texas as a new empire, inscribed on the books of the treasury. These tables, in the treasury reports of our exports to Texas, exhibit the following result:

Our exports to Texas in	1837	-	$1,007,928
"	"	1838	-	1,247,880
"	"	1839	-	1,687,082
"	"	1840	-	1,218,271
"	"	1841	-	808,296
"	"	1842	-	406,929
"	"	1843	-	190,604

If our exports to Texas had augmented from 1839 to 1843, as they had done from 1837 to 1839, and as they must have done with her great increase of business and population, but for her being placed towards us, in the mean time, in the attitude of a foreign state, they would have amounted, in 1843, to $3,047,000, instead of $190,000. Such has been the immense reduction in our exports to Texas, created by her recognition by other nations, and commercial treaties with them, since 1839. But great as were our exports to Texas in 1839, they were by no means so large as if she had then been a State of the Union; for she then had, and still has, in force a tariff on imports, varying on most articles from 10 to 50 per cent., which must have prohibited some of our exports there, and diminished others. Our tariff, also, did not embrace Texas, and secure to our manufactures almost a monopoly in her supply. Had all these causes combined, as they would have done, had Texas been a State of the Union, our exports there of domestic articles must have reached, in 1843, $7,164,139, as I shall proceed to demonstrate:

The products of Louisiana, by the census of 1840, were $35,044,959, of which there was, in sugar and cotton, $15,476,783; and of this, there was of sugar, $4,797,908; of which sugar, if we deduct $476,783, as consumed in the State, being more than double her proportionate consumption, it would leave $15,000,000 of products raised and exported by Louisiana in 1840, when her population was 352,411; and Texas, producing now in the same proportion to her present population of 200,000, would produce $19,886,360, and of exports for sale beyond her limits, $8,522,724; and deducting from this $1,258,585, the proportion of her products employed in the purchase of foreign products for her use, would leave $7,164,139 of the products of Texas used in the purchase of articles from other States of the Union. But if reannexed to the Union, in ten years thereafter, how much would she purchase of the products of other States of the Union? If we allow Texas to increase in the same ratio to the square mile as the State of Louisiana after the first census succeeding the purchase from 1810 to 1820, the population, in ten years, occupying the 318,000 square miles of Texas, would exceed two millions; and the increase in many States has been much more rapid. But estimated at two millions, Texas would then, according to the above proportion, consume $71,641,390 per annum of the products of other States, which consumption would be rapidly increasing every year; and her annual products then would be $198,863,600; which, also, would be greatly and constantly augmenting. Such is the wealth we are about cast from us, and the *home market* we are asked to abandon; for when we see that, by the failuree of reannexation, our domestic exports in 1843, to Texas, had fallen to $140,320; and this, multiplied by ten, would give the consumption, at the end of ten years, of our products by Texas, $1,403,200, it makes an annual loss of a market for our products to the amount of $70,238,190; and the loss would be greater, if Texas then, as a foreign State, consumed of our exports in proportion to their consumption by the rest of the world, which would reduce her purchase of our products to $230,000, and make our loss $71,411,390 per annum; and if we add to this the loss of revenue from the duties on imports, and the loss of the proceeds of the sales of her public lands, estimated at $170,139,158, which would all be ours by reannexation, the national loss, by the rejection of Texas, must be estimated by hundreds of millions. Nor is it the trade of Texas only that would be lost, but that of Santa Fe, and all the northern States of Mexico, which, with the possession by us of Texas and the Del Norte, would become consumers of immense amounts of our manufactures and other products, and would pay us to a great extent in silver, which is their great staple. Texas, also, has valuable mines of gold and silver, and this also would be one of her great exports, with which she would purchase our products; and thus, by her specie infused into our circulation, render our currency more secure, and subject us to less danger of being drained to too great an extent of gold and silver. Our exports of domestic products, by the treasury report of 1840, amounted to $103,533,896, deducting which from our whole products by the census of 1840, would leave $959,600,845 of our own products, consumed that year by our own population of 17,062,453; and the consumption of our domestic products, ($103,533,896,) by the population of the world, (900,000,000,) would make an average consumption of $56 in value of our products consumed by each one of our own people, and *eleven cents* in value of our products consumed on the average by each person beyond our limits: and thus, it appears that one person within our limits consumes as much of our own products as 509 persons beyond our limits; thus proving the wonderful difference, as regards the consumption of the products of the Union, between Texas now and in all time to come, as a foreign country, *or as a part of the Union.* When we reflect, also, that the products of Texas are chiefly of those articles among the few which find a market abroad, it furnishes her with the means to purchase, with the proceeds of those exports, the surplus products of other States, which do not produce these exports; and therefore, the accession of such a country to the Union is vastly more important to the great manufacturing interest than if Texas did not raise such exports, but became a rival producer of our own domestic manufactures. Hence it must be obvious, independent of the proof here exhibited, that the New England States, the middle and northwestern States, would derive the principal profit from the reannexation of Texas. Pennsylvania standing first, and then Massachusetts and New

York; and of the cities, Pittsburg, Cincinnati, and New Orleans, Boston, New York, Baltimore, and Philadelphia. The city which will derive the greatest advantage, in proportion to her population, undoubtedly will be Pittsburg, not only from the wonderful extent and variety of her manufactures, but also from her position. The same steamboat, constructed by her skilful workmen, which starts from Pittsburg, at the head of the Ohio, freighted with her manufactures, can ascend the Red river for many hundred miles, into one of the most fertile regions of Texas, and return to the iron city with a cargo of cotton, there to be manufactured for sale in Texas, and other sections of the Union. The steamboats of Pittsburg, also, can descend the Mississippi to the gulf, and, coasting along its shores to Galveston, Matagorda, and the other ports of Texas, there dispose of their cargoes of manufactures, and bring back the cotton and sugar of Texas, and also the gold and silver, which will be furnished by her mines in great abundance, whenever they are worked with sufficient skill and capital. Pittsburg is a great *western city;* and whether she shall soon be the greatest manufacturing city of the world, depends upon the markets of the west, and especially on the market of Texas —which, we have seen, can alone be secured by reannexation, and, without it, must be lost forever. And shall Pittsburg complain that new States are to be added in the West? Why, the new States of the West have made Pittsburg all that she is, and all that she ever will be; and each addition to their number will only still more rapidly augment her markets, her business, her wealth, and population. Nor can Pittsburg advance without the correspondent improvement of Philadelphia, and of all the great interior of Pennsylvania, throughout the whole line of internal communication that binds together the two great cities of the Keystone State. While it is true that New England and the middle and northwestern States, will derive the greatest profit directly from the reannexation of Texas, the South and Southwest, from the augmentation of the wealth and business of the North—produced, not by restrictions on the South and Southwest, but in reciprocal free trade with Texas and all the States—will then also find in New England, and in the middle and northwestern States, a larger and more able purchaser, and more extensive and better markets for all their exports. Indeed, so great will be the mutual benefits from this measure, that I do not hesitate to record the opinion that, in ten years succeeding the reannexation, with just and fair legislation. there will be more American cotton then manufactured in this Union than now is, or then will be, in England; and we shall begin to look to the prices current of our own cities to regulate the market, and not to England, to raise or depress, at her pleasure, the value of the great American staple. The North wants more markets at home for the products of her industry, and attempts to secure those of the South and Southwest by the tariff; while they complain that this most certainly depresses the price of their great staple, and as surely deprives them of the means of purchasing the products and manufactures of the North. But, upon grounds undisputed by the friends or opponents of a tariff, Texas must furnish, as a part of the Union, in any event, a vast market for many of its products, upon the principle of reciprocal free trade among the States—that great principle which led to the adoption of the constitution, and which has done more than all other causes combined to advance our interest.

Upon the rejection of reannexation, it will be utterly impossible to prevent the smuggling of British and foreign goods, to an almost incalculable extent, through Texas into the Union, thus not only depriving our manufacturers of the markets of Texas, but also of the markets of the whole valley of the West. This difficulty is already experienced to a small extent in Canada, although we have mostly a dense population upon our side, and located in a region of the north, generally highly favorable to the tariff, and deeply interested, as they suppose, in detecting and preventing smuggling. But the difficulty in Texas will be far greater. There, the line of division is, first the Sabine—a very narrow stream, far different form the lakes of the North, and the great St. Lawrence—as a boundary; and from the Sabine, for a long distance, a mere geographical line to the Red river, along that stream for many hundred miles, and then another long geographical line to the Arkansas, and thence many hundred miles along that stream to its source, and thence to latitude 42. Here is a boundary of fifteen hundred miles, and a very large portion of it mere geographical lines, running through the very centre of the great valley of the Mississippi. Could an army of revenue officers, even if all were honest and above temptation, guard such a distance, and such a frontier, against the smuggler, and that, too, in the midst of a population on both sides deeply hostile to the tariff; many of them regarding it as unconstitutional, and therefore that it is right, in their judgment, to evade its operation? These difficulties were foreseen by Mr. Van Buren, and constitute a strong argument, urged by him in his despatch of 1829, in favor of the reannexation of Texas. He there urges the difficulty of establishing a proper custom-house at the mouth of the Sabine, without which, he says, even in that direction, "it is impossible to prevent that frontier from becoming the seat of an EXTENSIVE SYSTEM OF SMUGGLING." It is true, that a custom-house on our side of the Sabine, and with numerous and faithful officers, might diminish smuggling in that direction; but as by the treaty, now in force with Texas, all vessels entering Texas through the Sabine, must pass unmolested, and land their cargoes at any point on the Sabine, could smuggling be prevented in that direction?

But if smuggling could be prevented through the Sabine, there is the harbor of Galveston, entirely in Texas, and with a depth equal to that at the mouth of the Mississippi; and there is the river Trinity (emptying into that harbor) also entirely in Texas, and navigable to a point not far from Red river, within the boundaries of Texas; and up and through these streams into Arkansas and Louisiana, and the valley of the West, it would be utterly impossible to prevent smuggling. The duties upon many articles under our present tariff, range from 50 to 250 per cent. Upon India cotton bagging they amount to 250 per cent. on the foreign price current; on many articles of iron to 100 per cent.; and upon glass, and nearly all low-priced goods affected by the minimum principle, there are very high duties. With these articles introduced into Texas free of duty, can they be kept out of the adjacent States, when the facilities and temptation to smuggling will be so very great? This smuggling will be encouraged by the manufacturers of England, and their agents and merchants in Texas, whose cities would be built up as the entrepots of such a traffic. What English manufacturers will do, by an organized system of fraudulent invoices and perjury, to evade our duties, was proved in the late investigation in New York. British courts, also, have refused to notice offences against our revenue laws; and the high au-

thority of Sir William Blackstone has been invoked, where he says, in reference to this subject, "These prohibitory laws do not make the transgression a moral offence, or sin: the only obligation in conscience is to submit to the penalty if levied." And such is the opinion of thousands of our countrymen; and many thousand more believe that the present tariff is unconstitutional, and hence that it is of no force or validity, and that it is not criminal to disregard its provisions. However strong, then, might be my opposition to smuggling, there are hundreds of thousands, both in England and America, who believe it is not criminal; and their number will be greatly augmented, when goods, free of duty, may be introduced into Texas, and premiums, under our tariff, from 50 to 250 per cent. are offered, to induce the illicit traffic. Most certainly then, the refusal of reannexation will REPEAL THE TARIFF, by the substitution of smuggled goods in place of American manufactures; the fair trader will be undersold and driven out of the market by the illicit traffic and smuggling become almost universal, and the commerce of the country transferred from New York and the ports of the North, to the free ports of Texas. This disregard of the laws would bring the government into contempt, and finally endanger the Union, if, indeed, it did not induce a degeneracy and demoralization, always fatal to the permanence of free institutions. Nor is it necessary, to effect these results, that Texas should become a colony, or even a commercial dependency of England; nor yet that there should be between these powers a treaty of reciprocal free trade. Texas (there being no separate States, and but one government to support, and having no expense of any revenue system) may maintain her single government at an annual expense of $300,000, which sum she can, as is now clearly ascertained, derive from the sales of her magnificent public domain, embracing, as we have seen, 136,000,000 of acres. Let it be known, then, and proclaimed as a certain truth, and as a result which can never hereafter be changed or recalled, that, upon the refusal of reannexation, now and in all time to come, THE TARIFF, AS A PRACTICAL MEASURE, FALLS WHOLLY AND FOREVER; and we shall thereafter be compelled to resort to direct taxes to support the government. Desirable as such a result (the overthrow not only of a protective, but even of a revenue tariff, and the substitution of direct taxation) might be to many in the South and Southwest, yet the dreadful consequences which would flow from this illicit traffic to the cause of morals, of the Union, and of free government, cannot be contemplated without horror and dismay.

Having now, gentlemen, fully replied to your communication, let me assure you that I shall persevere in the use of all honorable means to accomplish this great measure, so well calculated to advance the interests and secure the perpetuity of the American Union. That Union, and all its parts, (for they are all a portion of our common country,) I love with the intensity of filial affection; and never could my heart conceive, or my hand be raised to execute, any project which could effect its overthrow. I have ever regarded the dissolution of this Union as a calamity equal to a second fall of mankind—not, it is true, introducing, like the first, sin and death into the world, but greatly augmenting all their direful influences. Such an event it would not be my wish to survive, to behold or participate in the scenes which would follow; and, among the reasons which induce me to advocate so warmly the reannexation of Texas, is the deep conviction, long entertained, that this great measure is essential to the security of the South, the defence of the West, and highly conducive to the welfare and perpetuity of the whole Union. As regards the division of Texas into States, to which you refer, it seems to me most wise first to get the territory; and, when we have rescued it from England, and secured it to ourselves, its future disposition must then be determined by the joint action of both Houses of Congress; which, from their organization, will decide all these questions in that spirit of justice and equity in which the constitution was framed, and all its powers should be administered. I perceive that your meeting and your committee was composed of both the great parties which divide the country, and that you propose that the reannexation of Texas should not be made a sectional or a party question. Most fortunate would be such a result; for this is, indeed, a great question of national interests, too large and comprehensive to embrace any party or section less than the whole American people.

Accept, gentlemen of the committee, for yourselves, and that portion of the people of the great and patriotic Commonwealth of Kentucky whom you represent on this occasion, and in reply to whose call upon me this answer has been given, the assurances of the respect and consideration of

Your fellow-citizen,

R. J. WALKER.

To Messrs. Geo. N. Sanders, Henry Ramey, jr., F. Bledsoe, W. B. Lindsay, James P. Cox, &c., *Committee.*

TABLES APPENDED TO MR. WALKER'S LETTER.

Table No. 1, *compiled from census of* 1840, *of deaf and dumb, blind, idiots, and insane.*

States and Territories.	White population.	Colored population.	White.			Colored.			Deaf & dumb, blind, insane, and idiots.	In prisons, and paupers.
			Deaf & dumb.	Blind.	Insane & idiots.	Deaf & dumb.	Blind.	Insane & idiots.		
Maine -	500,438	1,355	222	180	537	13	10	94	117	
New Hampshire - -	284,036	538	181	153	486	9	3	19	31	
Massachusetts	729,030	8,669	283	308	1,071	17	22	200	239	
Rhode Island -	105,587	3,243	74	63	203	3	1	13	17	
Connecticut -	301,856	8,159	309	143	498	8	13	44	65	
Vermont -	291,218	730	135	101	398	2	2	13	17	
New York - -	2,378,890	50,031	1,039	875	2,146	68	91	194	353	
New Jersey -	351,588	21,718	164	126	369	15	26	73	114	
Pennsylvania -	1,676,115	47,918	781	540	1,946	51	96	187	334	
Ohio -	1,502,122	17,345	559	372	1,195	33	33	165	231	
Indiana -	678,698	7,168	297	135	487	15	19	75	109	
Illinois -	472,254	3,929	155	86	213	24	10	79	113	
Michigan -	211,560	707	31	25	39	2	4	26	32	
Wisconsin -	30,749	196	5	9	8	–	–	3	3	
Iowa -	42,924	188	10	3	7	4	3	4	11	
	9,557,055	171,892	4,233	3,219	9,599	262	333	1,191	1,786	24,556
Delaware -	58,561	19,524	45	15	52	8	18	28	54	
Maryland -	317,717	151,515	178	165	387	68	101	149	318	
Virginia -	740,968	498,829	443	426	1,052	150	466	381	997	
North Carolina	484,870	268,549	280	223	580	74	167	221	462	
South Carolina	259,084	335,314	140	133	376	78	156	137	371	
Georgia -	407,695	283,697	193	136	294	64	151	134	349	
Alabama -	335,185	255,571	173	113	232	53	96	125	274	
Mississippi -	179,074	196,577	64	43	116	28	69	82	179	
Louisiana -	158,457	193,954	42	37	55	17	36	45	98	
Tennessee -	640,627	188,583	291	255	699	67	99	162	328	
Kentucky -	590,253	189,575	400	236	795	77	141	180	398	
Missouri -	323,888	59,814	126	82	202	27	42	68	137	
Arkansas -	77,174	20,400	40	26	45	2	8	21	31	
Florida -	27,943	26,534	14	9	10	2	10	12	24	
District of Columbia	30,657	13,155	8	6	14	4	9	7	20	
	4,632,053	2,701,566	2,449	1,805	4,909	715	1,559	1,734	4,020	13,507
	14,189,108	2,873,458	6,682	5,024	14,508	977	1,892	2,926	5,806	

Table No. 2, *showing the annual products of each State, according to census of* 1840.

States and Territories.	Value of annual products from						
	Agriculture.	Manufactures.	Commerce.	Mining.	Forest.	Fisheries.	Total.
	Dollars.	*Dollars.*	*Dollars.*	*Dollars.*	*Dollars.*	*Dollars.*	*Dollars.*
Maine - -	15,856,270	5,615,303	1,505,380	327,376	1,877,663	1,280,713	26,462,705
New Hampshire	11,377,752	6,545,811	1,001,533	88,373	449,861	92,811	19,556,141
Vermont - -	17,879,155	5,685,425	758,899	389,488	430,224	–	25,143,191
Massachusetts -	16,065,627	43,518,057	7,004,691	2,020,572	377,354	6,483,996	75,470,297
Rhode Island -	2,199,309	8,640,626	1,294,956	162,410	44,610	659,312	13,001,223
Connecticut -	11,371,776	12,778,963	1,963,281	820,419	181,575	907,723	28,023,737
New England S.	74,749,889	82,784,185	13,528,740	3,808,638	3,361,287	9,424,555	187,657,294
New York -	108,275,281	47,454,514	24,311,715	7,408,070	5,040,781	1,316,072	193,806,433
New Jersey -	16,209,853	10,696,257	1,206,929	1,073,921	361,326	124,140	29,672,426
Pennsylvania -	68,180,924	33,354,279	10,593,368	17,666,146	1,203,578	35,360	131,033,655
Delaware -	3,198,440	1,538,879	266,257	54,555	13,119	181,285	5,252,535
Maryland -	17,586,720	6,212,677	3,499,087	1,056,210	241,194	225,773	28,821,661
Dist. of Columbia	176,942	904,526	802,725	–	–	87,400	1,971,593
Middle States -	213,628,160	100,161,132	40,680,081	27,258,902	6,859,998	1,970,030	390,558,303
Virginia - -	59,085,821	8,349,218	5,299,451	3,321,629	617,760	95,173	76,769,053
North Carolina -	26,975,831	2,053,697	1,322,284	372,486	1,446,108	251,792	32,422,198
outh Carolina -	21,553,691	2,248,915	2,632,421	187,608	549,626	1,275	27,173,536
Georgia - -	31,468,271	1,953,950	2,248,488	191,631	117,439	584	35,980,363
Florida - -	1,834,237	434,544	464,637	2,700	27,350	213,219	2,976,687
Southern States	140,917,851	15,040,324	11,967,281	4,076,054	2,758,283	562,043	175,321,836
Alabama -	24,696,513	1,732,770	2,273,267	81,310	177,465	–	28,961,325
Mississippi -	26,494,565	1,585,790	1,453,686	–	205,297	–	29,739,338
Louisiana -	22,851,375	4,087,655	7,868,898	165,280	71,751	–	35,044,959
Arkansas -	5,086,757	1,145,309	420,635	18,225	217,469	–	6,888,395
Tennessee -	31,660,180	2,477,193	2,239,478	1,371,331	225,179	–	37,973,360
Southwestern S.	110,789,390	11,028,717	14,255,964	1,636,146	897,161	–	138,607,378
Missouri - -	10,484,263	2,360,708	2,349,245	187,669	448,559	–	15,830,444
Kentucky -	29,226,545	5,092,353	2,580,575	1,539,919	184,799	–	38,624,191
Ohio - -	37,802,001	14,588,091	8,050,316	2,442,682	1,013,063	10,525	63,906,678
Indiana - -	17,247,743	3,676,705	1,866,155	660,836	80,000	1,192	23,532,631
Illinois - -	13,701,466	3,243,981	1,493,425	293,272	249,841	–	18,981,985
Michigan -	4,502,889	1,376,249	622,822	56,790	467,540	–	7,026,390
Wisconsin -	568,105	304,692	189,957	384,603	430,580	27,663	1,905,600
Iowa - -	769,295	179,087	136,525	13,250	83,949	–	1,132,106
Northwestern S.	114,302,307	30,821,866	17,289,020	5,579,011	2,958,331	39,380	170,989,925
Total -	654,387,597	239,836,224	79,721,086	42,358,761	16,835,060	11,996,008	1,063,134,736

Table No. 3, showing the number of persons engaged in mining, agriculture, commerce, manufactures navigating the ocean, and internal navigation.

States and Territories.	Mining.	Agriculture.	Commerce.	Manufactures	Navigating the ocean.	Internal navigation.
Maine - - -	36	101,630	2,921	21,879	10,091	539
New Hampshire -	13	77,949	1,379	17,826	452	198
Vermont - -	77	73,150	1,303	13,174	41	146
Massachusetts - -	499	87,837	8,063	85,176	27,153	373
Rhode Island - -	35	16,617	1,348	21,271	1,717	228
Connecticut - -	151	56,955	2,743	27,932	2,700	431
New England States	811	414,138	17,757	187,258	42,154	1,914
New York - -	1,898	455,954	28,468	173,193	5,511	10,167
New Jersey - -	266	56,701	2,283	27,004	1,143	1,625
Pennsylvania - -	4,603	207,533	15,338	105,883	1,815	3,951
Delaware - -	5	16,015	467	4,060	401	235
Maryland -	320	72,046	3,281	21,529	717	1,528
District of Columbia -	–	384	240	2,278	126	80
Middle States -	7,092	808,633	50,077	333,947	9,713	17,586
Virginia - -	1,995	318,771	6,361	54,147	582	2,952
North Carolina -	589	217,095	1,734	14,322	327	379
South Carolina -	51	198,363	1,958	10,325	381	348
Georgia - -	574	209,383	2,428	7,984	262	352
Florida - -	1	12,117	481	1,177	435	118
Southern States -	3,210	955,729	12,962	87,955	1,987	4,149
Alabama - -	96	177,439	2,212	7,195	256	758
Mississippi - -	14	139,724	1,303	4,151	33	100
Louisiana - -	1	79,289	8,549	7,565	1,322	662
Arkansas - -	41	26,355	215	1,173	3	39
Tennessee - -	103	227,739	2,217	17,815	55	302
Southwestern States	255	650,546	14,496	37,899	1,669	1,861
Missouri - -	742	92,408	2,522	11,100	39	1,885
Kentucky - -	331	197,738	3,448	23,217	44	968
Ohio - -	704	272,579	9,201	66,265	212	3,323
Indiana - -	233	148,806	3,076	20,590	89	627
Illinois - -	782	105,337	2,506	13,185	63	310
Michigan - -	40	56,521	728	6,890	24	166
Wisconsin - -	794	7,047	479	1,814	14	209
Iowa - - -	217	10,469	355	1,629	13	78
Northwestern States	3,843	890,905	22,315	144,690	498	7,566
Total - -	15,211	3,719,951	117,607	791,749	56,021	33,076

Table No. 4 from the Treasury report of 1840, for the year 1839.

States and Territories.	Imports into each State.	American vessels entered each State.	Foreign vessels entered each State.	American vessels cleared from each State.	Foreign vessels cleared from each State.	Vessels built in each State.	Tonnage owned in each State.	American crews cleared from each State.	American crews entered each State.	Domestic produce exported from each State.	Foreign produce exported from each State.	Total of domestic and foreign produce exported from each State.
							Tons. 95ths.					
Maine -	$982,724	351	926	459	921	145	282,296.40	3,358	2,581	$878,434	$17,051	$895,485
New Hampshire -	51,407	21	10	18	10	7	29,224.07	159	230	74,914	7,030	81,944
Vermont -	413,513	186	—	185	—	—	4,232.37	1,275	1,268	193,886	—	193,886
Massachusetts -	19,385,223	1,222	606	980	612	146	506,374.21	9,247	12,780	5,526,455	3,749,630	9,276,085
Rhode Island -	612,057	137	6	125	3	9	44,573.16	1,180	1,303	175,808	9,426	185,234
Connecticut -	446,191	129	—	136	9	35	82,914.34	1,746	1,596	583,226	—	583,226
New York -	99,882,438	4,006	1,805	3,604	1,728	106	468,410.58	29,612	32,810	23,296,995	9,971,104	33,268,099
New Jersey -	4,182	9	1	19	2	72	62,740.87	184	58	78,434	19,645	98,079
Pennsylvania -	15,050,715	453	78	333	72	49	112,359.17	3,169	4,518	4,148,211	1,151,204	5,299,415
Delaware -						16	19,303.19			8,680		8,680
Maryland -	6,995,285	339	90	311	89	129	116,204.00	2,491	2,648	4,313,189	263,372	4,576,561
District of Columbia -	132,511	23	11	46	11	14	23,142.26	341	243	497,965	5,752	503,717
Virginia -	913,462	87	37	192	50	10	51,886.39	1,813	674	5,183,424	3,772	5,187,196
North Carolina -	229,233	153	30	344	37	25	40,901.11	2,205	984	426,934	992	427,926
South Carolina -	3,086,077	146	94	212	102	4	33,414.21	2,263	1,318	10,318,822	66,604	10,385,426
Georgia -	413,687	56	50	111	50	7	20,992.83	1,943	450	5,970,443	—	5,970,443
Alabama -	895,201	128	45	200	44	—	21,742.00	2,077	1,053	10,338,159	—	10,338,159
Mississippi -												
Louisiana -	12,064,942	603	219	684	208	11	109,076.36	7,565	5,813	30,995,936	2,185,231	33,181,167
Ohio -	19,250	64	34	76	36	44	23,925.55	208	200	95,854	—	95,854
Kentucky -	10,480	—	—	—	—	11	8,125.87	—	—	3,723	—	3,723
Tennessee -	146	—	—	—	—	3	4,240.94	—	—			
Michigan -	176,221	43	39	78	34	7	10,999.29	156	96	133,305		133,305
Florida -	279,893	180	14	199	18	3	9,672.68	1,055	913	291,094	43,712	334,806
Missouri -	46,964	—	—	—	—	5	9,735.00	—	—			
Indiana -												
Illinois -												
Arkansas Territory -												
Wisconsin Territory -												
Iowa Territory -												
Total -	143,874,252	8,336	4,105	8,312	4,036	858	2,096,478.81	71,352	71,536	103,533,891	17,494,525	121,028,416

Table No. 5, for year 1839, from Treasury report of 1840.

	Where exported to.	Domestic exports.	American vessels cleared.	American vessels entered.	Foreign exports.	Total foreign and domestic exports.	Imports.	Excess of exports over imports.
1	Russia	$434,587	29	49	$804,659	$1,239,246	$2,393,894	
2	Prussia	29,313	4	2	43,500	72,813	70,412	$2,401
3	Sweden and Norway	337,000	3	34	26,502	363,502	1,553,684	
4	Swedish West Indies	103,282	22	6	4,130	107,412	12,458	94,950
5	Denmark	50,634	3	1	38,177	88,811	80,997	7,814
6	Danish West Indies	1,014,381	215	155	303,154	1,317,535	1,465,761	
7	Hanse Towns and ports of Germany	2,067,608	17	39	733,459	2,801,067	4,489,150	
8	Holland	1,677,352	40	54	295,651	1,973,003	2,149,732	
9	Dutch East Indies	86,619	24	12	396,934	483,553	692,196	
10	Dutch West Indies	282,042	26	67	70,975	353,017	582,284	
11	Dutch Guiana	58,863	36	35	2,803	61,666	49,008	12,658
12	Belgium	541,641	8	17	66,269	607,910	465,701	142,209
13	England	54,615,327	539	578	3,953,108	58,568,435	64,863,716	
14	Scotland	1,025,832	8	15	1,256	1,027,088	950,183	76,905
15	Ireland	380,719	4	4		330,719	150,689	180,030
16	Gibraltar	902,247	66	9	148,387	1,050,634	99,178	951,456
17	Malta	65,870	9	5	34,126	99,996	24,943	75,053
18	Mauritius	30,466	3	1	1,500	31,966		31,966
19	Cape of Good Hope	88,379	7	4	5,020	93,399	43,059	50,340
20	British East Indies	246,845	29	25	337,597	584,442	2,135,152	
21	British West Indies	2,472,833	501	285	90,642	2,563,475	941,699	1,621,776
22	British Guiana	34,906	31	7	218	35,124	14,215	20,909
23	British Honduras	181,861	41	22	29,339	211,200	164,027	47,173
24	British North American Colonies	3,418,770	3,313	3,361	144,684	3,563,454	2,155,146	1,408,308
25	Australia	6,790	3	2		6,790	58,344	
26	Other British Colonies				2,360	2,360		2,360
27	France on the Atlantic	14,919,848	207	186	2,088,655	17,008,503	30,918,450	
28	France on the Mediterranean	1,046,260	37	26	176,186	1,222,446	1,612,871	
29	French West Indies	585,916	186	155	105,905	691,821	702,798	
30	French Guiana	1,643	17	21		1,643		1,643
31	Spain on the Atlantic	316,144	58	23	82,014	348,158	263,193	
32	Spain on the Mediterranean	209,724	31	85	19,000	228,724	1,597,978	
33	Teneriffe and other Canaries	15,572	8	19	11,939	27,511	196,755	
34	Manilla and Philippine Islands	99,553	4	22	38,255	136,808	876,477	
35	Cuba	5,025,626	1,240	1,247	1,091,205	6,116,831	12,599,843	84,965

No.								
36	Porto Rico	779,049	153	411	87,348	866,397	3,742,549	
37	Portugal	59,711	17	48	6,093	65,804	587,778	
38	Madeira	64,082	24	11	15,045	79,128	539,800	
39	Fayal and other Azores	9,130	5	2	8,415	13,869	15,222	
40	Cape de Verd Islands	77,138	16	2	4,739	85,553	39,523	46,030
41	Italy	315,399	9	17	122,753	438,152	1,182,297	
42	Sicily	192,462	9	62	84,607	277,069	592,951	
43	Sardinia	—	—	—	—	—	1,348	
44	Trieste	429,578	11	18	162,671	592,249	477,539	114,710
45	Turkey, Levant, &c.	83,320	12	17	266,054	349,374	629,190	
46	Morocco and Barbary States	—	—	2	—	—	96,493	
47	Hayti	991,265	159	174	131,294	1,122,599	1,377,989	1,368,966
48	Texas	1,379,065	339	269	308,017	1,687,082	318,116	
49	Mexico	816,660	142	143	1,970,702	2,787,362	3,127,153	23,397
50	Central Republic of America	111,752	4	6	104,490	216,242	192,845	
51	New Grenada	35,219	8	14	29,585	64,804	90,514	
52	Venezuela	413,245	66	110	272,736	685,981	1,982,702	
53	Brazil	2,133,997	179	158	503,488	2,637,485	5,292,955	
54	Cisplatine Republic	50,998	37	30	38,302	89,300	625,432	
55	Argentine Republic	223,593	3	3	142,470	376,063	521,114	
56	Chili	1,307,143	22	13	487,410	1,794,553	1,186,641	607,912
57	Peru	—	4	—	—	—	242,813	
58	South America generally	23,618	—	7	27,257	50,875	3,678,509	50,875
59	China	430,464	15	18	1,103,137	1,533,601		
60	Europe generally	128,105	2	—	—	128,105		128,105
61	Asia generally	158,321	13	7	400,431	558,752	63,525	495,227
62	Africa generally	443,218	31	32	47,061	490,279	419,054	71,225
63	West Indies generally	457,968	134	9	33,060	491,028		491,028
64	South Seas	85,938	127	179	39,750	125,688	318,143	
65	Atlantic Ocean	—	1	8	—	—		
66	Uncertain places	—	1	—	—	—		
		103,533,891	8,312	8,336	17,494,525	121,028,416	162,092,132	

[*From the Treasury Report of* 1840.]
No. 6.—EXPORTS OF OUR DOMESTIC PRO-
DUCTS TO TEXAS IN 1839.
1. *Products of the fisheries.*

Dried or smoked and pickled fish - -	$3,137
Spermaceti oil and candles, whale and other fish oil - - - - -	7,057
Non-enumerated - - -	33,232
Total exports products of the fisheries -	43,426

2. *Products of the forest.*

Staves, heading, shingles, boards, plank, and scantling - - -	48,504
Other lumber - - -	22,267
Oak bark, and other dye - -	599
All manufactures of wood - -	51,112
Tar, pitch, rosin and turpentine - -	1,471
Ashes—pot and pearl - -	64
Skins and furs - - -	225
Non-enumerated - - -	33,232
Total exports products of the forest	157,474

3. *Products of agriculture.*

Beef - - - -	3,587
Pork, ham, bacon and lard - -	62,132
Butter and cheese - - -	13,028
Horses - - - -	700
Flour - - - -	55,091
Indian corn - - -	15,981
Indian meal - - - -	1,151
Rye, oats, and other small grain, and pulse	6,902
Biscuit, or ship bread - - -	12,701
Potatoes - - - -	5,145
Apples - - - -	1,040
Rice - - - -	5,743
Tobacco - - - -	1,509
Brown sugar - - -	27,900
Molasses - - -	3,250
Non-enumerated - - -	33,234
Total exports products of agriculture	239,092

4. *Exports of domestic manufactures.*

Household furniture - -	58,571
Coaches and other carriages - -	11,410
Hats - - - - -	19,055
Saddlery - - - -	14,063
Beer, porter, cider and spirits, from grain -	50,508
Leather boots and shoes - -	64,308
Tallow candles and soap - -	6,676
Snuff and manufactured tobacco -	17,895
Linseed oil and spirits of turpentine -	1,530
Cables and cordage - -	4,262
Lead - - - -	1,104
Bar iron and nails -	14,441
Castings - - - -	11,540
All manufactures of iron, or of iron and steel	89,261
Spirits from molasses - -	9,848
Refined sugar - - -	8,844
Chocolate - - - -	13
Gunpowder - - -	4,659
Copper, brass, and copper manufactured -	395
Medical drugs - - -	7,990
Printed and colored piece goods of cotton	95,856
White piece goods of cotton -	138,603
Yarn and other threads - -	28
All other manufactures of cotton -	11,166
Bags, and other manufactures of flax	20
Wearing apparel - -	118,303
Combs and buttons - -	1,470
Brushes - - -	1,025
Billiard tables and apparatus -	413
Umbrellas and parasols -	485
Printing presses and type -	1,756
Musical instruments - -	950
Books and maps - -	3,061
Paper and other stationery -	25,032
Paints and varnish - -	8,663
Vinegar - - -	1,051
Earthern and stone ware -	6,541
Glass - - -	6,875
Tin - - -	4,775
Pewter and lead - -	407
Marble and stone - -	966
Gold, silver, and gold leaf -	150
Artificial flowers and jewelry -	1,577
Bricks and lime - -	2,796
Domestic salt - - -	664
Manufactured articles not enumerated	100,056
Total exports of domestic manufactures	929,071

Index